TRACKING THE

ELUSIVE HUMAN

VOLUME II

BOOKS BY JAMES AND TYRA ARRAJ

TRACKING THE ELUSIVE HUMAN
Volume I: A Practical Guide to
C.G. Jung's Psychological Types
W.H. Sheldon's Body and Temperament Types
and Their Integration

TRACKING THE ELUSIVE HUMAN
Volume II: An Advanced Guide to the Typological
Worlds of C.G. Jung, W.H. Sheldon, Their Integration
and the Biochemical Typology of the Future

ST. JOHN OF THE CROSS AND DR. C.G. JUNG
Christian Mysticism in the Light of
Jungian Psychology

A JUNGIAN PSYCHOLOGY RESOURCE GUIDE

THE INNER NATURE OF FAITH
A Mysterious Knowledge
Coming Through the Heart

GOD, ZEN AND THE INTUITION OF BEING

IS THERE A SOLUTION TO THE CATHOLIC
DEBATE ON CONTRACEPTION?

THE TREASURES OF SIMPLE LIVING
A Family's Search for a Simpler and More
Meaningful Life in the Middle of a Forest

TRACKING

THE

ELUSIVE

HUMAN

VOLUME II:
AN ADVANCED GUIDE TO THE
TYPOLOGICAL WORLDS OF
C.G. JUNG, W.H. SHELDON,
THEIR INTEGRATION, AND THE
BIOCHEMICAL TYPOLOGY
OF THE FUTURE

JAMES ARRAJ
INNER GROWTH BOOKS

Copyright © 1990 by James Arraj

Printed in the United States of America.

For ordering information on this and other titles see the back pages or write:

INNER GROWTH BOOKS
Box 520
Chiloquin, OR 97624

The author invites your comments through the above address.

This book is printed on acid free paper.

Library of Congress Cataloging-in-Publication Data

Arraj, James.
    Tracking the elusive human. Volume 2.

    Bibliography: v. 2 p.
    Includes index.
    Contents: v. 2. An advanced guide to the typological worlds of C.G. Jung, W.H. Sheldon, their integration, and the biochemical typology of the future.
    1. Typology (Psychology) 2. Jung, C.G. (Carl Gustav), 1875-1961. 3. Sheldon, William Herbert, 1898-1977. I. Title.
BF698.3.A77   1988   155.2'64   87-30213
ISBN 0-914073-36-2 (pbk. : v. 2 : alk. paper)

CONTENTS

Figures

Tables

List of Photographs

This book is dedicated to
C.G. Jung, William Sheldon and
their coworkers whose work has
created a real tool for inner growth

A SHORT ORIENTATION

Volume I stressed the practical character of type recognition and development, which provides the indispensable foundation for this volume.

Here we are going to explore:

Part I: The history and development of Jung's psychological types

Part II: Sheldon's life and work, and the controversies that surrounded them

Part III: The integration of Jung's and Sheldon's typologies

Part IV: The frontiers of typology where it meets new developments in biochemistry and genetics.

It would be soothing to think of the journey that lies ahead of us as a leisurely stroll through the world of typology. But our journey is, unfortunately, a much more rigorous one because of the difficulty of the terrain, and its vast extent. Without making any pretense at being exhaustive, we are going to examine a considerable amount of the literature that has grown up around the typologies of Jung and Sheldon in order to try to capture their fundamental principles, bring them together in an integrated typology, and glimpse what new dimensions the future might add to them. And this will not be an easy task. Each of these typologies culminates a long historical tradition, represents an important advance over what went before, and together they present us with the possibility of forging a superb instrument for the understanding of human differences. At the same time they are embroiled in controversies and obscured by misunderstandings.

In view of the difficulties that face us it is worth while to attempt to avoid at the outset some of the most obvious. No matter how much we are going to talk about the variability of human beings, there is only one human race, and the differences we experience among ourselves dwindle almost to insignificance when we compare ourselves to other forms of life. But if we are one human race, we are a plastic and variable one. It has been suggested the more we go up the evolutionary ladder, the more intraspecies variability increases. And the bulk of the differences between people are not the differences that exist between one race and another, but those that exist all around us in our families and friends and local communities. (B.D.H. Latter). Finally, it would be futile to continually try to categorize this journey into the world of typology in terms of nature or nurture even when we are stressing one or the other. They always go together. We are being effected by our environment from the instant of our conception, but at the same time we are very definite someones who are being effected. Inversely, our distinctive individual nature has an infinity of developmental pathways it can follow, but it is inclined or predisposed to follow certain ones rather than others.

This world of typology is so extensive that there are other whole journeys to take besides the one on which we are about to embark. We could, for example, explore the historical roots of typology which stretch back thousands of years, or devote our time principally to the factor analytic school. Instead, although we will cross some of these paths as we proceed, our main energies will be concentrated on the typologies of Jung and Sheldon, their integration and its implications, and the biochemical typology of the future.

PART I

C.G. JUNG'S
PSYCHOLOGICAL TYPES

CHAPTER 1
THE ORIGINS OF
PSYCHOLOGICAL TYPES

When Jung's **Psychological Types,** stretching nearly 500 pages, first appeared in 1921, it seemed to emerge from nowhere. It was a disconcerting volume that concealed as much as it revealed about the new Jung, or at least that's how it appeared on the surface. Jung had been relatively silent since 1913, and now this: an involuted dissertation on Tertullian and Origen, the problem of universals, ancient debates over Holy Communion, etc. What did it all really mean to Jung? Tracing its origins will give us some clues. Its remote roots were in his word-association tests. In 1904 he had set up a laboratory in Burghölzli, the mental hospital where he was working under the direction of Eugen Bleuler, and proceeded to measure the reactions of patients to different words with something like an early forerunner of the lie detectors of today. He noticed that their answers could be sorted into two large groups, one of which he called "egocentric" and the other "impersonal". And while he initially related them to the psychiatric classifications of hysteria and schizophrenia, he soon

saw that they had a wider application in the field
of normal psychology, and they were related to what
William James had called the "tough-minded" and the
"tender-minded". It was Jung's work with these word-
association experiments that helped create his reputation in America and led to his invitation by Stanley
Hall, together with Freud and some of the other
early psychoanalysts, to talk at Clark University in
Worcester, Massachusetts, in 1909.

In 1911 he wrote of two kinds of thinking in his
Transformation and Symbols of the Libido. And all
during this time his thought was diverging further and
further from that of Freud's, and the tension between
them was increasing. It was in Munich in 1912 that
the famous incident of Freud fainting took place during a discussion about the theme of the death of the
father, and it was again in Munich the next year
that we find the formal beginnings of typology when
Jung delivered a paper to the 4th International Psychoanalytic Congress entitled, "A Contribution to the
Study of Psychological Types". This paper is a microcosm of much of what was to appear in expanded
form in **Psychological Types.** It describes the nature
of extraversion and introversion, and the need of psychology to take into account these distinctly different viewpoints. The "hysteric" exhibits exaggerated
emotivity, while the "schizophrenic" shows extreme
apathy. But Jung does not restrict the application of
these attitudes to pathology. His attention is drawn
more and more to the role they play in normal psychology. He is already amassing his amplifications of
how introversion and extraversion under various guises
appeared in the past, amplifications that were to fill
so much of his **Psychological Types.** He cites William
James at length and goes on to examine poetry,
language and psychiatry in the work of Schiller, Nietzsche, Worringer and Gross. Then he takes the bull
by the horns and boldly announces in the presence
of Freud that Freud's work represents an extraverted

psychoanalysis, while Adler's is an introverted one. And he concludes with a line that can be taken as an embryonic program for his own psychology:

"The difficult task of creating a psychology which will be equally fair to both types must be reserved for the future." (**Collected Works,** Vol. 6, n. 882, p. 509).

Just what this means he has hinted at in the body of his paper several times. The first time occurs when he is discussing the hysteric and the schizophrenic. The hysteric's exaggerated outward flow of energy is compensated by a regressive introversion: "The patients cease to partake in the common life, are wrapped up in their daydreams, keep to their beds, remain shut up in their sickrooms, etc." (859/ 500).

The schizophrenic, in his turn, exhibits his own peculiar kind of extraversion: "...he seems constrained to draw attention to himself, to force himself upon the notice of those around him, by his extravagant, insupportable, or directly aggressive behavior." (859/ 500)

What he is suggesting is that both introversion and extraversion are intimately connected in the individual in one energetic system. This becomes clear when he is describing Schiller's two kinds of poets. There is the "naive" extraverted poet who is contrasted with the "sentimental" introverted poet, and he adds: "But Schiller also saw that these two types result from the predominance of psychological mechanisms which might be present in the same individual." (875/506)

This manifesto of independence couched in typological form represented the beginning of Jung's open break with Freud. It could not be published in German in the normal psychoanalytic circles and after the Congress at Munich, Freud and Jung never met again.

Later, in the fall of this fateful year of 1913 Jung asked himself, "What is your myth by which you live?" And he had no answer. He stopped lecturing at the University of Zurich in order to focus his attention on this question, and he leaves us the exact date of Dec. 12, 1913, when he gathered up his courage and took the decisive step down into the inner world of the unconscious on a voyage of self-discovery. He was 38 years old and this adventure was to last until 1918-19. Jung was going through what he was later to call the process of individuation, and he was going through it alone without chart or guide. He was travelling towards the self. He had painted his first mandala in 1916, but he had not understood it. It was not until 1918-19 that he began to grasp the central meaning of the self. He says,

"During those years between 1918 and 1920 I began to understand the goal of psychic development is the self...This insight gave me stability and gradually my inner peace returned. I knew that in finding the mandala as an expression of the self I had attained what was for me the ultimate." (1961, p. 196-7)

But what particularly interests us here is not the individuation process directly, which was to so dominate Jung's later thought, but the fact that this process of individuation was directly connected with Jung's formation of his typology. There are two interwoven strands that gave birth to **Psychological Types.** One was interpersonal, as for example when Jung attempted to distinguish his own point of view from that of Freud and Adler, and the other was intrapsychic, or personal, when he confronted the unconscious. And in Jung's mind they were both connected. He did not want to simply add a third position to Freud's and Adler's, but effect a reconciliation. The differences that existed as typical differences manifested in individuals existed within himself, and needed to be reconciled there. In the next

few years Jung worked on the structure of his typology by striking out on the voyage of individuation,
dealing with his patients, and collaborating with his
colleagues. C.A. Meier in his seminal paper, "Psychological Types and Individuation", describes this outer
collaboration:

"In many a paper read to the Psychological Club
in Zurich and subsequent discussions with his friends,
colleagues and pupils, Jung's concept was clarified
step by step. It was particularly Dr. Hans Schmid-
Guisan who made it clear to Jung that extraversion
was not of necessity correlated to feeling as he had
originally been advocating, and Toni Wolff was highly
instrumental in introducing sensation and intuition as
two indispensable orienting functions of consciousness.
In particular, intuition was dealt with more critically
in those days by Dr. Emil Medtner." (p. 278)

The correspondence between Schmid, a Swiss psychiatrist, and Jung during 1915-16, which had been
excluded from Jung's published letters, later appeared
in a book by Hans Iselin. Despite their attempts,
Jung and Schmid, who considered himself an extravert, could not overcome their typological differences. In one place Schmid says, "Without the object
I cannot develop myself." And he cites Goethe in his
support: "With all striving after self-knowledge...we
do not go further in life." (p. 140) By calling Goethe
to his aid he anticipates a theme which was to
appear in **Psychological Types** itself, as we shall see.
After their relationship became deadlocked and their
correspondence was about to cease, he wrote to
Jung: "In a tower on the upper lake you sit and have
taken Nietzsche's inheritance. No father, no friend,
you, yourself, sufficient." (p. 141)

This break with Schmid, following the loss of his
relationship with Freud and most of his psychoanalytic colleagues recalls Jung's remark, as Iselin notes,
that after his break with Freud all his friends and
acquaintances fell away. Even during his emergence

from his confrontation with the unconscious, he broke with a woman, whom he leaves unnamed, who was determined that he should give these interior fantasies an artistic meaning.

When the massive volume of **Psychological Types** appeared, it was, then, hardly a question of a miraculous birth. **Psychological Types** represented the compass that Jung was fashioning as he went on the process of individuation, and it is the first major crystallization out of the fiery magma of his journey into the unconscious. Therefore, it is not surprising to find that there is a chapter where he defines his basic terms, nor to find one of the first uses of the term "the self". When H.G. Baynes translated the book into English in 1923 bearing the subtitle "The Psychology of Individuation", this was no exaggeration. In fact, the subtitle had been suggested by Jung himself. The point here is not to get lost in a thicket of historical details, but for us to concretely grasp a point of overriding importance. Typology was always in its very inception and development intimately connected with individuation. It is a certain visibility of the individuation process, a view of individuation from the point of view of the psychology of consciousness, and if we fail to grasp this it loses its real depth of meaning.

Let's take a closer look at the book itself. There is no escaping the fact that for most readers the book divides itself into two parts. There is Chapter X, the general description of types, and then there is the rest, honored more in the breach than actually read. And this kind of division is very understandable, for Chapter X is much more accessible than the rest of the book. But this is a fact that always upset Jung. He says, for example, in the "Forward to the Argentine Edition" that the reader who really wants to understand his book should: "Immerse himself first of all in chapters II and V" and "Far too many readers have succumbed to the error of thinking that Chapter X represents the essential content and purpose of the book in the sense that it provides a system of classification and a practical guide to a good judgment of human character."

The import of these remarks will only become clear if we bear in mind the intimate relationship between typology and individuation and spend a few moments looking at these chapters that Jung laid so much emphasis on. In Chapter I Jung had shown how introversion and extraversion had existed in ancient and medieval times. But Chapter II is different. It is an examination of the dynamics that connect the superior and inferior functions, and Jung does this by describing Schiller, an introverted thinking type, and his psychological counterpart, Goethe, an extraverted feeling type, and these were not merely handy literary examples used to dress up the "typical conflict of the introverted thinking type". Rather, they were Jung's alter-egos, the way he could impersonally describe the process of individuation he had been going through. He felt he was, himself, an introverted thinking type, and Goethe played and was to play a large role in Jung's inner drama both as the author of **Faust** and as a putative ancestor which symbolized, in Jung's mind, not so much a connection of flesh and blood, but a deep symbolic link to the unconscious. So when Jung says the reader should turn to Chapter II, he is saying, in essence, typology is not a classification of the visible consciousness of a person, but it is a way to explore the inner dynamics of the psyche, and he is also saying, "What I am speaking of here is derived from my own experience." If Jung was an introverted thinking type, this would help explain his earlier identification of introversion and thinking and extraversion and feeling, and it would also help explain why it would be extremely difficult for Jung to express this process of individuation except in a veiled manner, for Jung was really exposing his greatest discovery, the process of individuation, and along with it his emergent extraverted feeling and all the sensitivity that must have existed with this function. In Chapter V he is again describing the interrelationship between conscious and unconscious that will ultimately lead to the self. And, again, he does so in highly involuted and difficult language, but the message is there, and it is rooted not in deductions made academically from literary works, but in his own experience of the process. If this does not come across clearly in the text, it is certainly clear in Chapter X, and Jung tries to make it explicit at the very beginning in the "Forward to the First Swiss Edition":

"This book is the fruit of nearly twenty years' work in the domain of practical psychology. It grew gradually in my thoughts, taking shape from the countless impressions and experiences of a psychiatrist in the treatment of nervous illnesses, from the intercourse with men and women of all social levels, from my personal dealings with friend and foe alike, and finally from a critique of my own psychological peculiarity." (1921, p. xi)

This personal psychological peculiarity is in part Jung's own type, and the emergence of his extraverted feeling. This is why the intellectual thinking ramparts of the book tower so high, as if to protect the delicacy of this new birth, which is not only the inferior function with all its sensitiveness, but the inferior function as the gateway to individuation and the self. Under these conditions Jung must have certainly wished for a warm reception for this newborn child being presented to the public for the first time in his **Psychological Types.** What he got instead was summed up by Spittler's reaction, whose **Prometheus and Epimetheus** featured largely in what Jung felt to be a critical chapter, "The Type Problem in Poetry". Jung writes in **Memories, Dreams, Reflections:**

"I was presumptuous enough to send a copy of my

book to Spittler. He did not answer me, but shortly afterward delivered a lecture in which he declared positively that this **Prometheus and Epimetheus** 'meant' nothing, that he might just as well have sung 'Spring is come, tra-la-la-la.'" (p. 207)

It would not be surprising if Spittler, himself, was a fourth-function feeler, and just as Jung had honed in on Schiller because there was a certain coincidence of typological perspective, he might have penetrated into the psychological background of Spittler's work for the same reason, but in doing so set off a reaction from Spittler's unconscious.

In the medical world Jung felt unjustly accused of having invented psychological types as a kind of intellectual parlor game, and then using it to stick superficial labels on people. This continued to bother him for a long time. Fourteen years later he says:

"...it is not the case at all that I begin by classifying my patients into types and then give them the corresponding advice as a colleague of mine whom God has endowed with a peculiar wit once asserted." (**Letters**, v. I, p. 186)

When he sees his own journey to individuation trivialized by such an accusation and the whole inner meaning of types destroyed, he seems to say, "Let these people go crack their heads on Chapters II and V. That, if it won't cure them, might at least silence them."

There were exceptions to the indifferent or hostile reception of Jung's book. C.A. Meier says:

"When I read the book on types in 1922, it simply hit me between the eyes. It had such an impact that I could not help telling Jung immediately. He could hardly understand my reaction, for so far all the reviews of the book had been more than cool and totally lacking a deeper understanding. When he asked me what it was that had moved me so deeply, I said I thought that he had given nothing less than the clearest pattern for simply all the **dynamics** of the

human soul. Then he said that this was exactly what
he had intended to do, but so far nobody seemed to
have noticed." (p. 278-9)

All this helps make it clear why Jung did not
spend a great deal of energy developing the typological aspects of his thought further. He at once was
pursuing typology by exploring individuation, and at
the same time he was deterred from explicitly developing typology because it was so prone to misinter-
pretation, and the initial lesson, **Psychological Types**
itself, had not been adequately fathomed.

In 1937, writing in the "Forward to the Seventh
Swiss Edition", he says: "In particular the somewhat
terse descriptions of the types could have been expanded." But among his reasons for not doing so he
states, "...there is little practical purpose in making
the problems of typology still more complicated when
not even the elements have been properly understood." Elements in this context should not be understood in terms of the basic descriptions of introversion and extraversion and the four functions, but how
these elements combine in a dynamic view of the
psyche, which is no different from the process of individuation itself. Jung goes on and vents some of
his irritation at the superficial criticisms leveled at
his work, which failed to see how typology has not
been imposed on empirical material, but has emerged
out of it:

"What I have to say in this book, therefore, has,
sentence by sentence, been tested a hundredfold in
the practical treatment of the sick and originated
with them in the first place." And he scolds his critics for a lack of experience which is at the root
of their failure to understand what he was saying.

It is possible to imagine that this mixed reception
together with the difficulty that exists in grasping
the dynamic nature of typology made Jung, himself,
give up on his own typology. That this is untrue can
be demonstrated by a brief examination of his writings. Jung wrote three subsequent essays on psycholo-

gical types in the years 1923, 1931 and 1936. And these essays are not at all apologetic or merely derivative. In them Jung considers the matter of typology, finds it as valuable as ever, but open to misunderstanding. For example, in his 1931 essay, delivered first at a congress of Swiss psychiatrists in Zurich in 1928, he remarks on the many years in which he had treated innumerable married couples trying to explain their typical differences to them, and he goes on to recount how he was led to go beyond his initial formulations of introversion and extraversion. Certainly this is not a setting that Jung would have chosen to talk about psychological types if he had become hesitant and doubtful about them. He writes: "...scarcely had I published the first formulation of my criteria when I discovered to my dismay that somehow or other I had been taken in by them. Something was amiss. I had tried to explain too much in too simple a way, as often happens in the first joy of discovery.

"What struck me now was the undeniable fact while people may be classed as introverts or extraverts, this does not account for the tremendous differences between individuals in either class. So great, indeed, are these differences that I was forced to doubt whether I had observed correctly in the first place. It took nearly ten years of observation and comparison to clear up this doubt." (p. 535)

Types appear in his **Psychology of the Transference** (1946), and elsewhere throughout his writings. Even in 1957, towards the end of his life, we have a good example of his attitude about psychological types in his conversations with Richard Evans recorded in the Houston films. Jung discussed typology at length and, indeed, this is one of the principle topics of these filmed interviews. For example, he amplified how he differentiated the various functions: "...it took me quite a long time to discover that there is another type than the thinking type...There are, for in-

stance, feeling types. And after a while I discovered
that there are intuitive types. They gave me much
trouble. It took me over a year to become a bit
clearer about the existence of intuitive types. And
the last, and the most unexpected, was the sensation
type. And only later I saw that these are naturally
the four aspects of conscious orientation." (p. 341)
In short, Jung could honestly say about psychological
types: "but one thing I must confess: I would not for
anything dispense with this compass on my psychological voyages of discovery." (V. 6, p. 541)

Psychological Types, despite its initial reception,
went on to become one of Jung's most popular
books, especially in its English version. It was eventually translated into Dutch, French, Greek, Italian,
Japanese, Portuguese, Russian, Spanish and Swedish.
Something was getting through, and perhaps it was
the flavor of the experiences that Jung had built his
types upon, which gave promise to the reader that
he would actually be able to make sense of his own
life.

CHAPTER 2
THE USE OF
PSYCHOLOGICAL TYPES

With the publication of **Psychological Types** the terms introversion and extraversion came into general use and the book found three distinct audiences.

First, non-Jungian psychologists attempted to create written instruments to measure introversion and extraversion (while they ignored the four functions): Freyd (1924), Heidbreder (1926), Conklin (1923), Guthrie (1927), Campbell (1929), Ball (1932), etc. J.A. Browne has called this the early metric stage which was then followed by the more advanced metric stage of factor studies by Guilford, Cattell and Eysenck. This level has, in its turn, been superseded by what we may call the supermetric in which enormously complex analyses of questionnaires yield matrixes of 300 x 300 or 600 x 600 items which demand the use of sophisticated computers. This is a current of thought we will encounter only in passing.

The second audience for psychological types is in the circle of Jungian analysts. For example, Beatrice Hinkle, one of the first New York Jungians who had introduced Jung to America apart from Freud by translating his **Transformations and Symbols of the Libido,** described what she called objective, simple and subjective introverts and extraverts in her 1923, **The Recreating of the Individual:** A Study of Psychological Types and Their Relation to Wholeness. (Henderson, p. 11) Another early Jungian analyst in the United States, James Oppenheim, wrote a book which

appeared in 1931 entitled, **American Types.** It tried
to put types in an American perspective and made
an attempt to develop a physiognomy of the types
based on an equation of facial features with the various Jungian types.

The third audience were the creators and users
of distinctively Jungian psychological type tests. And
it is these last two groups that we will examine in
this chapter.

Typology in Professional Jungian Circles

It would be easy to assume that the process of
becoming a Jungian analyst would, by itself, produce
a typological expert. This is not the case. It could,
and does so in some instances, but it does not have
to. Individuation seen from the point of view of the
collective unconscious is not identical with individuation seen from the perspective of the different kinds
of consciousnesses. The experience of one does not
automatically confer the experience of the other,
though the training that the analyst undergoes could
easily blossom into a penetrating typological understanding.

In 1972 Plaut reported on the results of a survey
of 173 analysts. He found that about half (53%) of
the analysts found typology helpful in their analytic
practice, and this total was arrived at by combining
those who thought it often helpful with those who
thought it was sometimes helpful. Three-quarters of
the analysts were confident of their type, and three-
quarters thought it important in general psychology.
These results confirm the fact that typology and the
actual experience of analytical psychology are not
identical, and they can also be interpreted to mean
that since a greater number of analysts saw a role
for types in general psychology than saw one in their
own practice, there is something or some things in
the analytical process that discouraged the use of

typology. There are a number of possibilities of what these things might be:

1. Types have an easy affinity for explaining interpersonal relationships, while most analytic work is directed to the individual.

2. Creativity and neurosis, both common in those being analyzed, and both bringing up material from all parts of the psyche, make type recognition more difficult. If types have an affinity for interpersonal relationships, they also have a certain predilection for normalcy.

3. Types cannot be employed unless they are learned, and training analyses and the various lectures of the training program may or may not contain type material.

4. It is extremely difficult to understand types intrapsychically and explore their continuing relationship with the process of individuation. Even though Jung had to work out typology as his compass on the voyage of individuation, he did not spend much energy illustrating how situations within analysis could be understood typologically.

It is this last point that is critical for the future use of typology in analysis. Meier clearly presents the issue when, following one of Jung's early seminars, he draws a typological diagram in which both analyst and analysand are represented as circles or typological mandalas. He feels that it is important that the analyst be able to rotate his typological mandala "so as to produce a tension of opposites with regard to the system of the analysand, so that something really can happen and things can really be constellated and problems can really come to a head." ("Psychological Types and Individuation", p. 282-3) In this way he brings to life within the analytical situation his statement: "Individuation begins and ends with typology." (p. 276)

These perceptive comments of Meier were taken up by C.J. Groesbeck and combined with other indi-

cations in Jungian literature and given a more detailed and thorough development in his "Psychological
Types in the Analysis of the Transference". This
paper represents one of the most penetrating explan-
ations of the dynamic nature of typology. Groesbeck
carefully examines **Psychological Types,** especially
Chapter II, and explores its implications by using
types as a guide to the "vicissitudes of the transference on the way to individuation." (p. 31)

"Via types, one has available a virtually forgotten
compass to indicate what is happening within the
patient, between patient and analyst, and within the
analyst in the moment-to-moment, session-to-session
progress of analysis." (p. 30)

He demonstrates what this "analytical psychotypo-
logy" is in the concrete by taking up the diagram
used by Meier, and before him by Jung, and using
it to explain actual case material. In this way it
becomes much more comprehensible why certain projections take place, what the most promising pathway
to development is, and even what the strengths and
weaknesses of the analyst are in relationship to this
particular patient. Instead of seeing the analyst's particular typological weakness as a defect to be hidden, Groesbeck sees it as a golden opportunity for
both the analyst and the analysand:

"Could it be that in precisely acknowledging the
failure of the analysis, the door to the inferior functions can be opened to the archetypal levels of the
psyche and the symbol of the inner healer can be
constellated out of the uniting of the inferior functions of both analyst and patient?" (p. 41-2)

The dynamic role of the inferior function as the
gateway to the unconscious and the self is seen in
relationship to both analyst and analysand, and it is
out of the union of their inferior functions that can
come the fifth or transcendent function in which the
former typological struggles can be resolved. In this
connection he quotes Jung to point out that the

transcendent function is not to be understood as "a basic function but as a complex function made up of other functions" (p. 42), and demonstrates how the inferior functions unite by undertaking the extensive analysis of an actual case. This is a view of the actual working of the inferior function that we should keep in mind when we later come across the question of bi-polarity.

Another good example of types taken dynamically and within analysis can be seen in John Beebe's "Psychological Types in Transference, Countertransference and the Therapeutic Interaction", which we will look at in the next chapter. Unfortunately, typological work within analysis is all too rare and much more attention should be paid to it within Jungian circles.

Type Diagnosis

This short excursion into typology within analysis, far from being esoteric, is an ideal preparation for examining the most practical of all questions in typology, that of type diagnosis. How can I determine my own or someone else's type? Types viewed from the point of view of individuation give us a better idea of the complexity of the meeting of two typological beings. When I meet you I receive a highly complicated mass of impressions. I don't just see the superior function and its attitude, but rather, I am receiving many messages simultaneously and I must find some way of organizing them. I am picking up information about all the functions and both attitudes and their respective states of development, and I am receiving this information in its concrete embodiment in individual words and events. It is from this matrix that I must abstract my typological perceptions. Typology does not relieve me of the need to be in direct contact with the individual. Far from it. It is a guide or compass in making sense of the individual impressions I receive. I don't impose it on the material, but I use it to organize the material that is already present. This is what Jung was insisting upon in his various Forwards to **Psychological Types.** And much too often we underestimate the complexity of this material. I see your functions and attitudes and their state of development, but also the influence of your parents, education, the society you live in, the kind of work you do, the degree of your overall psychic integration, and the winds of your creativity in this moment, and habitually, which allow you, or even compel you, to show different sides of your personality.

But even this is a simplification, for I am only considering you and not myself. It would be more accurate to say the level of complexity must be doubled. Each impression I receive from you can be directed to various aspects of my own personality and provoke responses that condition my reception depending on my own type and its development, as well as its proclivities for projection, etc. Thus, Jung insists that without an understanding of my own personal equation I will scramble the messages and confuse what you are like with the way I imagine you to be. We could even try to describe the situation at a third level of complexity in which your words and actions provoke responses in me which, in turn, make you modify how you are relating to me, which, in turn, effects my reactions, and so forth and so on. But enough has been said to form the necessary backdrop against which to view the whole question of type diagnosis. It is also interesting to realize that over the years when Jung received letters about the question of types, he would insist, almost perversely at times, on their complexity. And this tendency came, I think, from his own keen understanding of how complex the whole matter is and how superficial some of our uses of typology have been.

The complexity of type can help us understand, for example, why we can type some people almost immediately and have our estimate confirmed by extensive contact, and then turn around and draw a complete blank with other people, or actually mistype them. We have our particular blind spots, and the people who we are typing can be setting off projections in us that effectively overwhelm the other impressions that we may be receiving about them. Or these people may be relatively undifferentiated or neurotic, and bewilder us with their perplexing barrage of material. Sometimes we make mistakes about those closest to us, or even ourselves, precisely because we are receiving material from all parts of the personality, and have not been able to adequately integrate it. The complexity of type precludes any easy solution to the question of type diagnosis. It would be nice to be able to appeal to the diagnostic powers of the Jungian analyst, but as we have seen, typological knowledge, especially in the practical order, is not identical with an understanding of the process of individuation. A. Plaut makes this clear in a description of his own tribulations:

"My former analyst thought that I could either be an intuitive-feeling type or possibly a thinking-sensation type. Before I filled in my questionnaire, I had been diagnosed by one highly intuitive senior colleague as a sensation type. Another senior analyst told me that I was a thinking type. (Could it be that the inferior function easily appears in the form of shadow projections, thus clouding our clinical judgments?) A third colleague thought that I was an intuitive-thinking type. Being therefore uncertain I did the Gray-Wheelwright test and came out as 'intuitive-thinking' (introvert). The Myers-Briggs Type Indicator, scored by a colleague, turned up quite unequivocally: INFP (introverted feeling perceptive with intuition, for short: introverted, feeling-intuition). As I dare not assume that I am fully integrated, I still prefer to rate myself as 'not sufficiently confident'. ("Analytical Psychologists and Psychological Types", p. 144)

It is this kind of diagnostic deadlock that has played a role in the creation of type tests and in attempts to put the whole issue of human differences on what would appear to be more secure scientific foundations. This brings us to our third audience for Jung's **Psychological Types,** the type test creators and users. And it is important to realize that the country we are entering differs from the analyst's consulting room. It belongs to another watershed. And this fact will become more and more apparent as we go on.

Psychological Type Tests

There are three major type tests that attempt to determine both attitude and function: the Gray-Wheelwright, the Myers-Briggs and the Singer-Loomis. (There are also experimental tests developed by Detloff, and Kingsbury and Skinner, etc.)

The Gray-Wheelwright

This test was developed by Joseph Wheelwright and Horace Gray. Wheelwright, one of the original San Francisco Jungians, had been initially attracted to Jungian psychology by typology, for he saw how useful it had been in his own marriage. He describes the origin of the test:

"Now, this type-test that I mentioned is a thing that Horace Gray and I spent a very long time working on during the war. And we involved Janie and, to a lesser extent, Joe Henderson in our struggles. Gray and I were actually perfect for the job, because I was an extraverted-intuitive-feeling type, and he was an introverted-sensation-thinking type; we figured that between us, we added up to one and we ought to be able to do it. So, we sat around, dreaming up questions. Feeling that charity began at home, the questions arose from our own conditions, as it were; then they were subjected to all kinds of testing out on people that had already been diagnosed clinically. Horace, who was a good mathematician, had stumbled on something that scientists seem to think a great deal of, called chi-square. This always made me very nervous, I don't know what chi-square means, and I'm determined that I never shall know. But he used it all the time, which apparently made the questions quite respectable." ("Psychological Types", p. 3)

All the participants in the creation of this test were Jungian analysts, and since it first appeared in 1944 it has gone through a series of revisions. The 15th of these revisions consists of 81 questions, all arranged in a forced-choice format where the test-taker must choose between extraversion and introversion, thinking and feeling, and sensation and intuition.

The initial use of the test generated a series of articles by Horace Gray, some of which were co-authored by Joseph Wheelwright. In "Jung's Psychological Types, Their Frequency of Occurrence", Gray and Wheelwright review some of the data generated by early questionnaires that had been developed to test introversion and extraversion. And then they look at the results of the first 200 people to take their own test, and find that introversion outweighs extraversion 54% to 46%. In "Jung's Psychological Types in Relation to Occupation, Race and Body Build", Gray describes their motivation in creating the test and how it should be employed.

"The difficulties found by many in classifying individuals, even with the aid of his stout volume on psychological types, led us three years ago to devise a questionnaire covering all three aspects: attitude, perception, judgment. Trials and errors have led to repeated revisions, and even after a dozen such, more must follow. A questionnaire makes no pretense of replacing psychiatric interviews, much less any deeper psychological analysis, but it is a device for diagnosis." (p. 100)

With 1,000 test results in hand, they again found

introversion 54% and extraversion 46%. Their results on the relationship between physical type and psychological type will occupy us later.

In "Jung's Psychological Types and Marriage" they studied 60 couples and found that 33% of them differed on all three measures, that is, extraversion-introversion, thinking-feeling and sensation-intuition. 30% differed in 2 measures, 27% in one, and 10% were alike in all three. They also plotted an intriguing balance:

"...if one partner is extremely marked for feeling-valuations, the other partner is not merely on the thinking side, but is near its extreme. Or, if one is moderately feeling, the other is apt to be only moderately thinking. The same balancing was found for introversion vs. extraversion, and for sensation vs. intuition; ...This choice of spouse, with amazingly quantitative strength of complement, must, in consequence of popular ignorance of this phenomenon, be unconscious." (p. 38-9)

In "Jung's Psychological Types: Ambiguous Scores and Their Interpretation", various difficulties in administering the test and interpreting their results are examined. True to his statement that the tests do not stand alone, Gray places them in a wider context. For example, the test results of 62 people are compared with evaluating interviews presumably given by Gray and Wheelwright themselves. In 52% of the cases all three basic judgments agree, leaving 48% in which there is a disagreement in one or more areas. The biggest discrepancy was in the area of introversion and extraversion. When exploring how answers on one of the measures can effect another, Gray describes extraverts who, when asked "How many friends do you have?", answer, "Few", if their thinking function is strong. And he describes introverts who talk so profusely that they give the impression of extraversion. Both of these keen observations demonstrate the amount of clinical experience that was the foundation for the test.

The Gray-Wheelwright test has been subjected to a factor-analytic evaluation by Baumann, Angst, Henne and Muser, who concluded that the extraversion-introversion scale was the most reliable, followed by the intuition-sensation, with the thinking-feeling faring poorly.

Mary Ann Mattoon in her **Jungian Psychology in Perspective** summarizes some other studies evaluating the Gray-Wheelwright. These include a split-half reliability study, another that relied on test-retest and validity against the criterion of self-typing, and studies by Bradway, and Bradway and Detloff, who compared the self-typing of Jungian analysts with their results on the Gray-Wheelwright Test. These last two studies will engage our attention later.

The Myers-Briggs Type Indicator

This is the most widely used of the full Jungian type tests, with a million answer sheets distributed by the end of 1979. It has appeared in various formats. Form F, for example, contains 166 questions, all of which are forced-choice and which include a number of word pairs, for example, which word would appeal to you more: active or intellectual? Once again the test had its origin in the practical circumstances of the test creator's marriage. When Isabel Briggs-Myers brought her prospective husband home, her mother, Katharine Briggs, concluded he was not like the other members of the family.

"She embarked on a project of reading biographies, and developed her own typology based on patterns she found. She identified meditative types, spontaneous types, executive types and sociable types (later identified in the MBTI as the I's, the EP's, the ETJ's and the EFJ's). When Katharine Briggs discovered C.G. Jung's book, **Psychological Types**, she reported to her daughter, "This is **it!**" and proceeded to study the book intensely. Mother and daughter became avid "type watchers" over the next twenty years." (MBTI News, Vol. 2, No. 4, p. 2)

From these beginnings the test slowly evolved over the course of 40 years, with Myers testing thousands of school children, and medical students. In 1962 Educational Testing Services published a research version. In 1975 Consulting Psychologist Press brought out a version for general use, and it has spread widely since then. In the 1970s Isabel Myers worked with Mary McCaulley developing a Center for Applications of Psychological Type with its library, data bank, publications, and a mailing list of over 16,000 names. The Association for Psychological Types now has over 2,000 members in 10 countries. It is involved in publishing the Bulletin of Psychological Types and the Journal of Psychological Types, holds national MBTI conferences, and so forth.

There has been an ever growing amount of literature about the use of this test. Let's pause for a moment and examine some examples of it to get its flavor.

James Hart, addressing himself to the question, "Are theoretical and methodological orientation an expression of psychology majors' personalities?", gave the MBTI and the theoretical orientation survey to 181 junior and senior psychology majors. He found that an objective orientation was related to high scores in extraversion, sensing, thinking and judging, while high scores in their opposites indicated a subjective orientation.

Alida Westman and Francis Canter in "Relationship Between Certain Circadian Behavior Patterns and Jungian Personality Types" had 24 adults rate themselves every two hours during the day on physical activity, concentration, and sociability, and gave these people the MBTI. Extraverts reported becoming more sociable from approximately 10 a.m. to noon to 2 p.m. and decreasing in their ability to concentrate between noon and 2 p.m. when they reported feeling happy, sociable and more relaxed.

In a more ambitious study John Ross compared the four scales of the MBTI with a battery of 32 different tests in 571 high school students. The first and most obvious factor that he derived, he felt, was one of general ability most manifest in a vocabulary test and also present negatively in the sensation-intuition scale. In another form of analysis he related liking to think with ENTJ, business information with ENTP, and gregariousness with ESFP.

In "Studies of Jungian Typology II: Representations of the Personal World" Rae Carlson, building on earlier work that found type differences in the performance of tasks involving short-term memory, the judgment of facial expressions and volunteer service, found: 1. the introverted thinking type and the extraverted feeling type differ in the quality of their affective memory; 2. thinking and feeling types differ in their emphasis on cognitive clarity vs. vividness of feeling; 3. sensation and intuitive types differ in their styles of self-description offered to an imagined foreign correspondent. In the last case the intuitives made direct or indirect references to the imagined other, while the sensing types introduced themselves in terms of their physical appearance.

James Witzig in "Jung's Typology and Classification of the Psychotherapies" tested 102 public health workers in such a way as to generate information about their own type preferences and how they would assign different hypothetical clients to different kinds of therapy. His questionnaire was based on items from the MBTI and generated results that supported his typological classification of therapies. In this classification:

"The individual approach is regarded as introversive and the group modality as extraversive. Psychotherapies are additionally classified according to function type: Thinking = Informational cognitive -

includes educational, psychanalytic, transactional and rational-emotive therapies; Intuition = Symbolic/intuitive - includes Jungian analysis, transcendental meditation and phantasy dominated procedures; Sensation = Sensory/experiential - includes Gestalt, bio-energetic, behavior modification, and most occupational therapies; Feeling = Confrontational/conative - includes psychodrama, client-centred and encounter methods." (p. 329)

Mattoon, in her **Jungian Psychology in Perspective,** concisely summarizes any number of studies which employ the MBTI. They include: changes in introversion and extraversion with age, whether friends are more similar or dissimilar in type, what types tend to marry each other, and how different types react in groups.

She also summarizes a number of studies that compare the MBTI with other introversion-extraversion tests, do split-half correlations, and other sorts of testing of the test similar to but more extensive to those that have accumulated around the Gray-Wheelwright Test.

A study by Stricker and Ross, "An Assessment of Some Structural Properties of the Jungian Personality Typology", turned up basically negative results when it found that the indicator scores did not have bimodal distributions and lacked other statistical attributes that they would have expected to accompany the existence of dichotomist types. The new edition of the MBTI manual, **A Guide to the Development and Use of the Myers-Briggs Type Indicator,** 1985, presents extensive information on attempts to test the validity of the MBTI.

The manual provides extensive comparisons between the MBTI and many other inventories including the Eysenck Personality Questionnaires, the Jungian Type Survey, the 16 Personality Factor Questionnaire (16 PF), Allport, Vernon and Lindsay's Study of Values, and the Strong-Campbell Interest Inventory. The

MBTI has found extensive use in school and business settings. (Moore, Keirsey and Bates, Lawrence, etc.)

This small sampling is dwarfed by the CAPT printout of MBTI studies which, when last I looked, contained over 1,100 items. Gille-Maisani briefly reviews dozens of studies on extraversion and introversion and psychological types in his **Types de Jung et tempéraments psychobiologiques.**

The Singer-Loomis Inventory of Personality

This is the work of two Jungian analysts, June Singer and Mary Loomis. It is not only the newest of the tests, but it is structured differently, for it does not make the assumption that the three measures of extraversion-introversion, thinking-feeling and sensation-intuition must be opposed to each other. The experimental edition has 120 questions grouped around 15 situations, and each question can be answered on a scale from 1 (never) to 5 (always). Situation 1, for example, states: "I have a free day coming up this week and will be able to do whatever I want. I would..." and then proceeds to name 8 possibilities, each to be answered on a scale from 1 to 5.

The 8 psychological types are viewed as independent cognitive modes, and the test attempts to measure their relative development in the individual. Since one type of development is not assumed to exclude another, the manual describes people with, for example, both introverted intuition and extraverted sensation highly developed. We will return to the question of bi-polarity when we look at new developments in the field of Jungian typology.

The development of these type tests and their application demonstrate the outward trajectory that **Psychological Types** has been following since its publication. The tests have arisen in large part in response to the diagnostic question, and they have

given prominence to the interpersonal nature of types
and brought Jung's ideas into the realm of the experimental psychologists.

Interpersonal Nature of Types

Outside professional Jungian circles it is clear
that the interpersonal nature of types holds center
stage, and there is no question that this kind of
development is legitimate. We have seen the interpersonal interactions that helped Jung formulate his
typology, and he, himself, used them to help explain
to his patients their family conflicts. Typology is
finding a fertile field of application in everything
from marriage counseling to vocational guidance, and
more people are probably being introduced to Jungian
psychology through typology, especially in the form
of type tests, than in any other way. Types are
ideally formulated for dealing with normal people who
will never see the inside of an analyst's office, but
are in dire need of some way to make sense of the
relationships they are involved in.

As positive as the development of this aspect of
typology is, and despite the enthusiastic reception it
is receiving in many quarters, it is important to look
beyond these new and exciting beginnings and try to
discern potential storm clouds forming on the far
horizon.

The first of these dangers is that the stress on
the interpersonal nature of types will make us lose
sight of, or never realize, the full meaning of the
intrapsychic nature of typology, which is the process
of individuation itself. We can discover our type and
be so caught up in discovering the types of those
around us and unraveling the implications of these
type differences that this genuine knowledge blinds
us from seeing the full depth of typology. We become
aware of our own typological configuration, but its
dynamic nature is evident principally in relationship

to other people and not as much in terms of our own development. Individuation, then, becomes foreshortened. It takes on the appearance of the broadening of the ego in which I balance my superior function with the auxiliaries. But this balance is very different from the balance produced by the self. It would be a shame if such a broadening and strengthening of the ego, as valuable as it is, were to be presented as a sort of ordinary man's individuation, instead of seeing that typology is an invitation to a new relationship between conscious and unconscious.

But typology seen as the doorway of individuation is not without its own problems, which it shares with Jungian analysis as a whole. In analysis there is a real and necessary concern with illness as well as health. The analyst must evaluate the potential danger the analytic process poses for the patient, especially in terms of latent psychosis. In discussing the dangers that face someone trying to go through a process of individuation by using active imagination Jung states that the most serious danger:

"is that the subliminal contents already possess such a high energy charge that when afforded an outlet by active imagination they may overpower the conscious mind and take possession of the personality." (1916/1957, p. 68)

This is the perspective in which he considers the question of lay analysis and says further of active imagination: "The method, therefore, is not without its dangers and should, if possible, not be employed except under expert supervision." (1916/1957, p. 68)

This is certainly a far different situation from administering a psychological type test, and then discussing with the test-taker the results and some of the practical applications it may have in his life. But we can't immediately say that the concerns of the analyst have nothing to do with this broader use of typology. There is something in the very nature of typology itself that leads to these issues, for typology is a visible manifestation of individuation. But what happens, then, if we begin to take typology seriously outside the analytic temenos and it leads us towards that fascinating and terrible night sea journey?

We are clearly caught in a dilemma to which there are no easy answers. If I say that typology will stay at the level of the ego and its development, I betray my misunderstanding of its real nature, but if I say that anyone who wishes to get seriously involved in typology should work with a Jungian analyst, I ignore certain practical realities: there are only a little more than 1,500 analysts in the world, they are clustered principally in large urban areas, at least in the United States, and they cost money. There is no way that they can contain the ever-growing interest in Jung's typology and through it, in his psychology, and put it in the analytic temenos in the narrow sense. To demand that everyone have direct access to a professional guide is equivalent to telling them that the most fruitful dimensions of typology and the most fundamental process of psychological development, which is individuation, must remain closed to them. Certainly people with particular and definite psychological problems should get professional help whenever possible, but the world of normal people is afflicted with serious problems that are so common they are perceived to be compatible with being normal: marriages being destroyed, conflicts between parents and children, our own mistaken attempts to fit societal norms that do not fit our type, and so forth. We are in desperate need of good psychological direction, and typology is one of the ideal ways to receive it.

The relationship between the growing world of typology and that of the professional Jungian analyst is comparable to that of the growing interest in nutrition and the small group of orthomolecular physicians and nutritionists that exists. These physicians and nutritionists, pioneering new treatments for everything from cancer to schizophrenia, cannot meet the enormous needs, and as a result, this sort of nutritional information circulates in non-professional circles and increasing numbers of people treat themselves as best they can. To call this an infringement on the medical profession would verge on hypocrisy, but this does not make it an ideal situation. The sick person and his family and friends are caught in a dilemma of either watching him die after traditional medicine has declared him terminal, or taking up in their inexpert hands the struggle for health not through drugs but through nutritional means. How happy they would be for an orthomolecular physician to walk through the door.

Typology is the psychological equivalent of good nutrition, and there is a tremendous need for it within marriage and family life, on the job, and so forth, as we have said. But we have to reckon with the fact that the more its use increases, the more it will open the door to the unconscious with its attendant dangers. The dangers have to be put in perspective in a world where illegal drugs are rampant and terrible psychological pressures are common, but the danger still exists. Typology should not be allowed to split into two different and separate worlds: the analyst dealing with its intrapsychic implications while others take up its interpersonal use. There is only one process of individuation viewed from different perspectives. If a temenos is not possible around each individual, then it should be erected, as far as possible, around the whole movement of typology. The professional Jungian community has to understand the extent to which Jung's work is spreading, and employ some of that intuition that it favors so much to head off some of the potential dangers by its own involvement in typological affairs, while the newly developing group of Jungian typologists have to be aware of the inner dynamics of typology that lead to the trials of individuation.

Using Psychological Type Tests

Can a psychological type test solve the diagnostic problem? There are two ways to look at the question. First of all, a great deal of effort has gone into the construction of these tests and their validation. They condense into usable form extensive experience in typology and make available to us a reservoir of good questions. Therefore, they can be an important aid in making an evaluation of type. The test can be a check on our subjective impressions that can be misled by preconceived ideas and projections. If the test and our personal evaluations radically disagree, it is time to reconsider the matter. The test can help us focus our typological knowledge and experience and bring it to bear on the case at hand. We can go beyond the simple administration and scoring of the test and take up the questions one by one with the client and use them as a point of departure for developing a full-fledged typological interview that will combine objective and subjective elements. The test then becomes an impetus to correlate our subjective evaluations with the test scores and the self-understanding of the test-taker.

But there is a second way of using the test, which is less commendable. In it the test results become automatically the final results. The test becomes the sole way we diagnose type. It is the single tool at our disposal. We don't see. The test sees for us. We simply administer the test and assume that solves the diagnostic problem. This is too much to ask from any type test. The test was originally dependent on personal experience. In the initial construction of the MBTI, for example, observation necessarily had to precede any numerical results. "The initial questions were tested first on a small criterion group of about twenty relatives and friends whose type preferences seemed to the authors to be clearly evident from long acquaintance, and from a twenty-year period of "type watching"." (MBTI Manual, 1985, p. 142) Its questions and answers had to be evaluated against the clinical judgment of what the test-taker's type actually was. The questions are forced to break up into pieces what is actually connected in reality. Extraversion and thinking, for example, in the extraverted thinker, are not two separate factors, but one and the same thing. Then the test has to confront the enormous complexity that we saw in types themselves, and do all this by means of the self-report of the test-takers. The validation of the test from a statistical point of view is not identical with their authentication individual by individual, which is precisely where the results are most important.

The test creators themselves are often keenly aware of how things could be different: questions rephrased, and answers scored in a different manner. Isabel Briggs-Myers, when discussing the potential uses of the MBTI, felt the test is applicable in many areas, and can be put to good use by many kinds of decision-makers, but only, she admonishes: "if they will remember they are dealing with a theory and that the hypothesis the Indicator provides about a given person must always be submitted to their own informed and critical judgment. The Indicator is no substitute for good judgment. Being a self-report instrument, in any given case it could be wrong, no matter how high the scores.

"The safe and proper way to use the Indicator is as a stimulus to the user's insight." (MBTI Manual, 1962, p. 5) Chapter 5 of the new MBTI manual presents a balanced approach to the problem entitled, "Initial Interpretation and Verification": "No questions, however accurate, can explain all human complexity. The MBTI results are a first step toward understanding the respondent's true preferences."

We have seen the quandry that A. Plaut landed in. Katherine Bradway gave the Gray-Wheelwright and the MBTI to 17 Jungian analysts who had typed themselves before the test. She compared the results without reference to the superior or auxiliary function (which, no doubt, would have made the results more dissimilar). The self-typing and the two tests agreed almost 100% on the evaluation of introversion and extraversion. This agreement falls to around 75% for sensation-intuition and a bit less for thinking and feeling. These results, which might be respectable from a statistical point of view, certainly can give us pause from a practical or clinical point of view. There is no reason to suppose that the analyst's judgments of themselves were completely correct, nor to imagine it was the tests or one of the tests which was completely accurate. Thirteen years later Bradway and Detloff looked at the issue again with 92 participants, this time just using the Gray-Wheelwright test. The results were similar. The classification of the whole type by self agreed with the Gray-Wheelwright results 58% of the time, and this is, again, combining the superior and auxiliary functions. Therefore, it becomes a question of how many times will the self-typing of the analyst and the results of the MBTI and Gray-Wheelwright and Singer-Loomis agree in typing a person?

A comparison between the MBTI and the Gray-Wheelwright highlights these difficulties in type testing, even when we make the admission that both tests are tapping into the same basic reality. In a study of 159 university students who took both tests, only 21% came out the same type on both instruments. In another study of 98 students the correlation between the different scores of the two tests were "E .68 ($p<.01$), I .66 ($p<.01$), S .54 ($p<.01$), N .47 ($p<.01$), T .33 ($p<.01$), and F .23 ($p<.05$)." (MBTI Manual, 1985, p. 209)

It would be unfair to appear to chastise the tests and leave the impression that diagnosis by Jungian analysts is better, even when it is a question of their own type. Introversion and intuition are outstanding in analysts' self-diagnosis and test-taking, but whether this is an actual fact or reflects their image of what they ought to be remains undecided. Probably it is some of both. The fundamental reason for not relying on the estimate of Jungian analysts is that their education in this area has often been sporatic at best. To return to our analogy between typology and nutrition, when we read Plaut's survey, we see that the Jungian analysts are like medical doctors when it comes to nutrition: some are profoundly immersed in it, others are distressingly ignorant, and in the profession as a whole it has not penetrated that nutrition is an integral and indispensible part of medicine. It may be that an analyst has learned typology through his own analysis, but if half the analysts find no great use for it in practice, there is no guarantee this will happen.

We have come to another dilemma. We can't rely implicitly either on self-reports or test results. There is no magic solution. We may decree that a person's type is whatever the tests say it is, but this decree need not coincide with reality. We have to hold on to the two horns of this dilemma: the clinical viewpoint and attempts to be more objective. Testing and observation by an experienced diagnostician should go together in order to accurately determine type. There are several principles that will aid successful diagnosis.

1. An intimate working knowledge of one's own type. This means not simply an accurate knowledge of what our type is, but the inner implications of this knowledge in terms of how it expresses itself in the myriad of details of our daily behavior, and especially how our inferior function, as well as the undeveloped aspects of the other functions, influence our conduct towards other people. Without a knowledge of our personal mechanisms of projection, how can we avoid them?

2. An extensive knowledge of the practical peculiarities of different types. This is an appreciation of the nuances and qualities that affect the function, not only when we consider whether it is introverted or extraverted, but the qualities it manifests in each of the four positions.

3. The use of a psychological type test in such a way that it becomes a key element in a typological interview that helps objectify our observations. This includes a dialogue with the client about what he considers his type to be. Naturally, the weight given to this self-report will have to vary with the degree that the person is informed about types. Someone who has just been introduced to typology can hardly be expected to render a definitive judgment that will bind himself and everyone else. Many people, however, do show a remarkable degree of insight after they have grasped the basic principles involved.

Type diagnosis becomes a three-way discussion between the person being diagnosed, the typologist and the objective testing. In this way we can limit the deficiencies that exist in each area. Though such a process is more time-consuming, in most situations where knowledge of type is to be the starting point for a process of self-development, even if an initial quick diagnosis is correct, it lacks the practical efficacious certitude that comes from a slower and more thorough process of typological discovery. If I am told I am an extraverted intuitive type, it does me little good as long as this remains a purely verbal definition, and I have generated no self-insight in how these typological principles can help me focus better on the actual course of my life.

The problem of diagnosis is a practical reflection of a wider issue in Jung's psychology and in psychology in general. What is the method that psychology ought to pursue? A divergence of method has already become apparent between the work of the analyst in his consulting room and the creators and users of the psychological type tests. It forms a microcosm of the differences that exist between Jungian psychology in general and experimental psychology. And this brings us back to the first audience who made use of the ideas of introversion and extraversion. Witzig reports that in the decade between 1966 to 1975 there were 692 experimentally designed studies of extraversion-introversion reviewed in **Psychological Abstracts.** But how many of these experimenters really read **Psychological Types?**

Two Conceptions of Psychological Science

Jung worked out of a medical and clinical background and relied heavily on personal contact and observation in order to discover the empirical facts upon which he based his typology. The experimental psychologists follow a model of science derived more closely from the physical sciences like chemistry and physics. Initial data is gathered through experimentation by a variety of techniques such as direct physical measurement and standardized written tests. And then it is submitted to mathematical analysis, especially factor analysis. This process yields a variety of factors which can explain the data and give rise to further experimentation, and it is natural that as Jungian typology became better known outside the analytic situation, it would undergo a process of objectification with the creation of various type tests, as we have seen.

But Jung conceived of his way of doing science somewhat differently. He based himself on the evidence of empirical facts, but he felt that evidence varied in kind from discipline to discipline. A fact in psychology, while it had to be empirical, i.e., observable, was not necessarily measurable by exact physical means: "The more we turn from spacial phenomena to the non-spaciality of the psyche, the more impossible it becomes to determine anything by exact physical measurement." (1931, p. 527) Nor could it always be determined by experimental means, for an experiment, he felt, imposed conditions on the psyche, and thus limited the range of the psyche's possible responses. He says:

"Experiment, however, consists in asking a definite question which excludes as far as possible anything disturbing and irrelevant. It makes conditions, imposes them on Nature, and in this way forces her to give an answer to a question devised by man. She is prevented from answering out of the fullness of her possibilities since these possibilities are restricted as far as practicable." (1952, p. 451)

It was not that Jung was unaware of experimental techniques, or completely ignored statistical methods. He realized at times it was extremely difficult to make the observations that supported his typology. But the only really adequate instrument for observing the whole psyche is the whole psyche itself.

Unfortunately, a sharp antagonism has grown up between what we can call the observational method and the experimental method. Instead of realizing the legitimate diversity of these methods, we attack one or the other. This is a form of epistemological imperialism that makes itself felt throughout all of psychology and has an impact on the development of Jung's typology. This imperialism is evident when Jung is portrayed as a myth-maker and mystic whose name is, unfortunately, connected with extraversion and introversion, and whose work forms a roadblock to the genuine scientific examination of this area. It is as if Jung, by some accident, stumbled on some typological ideas, which now must be taken up by real scientists, verified and developed.

This one-sided attitude has its counterpart, these days perhaps a more defensive one, on the part of more clinically-oriented people who ignore or write off attempts to construct a harder science of the human personality, and deride it as a technocratic fable which will find its culmination in rats instead of men. Neither attitude is justified. The first assumes there is only one method, which they possess, and whatever this method can embrace is psychology, and whatever falls outside it is unknowable. This becomes an accepted axiom, and mathematical technique begins to take the place of thought and generates a spate of studies which administer two tests, calculate the correlations, and state the results without attempting to see what these mathematical results mean in organic or real life terms.

On the other hand, the clinician, immersed in his own work, finds too little time and energy to ferret out the gems that exist in this flood of literature and translate them into a conceptual framework which will allow him to ask how they effect his own work. He can succumb to his own form of blindness in which his subjective opinion is elevated to the state of a dogma.

The question of method will return again and again as we proceed, but let's leave it for the moment and briefly look at something more congenial: some work that is being done in the field of experimental psychology. Many earlier studies were gathered in three volumes in **Readings in Extraversion-Introversion,** edited by Eysenck. They included articles on the higher sedation thresholds of introverts and their lower auditory and pain thresholds, as well as the higher pain tolerance of extraverts. Dicks-Mireaux summarizes some of the early experimental work on introversion and extraversion from a Jungian perspective, reviewing Eysenck, Cattell and Guilford. More bridge-building was done by Marshall in his "Extraversion and Libido in Jung and Cattell", and "The Four Functions, a Conceptual Analysis".

Eysenck in **The Structure of Human Personality** provides an extensive review of various theories in the field of human differences. After discussing Jor-

dan and Gross, both of whom Jung wrote about in
Psychological Types, he devotes a few pages to Jung
himself. He examines Jung's idea that the extravert
in cases of neurotic breakdown is predisposed to
hysteria, and the introvert to psychasthenia, a matter
which Eysenck studied experimentally. He recognizes
as implicit in Jung "a second factor additional to,
and independent of, that of extraversion-introversion.
This factor we may provisionally call "abnormality"
or "neuroticism"." (p. 24) And then Eysenck goes on
to add a third axis to the first two, which he calls
"psychotism", and he is concerned that this psychotic
factor will be mistakenly viewed only as an extreme
form of neuroticism, a view which he does not find
justifiable.

Let us simply list a few more articles that could
interest the Jungian typologist and perhaps inspire
him to develop Jung's work further. These include
the relationship between the AB blood group and
introversion, various studies about extraversion-introversion and the EEG, and a constant stream of
material appearing in **The Journal of Personality and
Individual Differences,** for example, "Intelligence and
Personality in Mate Choice and Marital Satisfaction",
"Delinquent Personality Types and the Situational
Contexts of their Crimes".

Jung's typology needs to be brought into relationship not only with the world of experimental psychology but beyond it to the world of literature, philosophy and art. William Willeford and James Hillman
make efforts to put Jung's typological thought in
a wider cultural perspective, and the ripples set off
by the publication of **Psychological Types** grow ever
wider as Jung's thought effects more and more people and they, in turn, relate it to more and more
areas. Two notable examples of this process can be
found in Hermann Rorschach's **Psychodiagnostik,** published in 1921, which tries to develop an objective
assessment of extraversion and introversion, and in

Roberto Assagioli's creation of psychosynthesis. A comparison of Rorschach and Jung was done by Brawer and Spiegelman. While Rorschach initially disclaimed any influence of Jung, Assagioli felt closest to Jung among all the modern psychotherapists, and he takes into account the four functions so neglected outside of Jungian circles. In his own schema of the psyche he groups six functions around the self and the will. In addition to the four Jungian functions we find imagination or fantasy, and a group of functions "that impel us towards action in the outside world". Perhaps it would not be amiss to recognize in these last two functions something of Jung's introversion and extraversion. (Keen, p. 98) Even Arnold Toynbee used Jung's theory of psychological types in his **Study of History** when he attempted to differentiate between the major world religions. He suggested that Hinduism represented a predominance of introverted thinking, Christianity extraverted feeling, Islam extraverted sensation and Buddhism introverted intuition.

It is well to pause for a moment and review where we have been before we come upon some of the most interesting sights in our exploration of Jung's typology: the new developments in type theory. We started with Jung's **Psychological Types** and proceeded to see how it had been taken up and developed in three distinctive ways: within analysis, by psychological type tests, and from an experimental point of view. We saw that interwoven in all these areas was a preoccupation with two major questions: type diagnosis and method. And it is well we have noticed this, for it will have sensitized us to recognize the important role these issues play in new type theories.

CHAPTER 3
NEW DIRECTIONS IN
PSYCHOLOGICAL TYPES THEORY

The theories that have developed in the field of psychological types after Jung can be roughly divided in the following categories: the relationship between the functions, reformulations of Jung's typology, and various refinements concerning bi-polarity, types and archetypes, and the inferior function.

The Relationship Between the Functions

This first development attempts to fill the gaps left by the very brief descriptions given in **Psychological Types** about the auxiliary functions. Wayne Detloff, for example, describes the relationship between the superior and auxiliary function:

"...the extravert's principle function is extraverted, but his auxiliary function is likely to have a cast of the introverted side. Thus, the extravert's auxiliary function helps him to relate to his inner world but, since it is his second best function, one can anticipate some difficulty. For the introvert, the principle function is introverted, but his outer adaptation is often complicated because his auxiliary function (second best) is more likely to appear in relation to the external world. Thus, outer adaptation more often manifests the introvert's difficulty." ("Psychological Types: Fifty Years After", p. 70)

This idea had appeared early in the development of the Myers-Briggs test, in fact, in the original formulations of Katharine Briggs after she had read

Psychological Types. Isabel Briggs-Myers felt that the practical utility of psychological types was unexplored because Jung failed to bring out this point with sufficient clarity:

"In view of Jung's deep appreciation of the introverts' value, it is ironical that he lets his passion for the abstract betray him into concentrating on cases of "pure" introversion. He not only describes people with no extraversion at all, but seems to present them as typical of introverts in general. By failing to convey that introverts with a good auxiliary **are** effective and play an indispensable part in the world, he opens the door for a general misunderstanding of his theory." (**Gifts Differing,** p. 18)

She attempted to remedy this reading of Jung - in itself highly debatable, for Jung always describes the introversion and extraversion of each type - by her judgment and perception scale. She explains this use of the auxiliary as follows:

"The basic principle that the auxiliary provides needed extraversion for the introverts and needed introversion for the extraverts is vitally important. The extraverts' auxiliary gives them access to their own inner life and to the world of ideas; the introverts' auxiliary gives them a means to adapt to the world of action and to deal with it effectively." (p. 19)

"Good type development thus demands that the auxiliary supplement the dominant process in two respects. It must supply a useful degree of balance not only between perception and judgment but **also between extraversion and introversion...** To live happily and effectively in both worlds, people need a **balancing** auxiliary that will make it possible to adapt in both directions - to the world around them and to their inner selves. (p. 21)

This idea has been amplified and developed by her close collaborator Mary McCaulley:

"When both the dominant and the auxiliary functions have become differentiated, the individual achieves a balance. He thereby avoids aimless drifting, which can come from total reliance on a dominant perceptive process, or a rigid reliance on form rather than content, which can come from total reliance on a dominant judgment process. In Jung's view, type development is a lifelong process. In midlife some rare individuals can develop to the point where they transcend their preferences and move easily from one function to another as the occasion demands. The MBTI, however, is concerned primarily with normal, rather than exceptional, personality development. In her characterizations of the sixteen types... Myers assumes that both dominant and auxiliary functions are well developed, but she also notes the typical problems to be expected if the auxiliary function is not developed." (1981, p. 301)

Despite the fact that Myers takes Jung to task for neglecting this principle, she feels he alludes to it cryptically in the following passages:

"The relatively unconscious functions of feeling, intuition and sensation, which counterbalance introverted thinking, are inferior in quality and have a primitive, extraverted character." (**Psychological Types,** 1923, p. 489) "When the mechanism of extraversion predominates... the most highly differentiated function has a constantly extraverted application, while the inferior functions are found in the service of introversion." (1923, p. 426) "For all the types appearing in practice, the principle holds good that besides the conscious main function there is also a relatively unconscious, auxiliary function which is in every respect different from the nature of the main function." (1923, p. 515)

These first two quotes appear to say nothing more than what Jung is continually saying throughout his Chapter X, that is, the conscious superior function is balanced by the other unconscious functions which differ in attitude from it. He realizes he is oversimplifying by not talking about the development of the auxiliary functions, but for clarity's sake he groups them in attitude with the inferior function.

The third passage appears to make a stronger case, but it has to be read in context. Then we see it comes in the middle of a discussion about the nature of the auxiliary function as a servant of the superior function:

"Hence the auxiliary function is possible and useful only in so far as it **serves** the dominant function, without making any claim to the autonomy of its own principle.

For all the types met with in practice, the rule holds good that besides the conscious, primary function there is a relatively unconscious, auxiliary function which is in every respect different from the nature of the primary function. The resulting combinations present the familiar picture of, for instance, practical thinking allied with sensation, speculative thinking forging ahead with intuition, ..." (Volume 6, p. 406)

Its whole tenor is not to give the auxiliary function a role separate from the superior, but precisely the opposite. If we understand "different in every respect" as a complete sort of opposition rather than a state of undevelopment, how can it serve and serve intimately the superior function, as in the case of practical thinking allied with sensation, etc.?

Furthermore, emphasis on the opposition between the superior and auxiliary function can easily be misconstrued as if their balancing created an individuation that is suitable for normal people while there is another kind of individuation which deals with the inferior function, and the arrival at the self which is reserved to exceptional cases.

Nor is it clear that opposition between the superior and auxiliary functions should be elevated into a universal principle. For example, we had contact for several years under varying circumstances with a man whom we concluded was an introverted sensation thinking type. In the course of a typological interview he also typed himself in this way and was happy with the fit of it. The administration of the MBTI, Form F, showed the predominance of introversion, sensation and thinking, and so was consistent with the other evaluations, but the judgment-perception preference would have made him an introverted thinking sensation type. This was not the case, and the same problem has arisen in other situations. Mary Ann Mattoon's opinion is:

"That they are of the same attitude seemed to be Jung's assumption, on the basis, perhaps, that the more conscious attitude is linked with the two more conscious functions, and the more unconscious attitude is linked with the more unconscious functions. My clinical experience generally supports this hypothesis." (**Jungian Psychology in Perspective**, p. 67)

On the other hand, Briggs and Myers noted the support for this principle in van der Hoop, and we have seen Detloff's comments, and more recently, Alex Quenk develops quite the same position in his **Psychological Types and Psychotherapy.** (p. 12-13) This kind of experience cannot be lightly discounted. Is it possible to find a way out of this dilemma? John Beebe in "Psychological Types in Transference, Countertransference and the Therapeutic Interaction" provides a direction in which to look for a solution. He accepts the opposition between the superior and auxiliary function, and extends it through the whole personality. An extraverted intuition thinking type would not only have introverted thinking but extraverted feeling, as well as introverted sensation: "My model extends the bipolar assumption to its logical conclusion, namely, that not only the functions but their attitudes as well are opposites along a given axis." (p. 153)

By extending the notion of bipolarity, Beebe creates type profiles useful in exploring different

kinds of transference and countertransference, and
he avoids the impression of limiting the perspective
of typology to the first two functions. He opens the
door to a wider view of the dynamic nature of typology. The type profile of the introverted intuition
thinking type would, according to Beebe, look like
this:

But it is clear that this profile represents only
half of the type. What is to prevent type development taking different pathways, depending on varying
circumstances and different natural inclinations? Another schema of development would look like this:

And a complete one would look like this:

This last model gives us a sense of the actual
complexity that we already saw in type diagnosis, and
which extends to the question of type development.
It alerts us to potential patterns of psychic energy
within the overall pattern formed by the superior and
inferior functions, and provides a framework for talking about how we deal with the shadow's side of our

superior function, that is, the same function with an opposite attitude, and how all these typological fragments can be related to the one personality and to the self. Here we might keep in mind the suggestive remark of Detloff: "The Self then might be conceived as having the potential for all the types." ("Psychological Types: Fifty Years After", p. 70)

Types and Archetypes

Scattered here and there in the literature of Jungian typology are interesting remarks about the relationship between types and archetypes. Groesbeck, commenting on a passage in Jung, states, "...in our shadow, anima, persona and ego figures we may find clues to our typological condition." (p. 32) And Beebe writes:
"...One has to recognize that characteristic archetypal personages carry the various functions according to their degree of differentiation within a given individual's type profile." (p. 157)
And he goes on to illustrate this principle by interpreting dreams typologically, a process which he finds can be aided even by the colors which appear in different dreams with blue representing thinking, red feeling, yellow intuition and green and sometimes brown sensation.
For von Franz if someone has only developed the superior function, then the shadow, animus and anima will appear in the auxiliaries as well as the inferior function. (**The Inferior Function,** p. 54) But she seems to imply that once the auxiliaries are developed, then these archetypal realities are mirrored in the inferior function. "In dreams, the inferior function relates to the shadow, the anima or animus, or the self, and it gives them a certain characteristic quality. For instance, the shadow in an intuitive type will often be personified by a sensation type... Then when one has become somewhat conscious of the shadow, the

inferior function will give the animus or anima figure a special quality." (p. 54-5) The same will happen with the self. Here we have a glimpse of the dynamic development of the psyche seen typologically, and perhaps it throws light on the question of the attitude of the auxiliary function. As we develop, we push back the frontiers of our conscious personality, and the archetypes we relate to and the psychological functions through which they approach us can change.

These interesting remarks could be the beginning of a careful evaluation of how dreams can be interpreted typologically and how typological development is reflected in them. If we have thinking or feeling as our third function and we have developed our auxiliary function, does this mean that the thinking and feeling will carry the anima and animus? Is there a special affinity between thinking and feeling and the anima and animus? Does the third function feeler relate to the anima more easily than the fourth function feeler? If a third function feeler relates to his feelings, does he thereby deal with the anima and constellate another archetype, or does the anima in some way shift and show a face of itself that is connected with the inferior function? It is possible to read Hillman's remarks about feeling and the anima in this connection (**The Feeling Function,** p. 121), or different remarks of Jung, for example, the vivid statement he made in a letter to Count Keyserling, who on one of his travels had activated his inferior function loaded with the contents of the collective unconscious: "Simultaneously the anima emerges in exemplary fashion from the primeval slime laden with all the pulpy and monstrous appendages of the deep!" (**Letters,** Vol. 1, p. 84)

Reformulations of Jung's Typology

Mann, Siegler and Osmond in "The Many Worlds

of Time" provide an excellent example of how the boundaries of psychological types can be extended. Invoking von Uexküll's **A Stroll Through the Worlds of Animals and Men,** which describes various umwelts or experiential worlds, they tried to understand what these experiential worlds would be in relationship to time and type. They suggest that the sensation type is present-oriented, the feeling type past-oriented, the intuitive type future-oriented and the thinking type linear, that is, someone who links past, present and future. And they illustrate these different perceptual worlds by abundant examples.

In "Typology Revisited: A New Perspective" Osmond, Siegler and Smoke attempt a more radical restructuring of typology, impelled by our old friend, the diagnostic problem:

"While Jung's typology has proved fruitful as a therapeutic instrument, it has been an unqualified failure as a reliable method of establishing people's types. There has been no growing file of agreed-upon examples of different types, no growing body of knowledge about the characteristics of each type." (p. 207)

In order to resolve this problem they propose a reorganization of the functions in which they will be linked in four pairs:

Thinking-sensation   Feeling-intuitive
Sensation-thinking   Intuitive-feeling

Intuitive-thinking   Feeling-sensation
Thinking-intuitive   Sensation-feeling

They call these pairs the "structural", "oceanic", "ethereal" and "experial", and then they go on to give descriptions of these four basic forms by which a person experiences the world. But while reading these interesting descriptions filled with typological analyses of famous people, the reader suddenly comes to himself and asks, "What happened to introversion and extraversion?" And the authors have given their answer right at the beginning of the exposition:

"We shall leave out the two attitudes, introversion and extraversion, which are independent variables of the functions." (p. 207)

Unfortunately, the functions are not really conceivable in this sort of vacuum. They are precisely Jung's attempts to more carefully delineate introversion and extraversion, and the four functions, themselves, appear very differently, whether they are introverted or extraverted. As Detloff puts it:

"It is very important to realize that the two attitudes (extraversion and introversion) so modify the appearance of each of the four functions that the terms are almost misleading. One can sometimes wish that a completely different term were used for a function when it is introverted from when it is extraverted, but, if one knows that the appearance of a given function is modified by introversion-extraversion and associated functions, changing of terms is unnecessary." ("Psychological Types: Fifty Years After", p. 70)

There is a real difference between sensing-thinking and thinking-sensing, as can be seen in an extreme way between an introverted sensation-thinking type and an extraverted thinking-sensing type. And when we make abstraction of introversion and extraversion, they have an uncanny way of creeping back into our descriptions. So our authors make statements like: "Oceanics learn to handle impersonal problems by subjectifying them, as Structurals learn to handle personal problems by objectifying them." (p. 211) Or, "What is real to the Ethereal is the psyche, experienced as synonymous with the mind, and the limitless possibilities offered by the mind." (p. 213)

The use of these compound categories was taken up by Michael Malone in **Psychetypes: A New Way of Exploring Personality.** But his efforts in this direc-

tion did not meet with the approval of its origina-
tors.

In "Towards a Reformulation of the Typology of
Functions" R. Metzner, C. Burney and A. Mahlberg
take up the quest, again, for an overhauled typology
that will not only solve the diagnostic problem, but
do justice to what they feel is evidence that points
to the non-bipolarity of the functions. This evidence
includes certain analyses of psychological type test
data and the self-reporting of analysts who decided
that their superior function was not opposite to their
inferior.

"We propose, in this paper, to examine the hypothesized bi-polarity of the four functions, and suggest
that perhaps the rigid dichotomizing inherent within
the functional typology as so far conceived, has
served as a kind of conceptual strait-jacket, inhibiting
growth and development of the model." (p. 33)

In this reformulation they leave aside extraversion
and introversion, and use both the primary and the
inferior functions to characterize 12 types, for example, thinking primary - inferior feeling, thinking
primary - inferior sensation, thinking primary - inferior intuition, etc. Though they are aware that introversion and extraversion must enter into this picture
to create 24 types, they ignore the fact that it is
difficult, if not impossible, to describe the functions
as if they were neutral, existing without introversion
or extraversion.

But there is an even more fundamental issue. The
bi-polarity of typology was, in Jung's mind, a reflection of the bi-polarity of the whole psyche. Therefore, if we eliminate it we are on the road to eliminating it from the whole relationship between the
conscious and the unconscious, and thus from Jung's
psychology as a whole, and this would be a complicated and thankless task. If typology were clearly
seen against the background of individuation, then the
relationship between the inferior function and the

superior has to be seen as the typological equivalent to the search for balance between the conscious and the unconscious.

The authors state: "the theory of the individuation process calls for this kind of balanced development of all the functions" (p. 34) and more explicitly, "The process of individuation consists, among other things, of bringing the least developed inferior function up to equal consciousness and strength with the other three, thus transforming the trinity into a quaternity." (p. 40) But this is not an understanding of the inferior function as Jung describes it and von Franz develops it. The inferior function does not lose its moorings in the unconscious and rise to the level of development of the other functions. If it did, individuation would be a broadening of the ego, but since the inferior function is rooted in the unconscious and maintains those roots despite the necessary task of developing it, it resists the ego usurping the functions, and makes it confront the unconscious as a partner in the quest for a new center, the self.

The authors have justly pointed to the diagnostic problem and the difficulty of developing statistical evidence, but when they say: "To what extent these 12 or 24-fold types actually occur in nature remains to be determined empirically" (p. 38) we can see that the word "empirical" has a very different meaning than it had in Jung. It is no longer the empirical facts of actual daily experience upon which he built his typology in the first place, but empirical taken in the sense of the evidence that mathematical analysis of test results might be able to produce. This is a very different kind of evidence than Jung would feel compelled to give, or Beebe when he says: "I have validated the bipolar assumption - that is, that thinking and feeling and sensation and intuition, are poles of a single axis - by studying psychological types in interactions, in dreams, and through inspection and empathy." ("Psychological Types in Transference...", p. 153)

We have returned to the problem of method in psychology and within Jungian psychology itself. Even Meier, that champion of typology, in making an impassioned plea for a more scientific approach to Jungian psychology, accentuates the statistical approach. He urges the universal use of the Gray-Wheelwright test, which he hopes will lead to the advancement of Jungian psychology in the academic world, and he says: "I would like to emphasize at this point that it is imperative that we support our own convictions by statistical evaluations as statistics are the closest we can come to the truth in psychology." ("Psychological Types and Individuation", p. 284)

If we understand this phrase that it is the closest we can come to the truth within the context of experimental psychology, and according to its norms and principles, there is no problem. But if we understand it more absolutely as the sole way psychology as a whole can proceed, then we are in an insoluble dilemma as far as Jung's psychology is concerned, for it would mean a virtual redoing of all Jung's work to "prove" it, as if it is unprovable in any other way, and we turn Jung into a dabbler who had many good intuitions but never proved anything, and we misunderstand the nature of the empirical evidence he is continually talking about. Finally, the most intriguing and interesting things of typology recede from sight because they are unknowable or as yet unknown by these statistical methods, as is illustrated by the general attitude of the experimental psychologists who consider Jung's four functions a fantasy.

Let's look at an attempt by Meier and Wozny to develop a better statistical basis to Jung's typology in their "An Empirical Study of Jungian Typology". They address themselves to the question: "What is the relationship between **living** Jungian types and those same types 'typed' by the Gray-Wheelwright test?" By Q-factor analysis they isolated specific groupings of analysts they felt would be equivalent to Jungian psychological types without assuming anything about what the Gray-Wheelwright scales actually measure.

"We correlated the response patterns, as recorded on each individual's score-sheet, with every other one for the 22 analysts, and then calculated which patterns were more similar to each other than to other patterns." (p. 227)

These types were compared with the self-typing of the analysts. They concluded:

"When we compared the 'self-knowledge' ratings with the types determined by the Gray-Wheelwright scores, we obtained little correspondence between them. Of the 22 analysts, 16 were found to have a conscious, typological appreciation of themselves that was different from (and, in some cases, opposite to) the way the Gray-Wheelwright types them" (p. 228) and this "...shed doubt on the advisability of using experiential judgments of Jungian analysts as possible criteria to evalutate the test's psychometric constructs." (p. 228)

In an attempt to overcome this problem they resorted to Q-factor analysis and found 8 distinct empirical subtypes which had no relationship with the self-typing and represented "8 distinct styles of responding to the test items." (p. 229) These empirical subtypes, they felt, could serve as the nuclei for the construction of a new test and concluded:

"...we would like to stress the importance of continued research on Jung's psychological types with methods that utilize objective, statistical designs. Only by using such procedures will we be able to separate fact from fiction and set Jungian typological test-constructs on firm empirical foundation." (p. 230)

Unfortunately, the use of sophisticated mathematical techniques does not create an unquestionable

objective foundation that all will agree on. Extensive
debates have and do rage among the factor analytic
schools involved in the study of human differences.
There is still the subjective factor of what data to
collect and what technique to analyze it with. Meier
and Wozny's study itself was soon challenged by N.
Quenk in "On Empirical Studies of Jungian Typology".
She underscored the difficulties in using Jungian analysts self-typing, and she found the use of Q-factor
analysis inappropriate both because it used too small
a sample and because this sort of factor analysis
itself was not the proper choice to begin with. She
compared it with R-factor analysis: "Unlike R-factor
analysis, which operates on correlations between
items or tests, Q-factor analysis operates on correlations between **individuals** over the range of a series
of items or tests." (p. 221) Q-factor analysis generates types but

"...though the prototype is a discrete entity, no
actual individual can be said to possess the characteristics of one type and one type only. A given individual is viewed as having more or less of the
characteristics associated with the type in a quantitative fashion."

The theory of psychological types, however, assumes that the types are discrete entities which are
qualitatively different, and that a given individual can
be said to possess the "...characteristics of one type
and one type only. Q-factor analysis therefore vio-
lates the assumptions of psychological type theory."
(p. 221)

Quenk considers construct validation a much
better way to proceed, a technique in which:

"...one must examine the theory of psychological
types, generate empirically testable hypotheses consistent with the theory, test these hypotheses using
appropriate research techniques, and finally examine
how well the empirical results correspond with theoretical predictions." (p. 221)

Meier and Wozny's study had been preceded by other Q-sort examinations of Jungian typology. Mattoon summarizes the work of Cook (1971), Gorlow, Simonson, and Krauss (1966) and Hill (1970). Cook and Gorlow, Simonson, and Krauss developed items based on psychological types and had the subjects sort them according to whether they fit them or not, and then examined these groupings to see if they were more like Jungian types than what would have happened by chance. Hill administered various tests, including the MBTI, and in all the cases there was moderate support for Jung's formulation of typology. The use of R- and Q-factor analysis in relationship to Jungian typology can be traced at least as far back as W. Stephenson's 1939 article, "Methodological Consideration of Jung's Typology".

The question of bipolarity was taken up in a distinctive way by Loomis and Singer in their "Testing the Bipolar Assumption in Jung's Typology". They reorganized the questions of the Gray-Wheelwright and the MBTI so bipolarity would not be written into the structure of the test:

For example, an item such as:

As a party, I
   (a) Like to talk.
   (b) Like to listen.

was replaced by two scaled items separated in the test:

At a party I like to talk.
At a party I like to listen.

120 people were given the original Gray-Wheelwright and the rewritten version. "The results showed that 86, or 72 per cent, of the subjects changed their superior function from one questionnaire to the other. Further, in the GW revised version, 66 subjects, or 55 per cent, did not have an inferior function that has the hypothesized opposite of their superior function." (p. 354)

In a similar test of 79 people with two versions

of the MBTI, 46% did not keep the same superior function, and 36% did not show the opposition between the superior function and the inferior. These results led the authors to abandon the assumption of bipolarity and the forced-choice format, and develop the Singer-Loomis Inventory.

In "A New Perspective for Jung's Typology" Loomis marshalls factor analysis support for their inventory, for "without substantiation by a factor analysis, no inventory measuring typology will ever have the solid empirical foundation required for experimental research or for clinical applications." (p. 59)

Instead of 8 factors emerging, corresponding to the 8 psychological types, 5 appeared: feeling, intuition, thinking, introverted sensation and extraverted sensation, with no ready explanation of why this happens.

The lack of bipolarity in their test data leads them to reflections on Jung's structuring of typology.

"The authors questioned the **conclusion** implied through the constructions of the inventories now in use, namely that it is impossible for individuals to transcend the bipolar opposites under any conditions. It would appear that one of the most important aspects of Jung's psychology is being violated here, that of the eventual union, or transcendence, of opposites." (**Interpretative Guide,** p. 19)

While this language is not as extreme as that of Metzner, Burney and Mahlberg's, it still raises the same question when Singer and Loomis say:

"We believe that in the individuation process that does occur, that people do learn to come to terms with functions and attitudes other than their 'superior' ones, that even the so-called 'inferior' function can and does reach a very high degree of differentiation in some individuals." (**Testing,** p. 352)

The issue, really, is what "a very high degree" means. They base part of their case on creative people, and it is true that substantial development of the inferior function can take place, but the whole idea of its creative role is based on the fact not only of its differentiation, but a differentiation still rooted in the unconscious, and therefore, being able to draw on the unconscious' creative energies. Even in its creative role it retains, according to Jung and von Franz, its inferior character, an issue that we should examine further by looking at the inferior function in more detail.

The Inferior Function

The role of the inferior function is central to how Jung conceives his typology. It is embedded in the very structure of his **Psychological Types** where he balances every description of a particular type with one of its other side, which is embodied in the inferior function. And this is not just a didactic device. The inferior function is the doorway to the unconscious, the way we see from the point of view of consciousness that we must come to terms with the unconscious. The inferior function is not just a theoretical construct that Jung created in order to extend his ideas about the polarity of psychic energy into the realm of typology. Rather, it was the actual experience of the inferior function both in himself and in others that helped him formulate the more general theory of polarity. Jung's formulations about the inferior function are about one of the most critical and practical psychological problems that we all face.

J.L. Henderson suggests this when he says, "...that a knowledge of the inferior function may contribute a most vital element to the formation of a psychology of the future by allowing psychotherapists to handle dynamically all those problems which do not properly speaking conform to the categories of the psychoneuroses or psychoses." ("The Inferior Function", p. 139)

The inferior function is not something that will be resolved like the challenges posed by the other functions. They are added to the ego and broaden and strengthen it; the inferior function will never be added in the same way. It is the stumbling block to complete ego aggrandizement. It prevents a total egocentricity for it makes it clear, often in a negative fashion, that the ego cannot control everything and therefore it presents the possibility of there being some dimension of the personality beyond the ego. If it presented this possibility as a theory it would join the large collection of things we "know" but don't truly understand and live. Instead, it involves us in our daily existence in an often painful and humiliating way in the recognition of our particular weakness.

Henderson continues:

"...analysis only provides a beginning for the self-knowledge required to trace the inferior function to its source in the whole process of life. It is only after analysis that the patient really comes to grips with it and has to work through the many stages of its integration into consciousness." (p. 139-40)

The inferior function is a constant opportunity for us to experience the dynamic nature of typology. In dealing with the inferior function we deal with individuation moment by moment. This is clearly expressed in Marie-Louise von Franz's **The Inferior Function**. This book, originally given as a series of lectures in 1961 at the C.G. Jung Institute in Zurich, has the flavor of experience. Here is someone who has actually come face to face with the inferior function again and again. And out of this concrete experience emerges a view of the inferior function which speaks powerfully to the issue of bipolarity. The fourth function can certainly be developed, but "when the fourth function comes up, however, the whole upper structure collapses. The more you pull up the fourth, the further the upper floor descends.

A mistake some people make is that they think they can pull up the inferior function onto the level of the other conscious functions. I can only say: "Well, if you wish to do so, try. But you can try forever!"" (p. 17)

The conscious has to go down in order to raise the fourth, and she calls where they meet the middle realm, which is the place where transformation takes place. If consciousness loses its former place in which it saw itself as the center of everything, if we lose our ego-centricity, then the polarity of the psyche is overcome in a certain way. "The ego can take up a particular function and put it down like a tool in an awareness of its own reality outside the system of the four functions... Going to it (the inferior function) and staying with it, not just taking a quick bath in it, effects a tremendous change in the structure of the personality." (p. 59)

This new kind of consciousness must initially appear strange to us. We are so used to pursuing our goals by means of the functions which are dominated by the ego that this ego-less-ness might first appear as a loss of life or a vacuum. We don't experience our desires as we did before. We are not driven by the same search for gratification and we miss that drive. But we can actually be more capable and creative than before. It is simply that we are not in our acts the same way. Our ego has withdrawn and lives more in another center in this middle realm.

"There is a complete standstill in a kind of inner centre, and the functions do not act automatically any more. You can bring them out at will, as for instance an airplane can let down the wheels in order to land and then draw them in again when it has to fly. At this stage the problem of the functions is no longer relevant; the functions have become instruments of a consciousness which is no longer rooted in them or driven by them." (p. 63)

It is "hellishly difficult" (p. 66) to stay with the inferior function. But if we do, we get our "very appropriate, private discipline - invisible to the outer world, but very disagreeable." (p. 66)

After reviewing these attempts at restructuring psychological types, it is clear that questions of both diagnosis and method play a large part. The very complexity of behavior from which Jung's typology has been abstracted leads to diagnostic problems which, in turn, leads to attempts at overhauling typology to solve the problem. But what if the problem does not lie in Jung's typology, as much as in the difficulty of the empirical material itself, as Jung indicated many times? No doubt, Jung's typology will be expanded and refined, but if we are to do this properly we have to share in his appreciation of the tremendous welter of empirical material. If we grasp something of this complexity, then we are in a position to grasp something of Jung's formulations which relate directly to that material. We have to see the individual behind and through his psychological types, for that is how he wrote them, and since we cannot see his case material, his individuals, we must see our own, day by day, in our own lives. Failure to do this will make us think of reformulating Jung's types before we have fully fathomed what he is actually saying. J.L. Henderson compares the inexperienced typologist to a child who has a fine watch but can't really tell time yet. He tells of his own misguided attempts with his first patient that resulted in a misdiagnosis and in his feeling:

"And so I thought that if I, who was a Jungian analyst with years of study and training behind me, could make such a glaring mistake, surely the type theory was unusable and must eventually be discarded as of any practical application in psychotherapy, to be kept only for its aesthetic enjoyment by a few superior minds." ("The Inferior Function", p. 135)

But he persisted, and not only used typology successfully, but developed some valuable principles concerning its use in general.

"Like all superior creations of the human mind it is more nearly perfect than its user, yet its only real function lies in its use. Such application requires a conscious awareness which is extremely hard to maintain until through practice it may become in a way habitual." (p. 134)

The use of the word "empirical" is highly ambivalent in relationship to Jung's typology, as we have mentioned before. It has become restricted to those results that could be supported by factor analysis, as if the actual contact we have with people and from which Jung derived his typology, is not empirical, that is, a direct experience of the concrete facts. Jung never limited the word "empirical" to statistical verification. Quite the contrary. He was convinced that certain things could simply not be handled this way, but this did not make them any less empirical. If extraversion and introversion can be statistically and experimentally demonstrated, it is because they are the most obvious and clear-cut of all the subjects that typology examines. But this does not mean that the four functions are illusions. They are refinements of introversion and extraversion, and as such, are more subtle and harder to measure. This is even more the case when it is a question of the relationship between the functions. If they cannot be measured by the standard statistical techniques, that is not because they do not exist, but rather, because the instruments we are using are not yet refined enough to see them. There is a value to refining these instruments and employing them in the field of typology where the dangers of projection are so great. But if we look at them as the only way we can know types, or know the individual, we will have succumbed to an equally great danger which is a misguided objectivism which concludes that since we cannot read braille with mittens on, the bumps

don't exist. The world of experimental psychology and
its sophisticated mathematics does not represent a
panacea for the problems that Jungian psychology
faces. A great deal of Jung's attraction today is precisely because he takes a broader view of things, and
to make him over in standard categories would eliminate much of what he has to offer. It would be to
succumb to an objectivism which represents only one
half of the psychological method. Even the harder
scientific approaches to human differences have their
own difficulties. In 1982 G.L. Mangan, concluding his
Biology of Human Conduct: East-West Models of
Temperament and Personality, a 450 page review of
Western and Russian literature, asks:

"What do we see in prospect for psychophysiology,
and in particular, for differential psychophysiology?
In both areas, there has been disappointingly little
progress during the past decade." (p. 452)

It is not a question of ignoring developments in
the experimental field or the use of sophisticated
techniques in the analysis of type tests, but rather,
of seeing that there is more than one way to arrive
at genuine typological knowledge.

What can be done about the diagnostic problem?
We cannot expect to be able to resolve it by reading
Psychological Types or taking a short course any
more than we would expect to become medical diag-
nosticians by reading the Merck Manual. We would
not trust ourselves to a second-year medical student,
but a typological diagnosis can be as demanding as
a physical one. We expect the medical doctor to be
trained not only theoretically, but on a practical
level through his internship, and this actual training
is carried out in analytical psychology through the
training analysis, an innovation of Jung's that spread
to psychoanalytic circles as well. But as we mentioned before, this is not equivalent to training in
psychological types. Typology is an integral part of
the process of individuation, but it is a distinctive

view of it. What we need is training directly geared to typology, and there is no such training. This is why typology languishes much more than any need to reformulate Jung's work. The only training that takes place now is individual by individual, through the slow accumulation of insight that comes through personal experience, and this accumulation, since it takes place in relative isolation, is subject to distortion coming from the individual's personal equation and his projections and to the snail-like progress that comes from trial and error.

However, it is possible to envision an actual training program in typology. For example, it could build on the way psychiatric cases are often demonstrated, with actual interviews with the patient and subsequent discussions. In a good typological interview there are literally dozens and dozens of clues to diagnosis which range from posture to facial expression, gestures, verbal responses, off-hand remarks, reactions to physical situations, and so forth. And when the moment comes when the diagnosis begins to coalesce, there is a tremendous surge of perception as all these details become integrated around the axes provided by psychological types. These typological interviews could take different forms depending on the audience. Some might be geared to the demonstration of the dynamic process of typology that takes place within the analytic context. Others could show how typological knowledge can be arrived at by the individual and related to the situations he finds himself in during the daily course of events. Equally interesting would be a typological interview of a married couple, or a family in which the dynamics between the members slowly becomes conscious as their awareness of typological differences increases.

This sort of training could be integrated with the administration of type tests, the latest results from the experimental sciences, and so forth, but there is one major obstacle to its coming about. It demands that we admit how limited and defective our present typological knowledge is, and that we then devote our energies to remedying this lack. As long as we hold on to one particular method, subjective or objective, as long as we hold on to our distinctive point of view as the universal one which all other people should conform to, then we demonstrate the very situation that typology was meant to remedy.

PART II

W.H. SHELDON'S SOMATOTYPES

In Part II we face a more difficult task than in Part I. The world of somatotypes (so-mắt-to-types) is much less known than the world of psychological types, and is much more obscured by controversy. If Jung's fame is increasing, Sheldon's seems to be decreasing. If Jung's work is being carried on by different audiences around the world, Sheldon's is by and large neglected. If Jung's life is well known through his autobiographical **Memories, Dreams, Reflections,** numerous biographies and the volumes of his published letters, Sheldon's is virtually unknown, without a single biography or even a full-fledged biographical essay. And most of all, if Jung's work is gaining increased recognition as a major advance in psychology, Sheldon's is under a cloud as if it has been somehow discredited.

This state of affairs is highly regrettable. Sheldon was, in fact, one of America's most talented psychologists, and his work provides an excellent complement to Jung's psychological types. In Chapter 4 we will look at the vision Sheldon had of a biologically founded constitutional psychology, and how far he advanced in creating one. In Chapter 5 we will examine the validity of the criticisms that surrounded his work, and in Chapter 6 the developments it inspired. And Chapter 7 asks just who was William Sheldon and whatever became of him?

CHAPTER 4
THE ORIGINS OF
SHELDON'S PSYCHOLOGY

Psychology and the Promethean Will

Let's examine briefly the basic principles that animate Sheldon's psychology. In 1936 he wrote **Psychology and the Promethean Will,** which gives an overview or blueprint of what he wanted to achieve. The book is an analysis of the human condition in five areas, or panels, as Sheldon called them: the economic, sociopolitical, sexual, religious and aesthetic. And it is the religious panel, which he defined as an orientation in time, that captures most of his attention. Sheldon was looking for a way in which psychology, religion and medicine could work together to solve human problems. He felt that psychology has never grown to its full stature. It suffered from an animectomy complex - his own take-off on the Freudian complexes - meaning a repressed fear of loss of soul. "For years psychologists have shouted down the soul with an intensity which recalls the Puritan shouting down his sexual consciousness", and it is religion in the terms of a Promethean foresight that must awaken us so we can prepare for the future. It is the role of religion to look to "the maintenance of harmony and mutual acceptability between the inner and outer world of awareness; between the world of human feeling and desire and the world of objective intellectual presentation." (p. 28) It is the religious mind if it is endowed with enthusiasm, intuitive insight and systemized factual equipment that will give a sorely needed sense of direction to the other panels of life.

What students of religion lacked, according to Sheldon, was this systemized factual equipment. They were eager to tackle human problems, but they had no grasp of just who, biologically speaking, they wanted to help. If a basic framework of descriptions could be erected - a schema of biological identification - then the insights of psychology, religion and medicine could be shared by means of a common language, and put to use in a concerted effort to tackle the seemingly intractable problems that face the human race. Sheldon wanted to create a biologically grounded study of man, or what he called a biological humanics. And this entailed a major refinement of the ways in which we can describe the individual. Only then, he felt, once we know in a more scientific manner what and who we were talking about, could we proceed to tackle the problems that faced the individual and the society, as well. In short, he wanted to start at the beginning and carefully describe people in terms of body and temperament.

This was certainly an ambitious project, and its religious framework undoubtedly owed something to Jung's thought, for Sheldon had been with Jung in Zurich just prior to his writing of this book. But, in actual fact, this plan was never developed as Sheldon first imagined it. The vast majority of his time and energy was to be devoted not to the religious aspects of the human personality, but to creating this more adequate way to describe men and women from the point of view of physique and temperament. This is the work that made him famous and is set forth in his Human Constitution Series: **The Varieties of Human Physique** (1940), **The Varieties of Temperament** (1942), **The Varieties of Delinquent Youth** (1949), and **The Atlas of Men** (1954).

The Varieties of Human Physique

The **Varieties of Human Physique** and **The Varieties of Temperament** were the fruits of Sheldon's
labors which began under the direction of L.L. Thurstone as he worked on his doctorate in psychology
at the University of Chicago in the mid 1920s. Together, they are comparable to Jung's psychological
types in the extensive research and practical experience that went into their creation. As a young man,
Sheldon had become enamored with the age-old questions; "Do those who look most alike behave most
alike? Does a particular sort of temperament go with
a definite physique? Can we predict a man's likes
and dislikes by measuring his body?" (**Varieties of
Human Physique,** p. 1) And at Chicago he began to
look in earnest for the answers. He studied the work
of Sante Naccarati, who was heir to the Italian anthropometric school of Viola and di Giovanni. They,
in turn, had come to prominence when the intuitive
phrenology of the past had been swept away by the
new scientific spirit, which relied on measurements
and statistics. Viola had developed a morphological
index, which measured the trunk of the body and
compared it with the limbs. The fruit of the work
of these older anthropometrists was "a low positive
relation between the preponderance of vertical measurements and mental ability, and also a low negative
relation between lateral or horizontal preponderance
and mental ability." (p. 14)

But these studies had been done on isolated body
parts and Naccarati wanted to improve on them by
making use of Viola's morphological index. In a
study of 75 male Columbia students he found a correlation of .36 between the index and intelligence
scores. And this is where Sheldon enters the scientific scene, not with wild suppositions or grand theories, but with the idea of replicating Naccarati's
work with a larger sample of 450 students. He used

Viola's index, intelligence tests and scholastic grades, and found a correlation of .14 between bodily measurements and test scores, and .12 between bodily measurements and scholastic achievements. Lower correlations than Naccarati, but still intriguing. He tried to dig further by comparing the various parts of the data with one another, but to no avail. There was no way to tease out the factors that were producing these correlations. This work lay the foundation for Sheldon's doctoral dissertaion, which inspired an article entitled, "Morphological Types and Mental Ability" in 1927. In another attack on the problem of constitution and behavior, he had the older members of a fraternity rate the younger ones on sociability, perserverance, leadership, aggressiveness and emotional excitability, and these ratings were compared to the bodily measurements. He found low correlations between measurements of width and aggressiveness, leadership and sociability, and he also found the general factor of bigness or heaviness showed a low positive correlation with these traits as well. Again, in 1927, he reported these results in "Social Traits and Morphological Types".

Next he turned to measurements of the head, for what better site for correlations between physique and mental behavior? In the past no high correlations had ever been found, but Sheldon reasoned that the problem might reside in the difficulty of making delicate measurements. To circumvent this problem he designed a special chair that held the subject's head in place, took photographs, projected them on a screen and measured them. Once again, the intriguing but frustrating low correlations appeared between the measurements, the social traits, and the mental ability. And once again, it was a global phenomenon, for the correlations could not be increased by selecting any particular measurements.

Sheldon had now arrived at a crossroads. He had refined the work of his predecessors and found the same sort of correlations, and we should note that they were lower than those of Naccarati. He was approaching 30 years of age and had the makings of a good academic career. All he had to do was accept the limitations that his measurements and statistics imposed upon him, and continue his work within those limits. But the "irritatingly persistent promise that deeper down lay something very interesting" (p. 20) kept on beckoning to him, and he saw "only too clearly that further progress on this particular trail alone could but complicate and obscure the picture." (p. 19) He made up his mind and chose a more intriguing but more difficult path:

"It had become clear that the missing vital link between psychology and physical anthropology was not to be found in anthropometry and statistical precision alone, however valuable these two aids might later prove to be.

"In the meantime another development had begun which seemed to offer greater prospect than had the correlation coefficient, the calipers, and the mental test. This was the method of clinical observation as employed by the psychiatrist Ernst Kretschmer." (p. 20)

It was this fateful decision that was to bear enormously interesting results, as well as embroil him in bitter controversy. His critics in later years would forget, or never knew, that Sheldon, far from being unacquainted with the normal methods of psychology, had pursued them until he became convinced that there was something vitally important that he had to pursue beyond their ability to grasp.

One of his first steps on this new path was the realization that he must become expert on the structure of the human body, and that meant, in his mind, training to become a medical doctor. He took up medical studies at the University of Chicago, received an MD in 1933, and interned at a children's hospital in Chicago. But he was never a doctor in the traditional sense. It was his vehicle for exploring the constitutional problem, and he began to examine Kretschmer's work with an eye to refining and extending it.

Ernst Kretschmer (1888-1964) is best known for his **Physique and Character** (1921), although he wrote on a wide range of psychiatric topics and was not adverse to exploring their ethical implications and their practical applications, whether in pedagogy, criminology and so forth. He was a privat dozent at Tübingen from 1918 to 1926, then professor of psychology and neurology at the University of Marburg, and he eventually returned to Tübingen as the director of its neurological clinic. It is interesting to see that his attraction to body types and character, like that of Joseph Wheelwright and Isabel Myers, is rooted in his own family situation. One of his noted students, Willi Enke, writes, "His mother was sensitive, humorous, artistic, and lively; while his father, a profound thinker and idealist philosopher, was so Spartan, sober, dry, and laconic that he appeared to lack aesthetic sensibility. It does seem significant that Kretschmer was initially most successful in elaborating the pyknic-cyclothymic group of types to which his mother belonged. Beyond this he did best in developing the contrast between cyclothymic and schizothymic temperaments; his father was an almost pure example of a schizothyme." (p. 451)

Kretschmer's initial work had been based on 260 cases divided into 85 circulars and 175 schizophrenes, and underlying these psychiatric disorders he discerned the cycloid and the schizoid temperaments. The cycloid was characterized as friendly, genial, cheerful and humorous. "..sociable, good-natured men, people with whom one can get on well, who understand a joke, and who take life as it comes. They give themselves naturally and openly, and one soon makes friends with them." (**Physique and Character**, p. 128) They have heart and are good natured, and

if they blow up they soon get over it. The schizoid,
in contrast, is "a man who stands in our way like a
question mark", sometimes bitingly sarcastic, sometimes timidly retiring, "like a mollusc without a
shell". (p. 150) The schizoids are unsociable, quiet,
reserved, timid, with fine feelings, sensitive, nervous,
and fond of nature and books. Kretschmer developed
these contrasting temperaments at great length, and
with a flare that engraved them in the minds of his
readers and inaugurated a new era of interest in
typology, and this is the most proximate raw material on which Sheldon drew.

Kretschmer had seen that most of his circular
psychotic patients, or manic-depressives, had a compact or pyknic build, while most of the schizophrenics had an asthenic one, meaning one without
strength. To these he added a third body type, the
athletic. There had been enthusiasms for, as well as
serious criticisms of Kretschmer's work, and Sheldon
saw them as a conflict between the logical and the
creative minds: "With Kretschmer, insight and the
observant eye came first, tools of quantification were
to be applied later." (**Varieties of Human Physique,**
p. 24)

And Sheldon hoped to handle the process of quantification at a new level of sophistication, and therefore avoid the reproaches directed at Kretschmer.
For him the key to this new approach lay in talking
not of types, which could not handle the infinite
variability of the human physique, but of fundamental
components which made up each physique and which
could be quantified. Sheldon had attempted to classify
400 male students at the University of Chicago according to Kretschmer's criteria, but had found that
72% of them were mixtures of the three types. Again
he reasoned that there must be a way to get at the
question of classification more directly. He had been
particularly impressed with a study by Wertheimer
and Hesketh, who had used a modified version of

Viola's index to measure 65 male patients who had been classified according to Kretschmer's method. Kretschmer's asthenics were microsplanchnic, or the more linear, while the manic-depressives were more lateral or macrosplanchnics. Something was there and he was determined to find it. He would look for the basic components, use more rigorous tools of measurement, but this time not allow technique to dominate his search as if the answer could come from technique alone. To this end he assembled the photographs of 4,000 male university students from 16 to 20 years of age, studied the pictures intently and looked for examples of the extreme variants. "...The procedure was strictly empirical and no a priori criteria were admitted." (p. 46) And this careful perusal yielded first two basic components, and eventually three. These three elements had a relationship to those of Kretschmer, but there was no exact correspondence. Instead of the pyknic or compact extreme, Sheldon found a round and soft one. He also found a muscular one, and a third, who was not necessarily asthenic, or weaker than the first, but fit Kretschmer's later terminology of the leptosomic, or the delicate-bodied. And Sheldon's response to why he describes three components parallels Jung's answer to why he describes four functions. That's what he saw in the empirical material, and that's what he expected we could find for ourselves if we examined the same or similar material.

While Sheldon was studying how these bodies actually appeared, he was also probing beneath the surface searching for a sense of why these different body types existed. He had begun attending autopsies and measuring and weighing the internal organs of each of the three types. He soon became aware that this was not a completely original idea.

Digging into the literature, he discovered that his results were confirmed by earlier studies of men like Goldthwait and Bryant who described the herbivorous and the carnivorous types, whose intestines were from 25' to 30', and from 10' to 15' respectively. He also found that starting in 1912 R.B. Bean had described the hypo-ontomorph, the meso-ontomorph, and the hyper-ontomorph, and Bean not only felt he could predict the length of the intestines from the body type, but described some of the other anatomical differences between them. Sheldon could not help but be impressed by the large intestines, stomach and liver of the round and soft extreme, the large hearts and arteries, muscles and bones of the muscular extreme, while the third extreme had brains and sense organs which were about the same size as the other types, but were proportionally larger because of this type's lower weight.

Sheldon realized that the stomach, intestines, liver, salivary glands, esophagus and so forth were derived from the endoderm or inner layer of the embryo. From the mesoderm, or middle layer, came the heart, blood, blood vessels, bone, muscles, adrenal glands, etc., and from the outer layer or ectoderm came the brain, spinal cord, skin, sensorial nerves, etc. Therefore, he settled on the names endomorph, mesomorph and ectomorph to describe those individuals in which the manifestations of each layer predominated. He concluded:

"We make the assumption that these individuals are extreme because they are dominated each by a different structural or morphological component." (p. 35-6)

What this means in the wider context of Sheldon's work is that he did not want to spend his days tracking transitory fluctuations in the shape and weight of his subjects, but wanted to make his measurements become the means by which he penetrated beneath these surface variations, and discovered a basic body structure or somatotype that endured through time. It was to be his lifelong task to refine the actual technique which would disclose this morphogenotype or fundamentally enduring somatotype, but the work that culminated in **The Varieties of Human Physique** provided Sheldon with one half of his biological identification system. The other major element was his study of temperament that was underway during these same years.

The Varieties of Temperament

It is revelatory of Sheldon's character and the ultimate intent of his Prometheus book that his work on temperament proceeded his study of somatotyptes, even though it was published later.

For Sheldon temperament was "the level of personality just above physiological function and below acquired attitudes and beliefs." (**The Varieties of Temperament,** p. 4) In fact, it was the behavior most intimately connected to the physical structure. It was somatotypes in action. And the way he went about discovering the basic components of temperament paralleled his somatotype work. He first collected 650 alleged traits of temperament and refined them down to 50, and proceeded to rate various people on them. His first group of subjects was 33 male graduate students, and he had 20 analytic interviews with each, was able to observe them in their daily routines and social relationships, and he wrote extensive notes on each one. For developing his somatotypes he wanted to avoid becoming submerged under an increasingly complicated collection of measurements which would obscure as much as it revealed about the human body. For his study of temperament he was quantifying ratings on specific traits, but with an eye to select the traits in such a way that the primary components of temperament would emerge. He examined the interrelationships between the 50 traits, looking for clusters of traits that would correlate in a positive fashion among themselves, but negatively with the other traits. Gradually three basic clusters emerged, despite his expectations there would be at least four, and 22 of his original 50 traits had survived, forming a first group of 6 traits, a second group of 7 traits, and a third group of 9 traits. This laborious process would have been more than enough for most of us, but Sheldon spent another four years reworking and adding to these three basic components until after 7 or 8 revisions he arrived at his Scale for Temperament which consisted of 20 traits for each basic component. After considering various possibilities he called these components viscerotonia, somatotonia and cerebrotonia. Now the scale was ready to be used. Sheldon lays down the proper conditions of its employment: "Observe the subject closely for at least a year in as many different situations as possible, conduct a series of not less than 20 analytic interviews with him..." (p. 27) and evaluate him and reevaluate him on every one of the 60 traits. And Sheldon is serious about this!

THE SCALE FOR TEMPERAMENT

Name	*Date*	*Photo No.*	*Scored by*

I VISCEROTONIA....	II SOMATOTONIA....	III CEREBROTONIA....
( ) 1. Relaxation in Posture and Movement	( ) 1. Assertiveness of Posture and Movement	( ) 1. Restraint in Posture and Movement, Tightness
( ) 2. Love of Physical Comfort	( ) 2. Love of Physical Adventure	— 2. Physiological Overresponse
( ) 3. Slow Reaction	( ) 3. The Energetic Characteristic	( ) 3. Overly Fast Reactions
— 4. Love of Eating	( ) 4. Need and Enjoyment of Exercise	( ) 4. Love of Privacy

THE SCALE FOR TEMPERAMENT

Name	*Date*	*Photo No.*	*Scored by*

I VISCEROTONIA....	II SOMATOTONIA....	III CEREBROTONIA....
— 5. Socialization of Eating	— 5. Love of Dominating, Lust for Power	( ) 5. Mental Overintensity, Hyperattentionality, Apprehensiveness
— 6. Pleasure in Digestion	( ) 6. Love of Risk and Chance	( ) 6. Secretiveness of Feeling, Emotional Restraint
( ) 7. Love of Polite Ceremony	( ) 7. Bold Directness of Manner	( ) 7. Self-Conscious Motility of the Eyes and Face
( ) 8. Sociophilia	( ) 8. Physical Courage for Combat	( ) 8. Sociophobia
— 9. Indiscriminate Amiability	( ) 9. Competitive Aggressiveness	( ) 9. Inhibited Social Address
— 10. Greed for Affection and Approval	— 10. Psychological Callousness	— 10. Resistance to Habit, and Poor Routinizing
— 11. Orientation to People	— 11. Claustrophobia	— 11. Agoraphobia
( ) 12. Evenness of Emotional Flow	— 12. Ruthlessness, Freedom from Squeamishness	— 12. Unpredictability of Attitude
( ) 13. Tolerance	( ) 13. The Unrestrained Voice	( ) 13. Vocal Restraint, and General Restraint of Noise
( ) 14. Complacency	— 14. Spartan Indifference to Pain	— 14. Hypersensitivity to Pain
— 15. Deep Sleep	— 15. General Noisiness	— 15. Poor Sleep Habits, Chronic Fatigue
( ) 16. The Untempered Characteristic	( ) 16. Overmaturity of Appearance	( ) 16. Youthful Intentness of Manner and Appearance
( ) 17. Smooth, Easy Communication of Feeling, Extraversion of Viscerotonia	— 17. Horizontal Mental Cleavage, Extraversion of Somatotonia	— 17. Vertical Mental Cleavage, Introversion
— 18. Relaxation and Sociophilia under Alcohol	— 18. Assertiveness and Aggression under Alcohol	— 18. Resistance to Alcohol, and to Other Depressant Drugs
— 19. Need of People When Troubled	— 19. Need of Action When Troubled	— 19. Need of Solitude When Troubled
— 20. Orientation Toward Childhood and Family Relationships	— 20. Orientation Toward Goals and Activities of Youth	— 20. Orientation Toward the Later Periods of Life

Note: The thirty traits with parentheses constitute collectively the short form of the scale.

The Varieties of Temperament, like The Varieties
of Human Physique, stresses the constitutional or biological side of the nature and nurture question. But
for Sheldon the whole question was framed in an inappropriate way. There is no nurture without a nature
to nurture. There is no nature that is not being continually influenced by a particular environment. The
Varieties of Temperament is really a book about
somatotype, temperament and environment. Even with
Sheldon's careful evaluation of both somatotype and
temperament, most of the 200 cases he describes
differ in these two classifications, and furthermore,
even people of the same somatotype and roughly the
same temperament index have widely different personalities when it comes to achievement. Sheldon
describes, for example, 8 men of the 2-3-5 somatotype, and gives their temperament indexes as 1-3-7,
2-4-4, 1-5-4, 1-4-5, 2-3-6, 3-4-4, 3-3-6, 3-3-5. These
evaluations of temperament fall in a circular range
around the position of the somatotype that well illus-
trates Sheldon's views on the question of heredity and
environment. There is a natural given represented by
the somatotype, but even on the level of physiologically conditioned behavior, that is, at Sheldon's temperament level, there is a large variety of different
paths of development that can be followed due to
different life circumstances, and an even wider range
of adjustment and adaptation. For example, one of
the 2-3-5s, temperamentally a 2-4-4, and with a very
high dysplasia, is one of the most promising men at
the university. The next case, temperamentally a
1-5-4, reverses his morphological predominance. In
other words, he appears to have drifted from his
biological moorings and created a personality at odds
with his natural predispositions. He has become highly
aggressive and violently disliked. And Sheldon has
doubts about how well he will fare in the future, and
classifies him "normal through effort".

Sheldon continues to analyze the relationship between somatotype and temperament in a variety of different ways. For example, he looks at the cases where there is perfect agreement between the two, and then those that show a radical disagreement, or where the index of temperament reverses a morphological predominance. He finds that endomorphs have the greatest chance of being normal, but not particularly distinguished in the academic community, nor is the endomorph likely to become a troublesome misfit. The mesomorph also has a good chance at normal adaptation, but he is more likely to become difficult if he fails to adapt. The ectomorph is lowest in the normal undistinguished category, and is highest in distinguished achievement. But if he is neither normal nor distinguished, he can run into a good deal of trouble.

But what captured readers' attention were the high correlations Sheldon found between the principle somatotype components, and the principle components of temperament. Between endomorphy and viscerotonia it was +.79. Between mesomorphy and somatotonia, +.82, and between ectomorphy and cerebrotonia +.83. Such correlations, Sheldon comments, "would suggest that morphology and temperament, as we measure them, may constitute expressions at their respective levels of essentially common components." (p. 401) In other words, Sheldon approaching the problem of the human constitution from two different directions felt he had finally arrived at discovering that something deeper down that he had been looking for for so many years.

He was too familiar, though, with the world of academic psychology to imagine these kinds of highly positive results would be readily accepted. But he probably underestimated how virulent these criticisms were to become. What upset his critics more than anything was that he had evaluated both temperament and somatotype himself. Some were even to go

so far as to consider that this fact alone constituted
an experimental error that vitiated his work. Even
before the fact, Sheldon was preparing his defense.
How, he asks, can he be expected, once he has deeply immersed himself in somatotypes, not to notice
the bodies of those he is evaluating for temperament? This whole issue will come to the forefront
when we evaluate some of the various criticisms
made of Sheldon's work. But some reflections are not
out of place here. Would it have made a great deal
of difference if one of Sheldon's professionally
trained colleagues had done the somatotyping? The
answer hinges on whether somatotyping is an objective procedure. Sheldon felt it was. In one experiment he and three other people evaluated the same
somatotype photos and compared these four ratings
to the results given by his somatotyping machine. The
average correlations between the machine and human
observers were .97. Later critics objected that the
various professional somatotypers had learned to sing
in harmony, as if this were a telling objection
against the objectivity of their observations. Are we
to imagine that the somatotype machine had learned
harmony as well? The problem of Sheldon rating both
somatotype and temperament was not an experimental error. Rather, it introduced the possibility of an
experimental error. But his critics, for the most
part, did not try to duplicate Sheldon's work as Sheldon initially did it. What they did was introduce various abbreviated versions of his temperament evaluation, and compared them with the somatotypes.

How objective was Sheldon's temperament rating?
He offers several experiments that try to come to
grips with this question, and their overall results
show that it is possible for observers to reach a
reasonable degree of agreement in evaluating temperament. For example, Sheldon and a psychiatrist used
a short form of the temperament scale with a group
of 50 subjects and found correlations between the

two evaluations of +.81 for the first component, +.89 for the second component, and +.87 for the third component.

The question of the objectivity of somatotypes and temperament were important issues. Sheldon made a serious attempt to address them, but they were not the only issues in the controversies that were to ensue. Behind them were the different methodological perspectives that we have already met in the field of psychological types and will see in the next chapter.

But there is something that such an examination of critics can never give us, and that is a sense of the intellectual adventure that must have pervaded Sheldon's life at this time. He knew the literature about body and temperament types, both old and new, that had started with the Greeks. He knew intimately the current efforts to put the clarification of physique and temperament on a solid scientific footing, and yet he realized that it is the empirical material itself that must take precedence. He pored over his stacks of photographs and rearranged them this way and that. He honed his Scale of Temperament and he studied his subjects exhaustively. Slowly he came to the conclusion that the three components of physique were the outer expression of the physical nature of the individual rooted in his very anatomy and physiology. And they, in turn, had a behavioral expression in the three components of temperament. In fact, they were but two reflections of the one human individual who was made of both body and psyche. He had finally arrived at that something, deeper down, that he had been searching for for so long.

The Varieties of Human Physique and **The Varieties of Temperament** represent an extraordinary advance in the field of typology, just as **Psychological Types** did. They were not Sheldon's first fruits, but his final fruits. And because they were the final

fruits of his years of labor they were open to misunderstanding, just as **Psychological Types** had been.
Sheldon had refined, polished and reworked his ideas
and language until he had his thoughts in a completed
form, and only then did he present them to the public. But who had or was willing to gain enough experience to properly evaluate them? Who would take
a year to conduct an evaluation of temperament, or
undergo the necessary apprenticeship to become a
professional somatotypist?

We could understand Sheldon's refinements of
Naccarati's work and the correlations he found. But
when Sheldon spent half a career probing deeper and
saying, in essence, that he has made a substantial
advance resolving the age-old question of the relationship between body and temperament, he loses us
by a shift of perspective. We are ready for the next
small incremental step, and instead we are confronted
with a substantial edifice. Our eyes cannot adjust.
We simply haven't learned to see in that way. In
fact, we have lost most of our hope in finding in
psychology that useful science to tackle concrete
human problems that Sheldon sought in his **Psychology
and the Promethean Will,** and we cannot believe that
his foundations for a schema of biological classification can be correct.

There are weaknesses in Sheldon's psychology. He
never did create the integral psychology he envision-
ed. And there are questions that can be raised about
his mathematical techniques, as we will see. And
finally he became embroiled in personal and professional conflicts that sapped his energy and prevented
his work from having the impact it could have had
- an issue that will occupy us in Chapter 7. But
when all is said and done, we have only to suspend
our disbelief and carefully read the brilliant case
studies that enliven **The Varieties of Temperament**
or page through photographic plates in **The Atlas of
Men** to realize that we are in the presence of one

of typology's most creative personalities.

What Sheldon has left us, then, is not a complete psychology like Jung's, but two powerful and inter-connected tools by which we can learn to see our bodies and the temperaments, and then apply this knowledge in countless different ways.

CHAPTER 5

SHELDON AND HIS CRITICS

When it comes to criticism it's best to confront the issue directly by loosely following Eysenck's extensive objections raised in **The Structure of the Human Personality.**

The first objection concerns Sheldon's mathematics. Sheldon did not use factor analysis, which was still developing when he wrote, but a less refined method called cluster analysis. Later investigators attempted to put his data in more mathematically sophisticated factorial forms. Eysenck cites Adcock (1948) and Lubin (1950) who found difficulties in understanding how Sheldon arrived at his conclusions from a mathematical point of view. A treatment of Sheldon's data led Ekman (1951) to the conclusion that it would be possible to represent Sheldon's three factors more parsimoniously by two orthogonal factors. And Hammond, in "The Status of Physical Types" (1957), reviews the two basic approaches to the study of body types, that is, both Sheldon's and the factor analytic approach, and describes the difficulties that he feels are found in each. For example, the elements in the somatotypes are complexly related and factor types offer no generally agreed solution. And then he reviews several studies of somatotypes by means of factor analysis in which Howells (1952), and Lauren Fields (1954) found two basic factors. One was endomorphy-ectomorphy with the endomorphs and the ectomorphs at the opposite ends of one continuum, and the second factor differentiated the mesomorphs from the endomorphs or ectomorphs. Hammond, himself, suggests a compromise based on Parnell's length, muscle and fat, "expressed by positive and negative numbers whose magnitude indicates general size and whose pattern shows the type distinction". (p. 240)

These lines of mathematical critique were pursued vociferously by Humphreys (1957) in his "Characteristics of Type Concepts with Special Reference to Sheldon's Typology". He was upset with Sheldon's way of discovering the three factors:

"...with regard to establishing the physical types, it is clear that the procedure was not empirically sound. The types originated in the arm chair. Sheldon did have large numbers of photographs spread out before him when he selected the types, but that hardly makes the procedure empirical." (p. 219)

He goes on to attempt to demonstrate on mathematical grounds alone "that Sheldon has evidence for no more than two independent (not necessarily valid) types of human physique." (p. 221) And he makes an interesting point meant as a thoroughgoing criticism, but which can be interpreted in a wider context, as we will do later. "Measurement entered later as a means of differentiating objectively the subjectively determined types. It was also shown that the choice of types to describe human physique and temperament automaticaly restricts the data in predictable ways." (p. 227)

Eysenck adds another category of criticism by accusing Sheldon of being derivative. According to him, Sheldon got his principle ideas from Kretschmer, his embryological notions from Bessonet-Favre (1910), Bauer (1923) and Castellino (1927), and his idea of separate factors from Plattner (1938). What Sheldon added was his photographic method. (p. 321-24). All this leaves the impression of Sheldon furtively scurrying about picking up bits and pieces and cobbling them together into a system. The facts are rather different. Eysenck glosses over the differences between Kretschmer and Sheldon, and ignores Sheldon's extensive familiarity with the history of typology. For example, Sheldon's chart of his predecessors is more extensive than the one Eysenck himself gives. Sheldon does mention Bauer and Plattner, as well as dozens of other people (but not Bessonet-Favre and Castellino) and is careful to indicate the origin of his ideas.

But there are more important objections in the offing. Do somatotypes really change? Eysenck cites Lasker (1947) who found differences in somatotype ratings before and after partial starvation, and Newman (1952) who found changes with age. He also cites Tanner (1956) who found little relationship between birth measurements and later measurements, but did find that childhood measurements and adult measurements were more strongly correlated. Hammond (1953) found some constancy in children over a period of several years, though a percentage of both the boys and the girls in his study had, according to him, changed their physical type. In a study by Zuk (1958) the somatotypes of male and female subjects were measured at 12, 17, and 33. Most of the correlations were fairly high, but different problems, for example, the estimation of endomorphy, were noted. Eysenck concludes "the evidence suggests that there is considerable stability of somatotypes but this is by no means as perfect as Sheldon would have us believe." (p. 329)

Next the issue on Eysenck's agenda was the close relationship Sheldon found between somatotype and temperament. There is a mainly negative study by Fiske (1944) and one with more positive results by Child (1950), which we should look at in more detail. A group of Yale students were somatotyped by Sheldon and some of them were given a questionnaire during a course, while the bulk of the subjects filled out the questionnaire after it was mailed to them. This procedure resulted in 414 actual subjects. Child had developed a whole series of predictions based on

Sheldon's system, and "of 96 predictions based on Sheldon's views 77 per cent are confirmed by the direction of relationship found in these data. Of the 74 correlations which are in the predicted direction, 20 reached significance at the 5 per cent level, whereas only 1 of the 21 correlations, contrary to prediction is significant at the 5 per cent level. The most marked contrast between the results which conform to prediction and those which do not is found in the number of instances of results significant at the 1 per cent level, where the contrast is between 10 and none." (p. 445)

Child concludes:

"It is thus possible, but not certain, that appropriate measures based on self-ratings such as were used here have a quite sizable relationship with dimensions of physique. It is reasonably certain that this relationship does not at all approach the magnitude of the relationships reported by Sheldon between dimensions of physique and his measures of temperament." (p. 447)

Results in the same direction can be seen in Davidson et al. (1957) who found a relationship between ectomorphy and the traits meticulous, fussy and conscientious, and Smith (1957) who compared somatotypes and MMPI scales and found many significant correlations, most of them as predicted from Sheldon, but the correlations were much lower than the ones Sheldon found.

A more positive study by Sheldon and Wittman of 155 psychotic male patients found higher correlations between the various psychiatric components and the components of physique. Eysenck found these results of considerable interest, and this is a study we will return to later in another connection. There are also studies by Fiske (1942), Smith (1949) and Janoff et al. (1950) where somatotypes were compared with objective tests of temperament, and these found extremely low correlations.

Eysenck concludes his examination by saying that Sheldon's contributions "probably contain sufficient truth and insight to be worthy of proper scientific investigation.

"Sheldon's analysis is essentially subjective; his types, as are those of Kretschmer and his predecessors, are derived from intuition and theory. It is obviously advantageous to have a more objective approach based on empirical data..." (p. 334)

Have we, then, reached the point where Sheldon has been exposed as an armchair theorist, as Humphreys would have it, or a derivative dabbler whose work must be redone at a proper scientific level? No. This is hardly the case. We are once again confronted with the problem of method in psychology, and this delicate theoretical problem is exacerbated by the attitudes of the combatants. Sheldon does employ various mathematical techniques, but he does it in such a way that at times it appears, as Eysenck says, "en passant", and has something of an off-hand sense of condescension for the less perceptive. This, of course, would be infuriating to those on the other side of the methodological fence, but they, in their turn, have their weak points. Humphreys, for example, wants to limit the empirical to what his mathematical methods can perceive, and thus relegates Sheldon to being an armchair theorist, which is not correct. Eysenck, himself, appears to picture his role as the difficult and laborious one of reconstructing psychology on more secure scientific foundations. This has a leveling effect. The intricate and fascinating typological edifice that Jung constructed on the basis of empirical material is limited to the ideas of introversion and extraversion. The four functions are ignored, as well as the dynamic relationship between the conscious and unconscious attitudes. The same process can be seen in relationship to Sheldon. Sheldon's highly perceptive insights, which he systematized into a new high point of the understanding of physique and behavior, are subjected to a similar process of leveling, which eliminates almost all of what is most interesting in Sheldon. It amounts to saying since our methods cannot achieve the results that Sheldon says he achieved, therefore Sheldon is wrong. No one is particularly interested in following Sheldon's methods. Eysenck says: "One difficulty in the way of a ready acceptance of Sheldon's work must be the difficulty of repetition. Few psychologists can observe their subjects for a whole year and give each one 20 or more analytic sessions before making a rating." (p. 141)

Sheldon's method is very different from that of his critics. At first glance he may appear to be employing exact measurement and mathematical analysis, but this is misleading. He is best understood when he is placed in Jung's company in terms of scientific methodology. L.L. Thurstone gives us an interesting criterion for trying to clarify this point, when in a talk to the Psychometric Society in 1936 on the establishment of psychology as a quantitative and rational science, he distinguishes the use of mathematics as an aid or tool from its use as the very language in which the psychologist thinks. No one would make the mistake of imagining that Jung thought in the language of mathematics, and while Sheldon used mathematics, a case could be made that he did not think in the language of mathematics. For example, even though he worked with Thurstone on his original attempt to mathematically represent his constitutional conclusions, they did not find favor with later factor analysis advocates. Further, Sheldon was apparently in no rush to try to objectify his somatotyping procedures. He moved from observation to measurement and back again. It was only with the urging from his long-standing associates Eugene McDermott and C. Wesley Dupertuis that he produced his final objective method.

Sheldon resisted developing completely objective

techniques, and part of the resistance has to be seen against our earlier discussion of the deadends that an overreliance on measurement and statistics had led him to early in his career. Perhaps he overreacted. He was annoyed at his colleague C.W. Dupertuis when in the course of their examinations of the thousands of mental patients Dupertuis wanted to take anthropometric measurements, for he felt he had tried them at one time but they didn't show what he was looking for.

Eventually he came around to the necessity of showing that his somatotyping could be done on a completely objective basis. But this came late in his career and went virtually unnoticed. We will examine this contribution a little later, but now let's turn to see what Eysenck and his factor analytic colleagues would put as the more objective structure that should replace Sheldon's. The various factor analytic studies of physique can be briefly summarized as having yielded two factors: one of body size and another of height and width. According to Eysenck:

"The major outcome of factorial analyses of body build appears to be that we may regard the body as a rectangle which can be described with fair accuracy in terms of two independent dimensions, to wit, height and width." (p. 339)

On this basis physique can be divided into three classes: the eurymorph, equivalent to Sheldon's endomorph and mesomorph, or the lateral physique, and the leptomorph, equivalent to the ectomorph, or linear physique, and a mesomorph which is not Sheldon's mesomorph, but which is simply someone in the middle from a statistical point of view. We have returned to the old dichotomy which originated with Hippocrates, but now in a more sophisticated form.

This is no place to take up a mathematical defense of Sheldon. Perhaps some day a highly impartial and mathematically gifted researcher will unravel this question, and I don't think Sheldon would object to this. Quite the contrary. C.J. Adcock, for example, in his factorial examination of Sheldon's types analyzes Sheldon's figures and concludes that a halo effect must be the explanation for the uniformity of Sheldon's correlations. "It's much too perfect. Nevertheless we feel that there is a sound basis to it all and that with all allowance made for the halo there is still something substantial left." (p. 318)

When Adcock writes "these correlations between S (somatotonia) and C (cerebrotonia) are too high which makes impossible a normal analysis of this data", Sheldon, in a margin of an offprint of his article responds, "Yes. The original error, of course, lay in the insufficient thickness of the assumed 3-dimensional plot of the S-types (76 S-types). With the current parameters and greater spread of S-types this difficulty vanishes and the 3 components are more nearly orthogonal". And he felt he corrected this original error with his later article "Psychotic Patterns".

It is important to note, however, that Sheldon's mathematics are built on the foundation of his observations. As Humphrey noted in another connection, this might automatically effect how the data is analyzed. Sheldon is trying to quantify something he has already seen, and so there is a constraint placed on the measurements he will choose and their analysis. The factor analysts are taking a series of measurements and seeing what emerges. Their mathematics suffers from fewer constraints, and therefore is clearer and more lucid. But at the same time is it not possible that they are flattening out what Sheldon saw, since their techniques cannot grasp it? Thus, skeletal measurements readily show a height and width factor, but have trouble dealing with the question of muscularity and fat, which stand out more sharply from an observational point of view. This does not mean there are no highly distinctive mesomorphs so that mesomorphy becomes just a statistical classification. It can also mean that different methods produce different results, somewhat of a truism which will take on flesh when we look at the work of Parnell, Dupertuis and others.

Let's return for a moment, though, to the results of factor analysis in other areas comparable to Sheldon's work. The eurymorph body build is connected with extraversion and manic-depressive disease, while the leptomorph is connected with introversion and schizophrenia. To this can be added the leptomorph's inclination to what Eysenck calls "dysthymic" kinds of neurosis, and the eurymorph to more hysterical disorders. All this parallels insights found both in Sheldon and Jung.

But what of the factor of size? Eysenck in a 1940 study compared 156 microsomatic, 156 macrosomatic and 688 mesosomatic male neurotic soldiers, that is, he compared the small-bodied to the large and medium-bodied. The small-bodied had the following characteristics: poor physical health, weak and dependent, inert, depressed, poor muscular tone, and so forth. "Altogether both mentally and physically he is what is popularly called a poor specimen." (p. 345-6) The reader of Sheldon would clearly recognize the parallel between the microsomatic and Sheldon's asthenic characteristics. The asthenic person was characterized by Sheldon, following Hooton, as "poor protoplasm, poorly put together".

What all this amounts to is that Sheldon is guilty of having rated his initial 200 subjects on both somatotype and temperament, and therefore could have let the results of one level influence the other. This does not mean that anyone has demonstrated that he did allow them to influence each other. Further, his mathematical analysis of the data is not ideal, a fact he would admit and worked to rectify. At the same time he was working at a time when the current factor techniques were still being developed. And he was determined not to let mathematical technique obscure the deeper realities he was trying to draw out.

There is a final issue that became a point of contention. What are the biological underpinnings both to Sheldon's work and to factor analysis? Eysenck finds support for the two factor theory in Lindegard's work in measuring the length of the long shaft bones and their thickness.

"The very extensive correlations reported by him suggest strongly that these two factors, derived from physiological and anatomical considerations, correspond closely to the length and width factors of the factor analyst, which thus find strong biological backing." (p. 341)

But when it comes to Sheldon's assumption that there is a connection between his three factors and the three layers of the embryo, Eysenck is convinced of the importance such a relationship would have if it could be proven, for "the observed intercorrelations among the types would be a cheap price to pay for the gain in understanding obtained through this relationship." (p. 326) But he has various reservations about this connection actually existing. He asserts that Sheldon fails to account for the complexity of the development of the germ layers, makes no deductions from his hypotheses, does not take into account the "mesenchyme", or a sort of intermediate layer between the other layers, and he cites an article by Hunt (1949) as evidence to the contrary for a relationship between the layers of the embryo and the different physiques. This is an issue of considerable importance which outweighs, as Eysenck makes clear, the various debates about two or three factors, and we will return to it in a later section.

All in all, there is a rather remarkable parallelism between the basic results of the two methods. If there were not such methodological bad blood, this common ground would be more to the forefront and more collaborative efforts would be taking place

between people involved in both methods. But this
excursion through Eysenck can still leave the impression that Sheldon's work has to be satisfied with
faint praise begrudgingly given. It is important, then
to spend some time looking at a variety of studies
in this chapter and the next which will help redress
the balance.

Among these studies pride of place should go to
Sheldon's final paper entitled, "Psychotic Patterns in
Physical Constitution", a 30-year follow-up of 3,800
psychiatric patients in New York State, which was
given at a symposium on schizophrenia in New York
in November, 1968. Unfortunately, by then, his critics
had dominated the field for so long that it must have
appeared to the psychological community that Sheldon
had nothing to say in his own defense, and this paper
did little to change that state of affairs. His critics,
if they heard about it, which was not too likely,
ignored it. This is unfortunate because it is a brilliant piece of work that is very much Sheldon at his
best, sharp and perceptive. It contains two sections:
one, a preliminary report on the psychiatric studies
that he and his colleagues had carried out over the
course of 30 years in various hospitals around New
York State. The other part was the final objectification of somatotyping. Sheldon reviews his previous
work, and then turns to the objections brought
against it, admitting that in his **Varieties of Human
Physique,** "a number of major problems were doubt-
less oversimplified and some were left unexplored -
or even worse, unmentioned." (p. 844) He summarizes
the objections under four headings: (1) the somatotype
changes (2) somatotyping is not objective (3) there
are only two, not three, primary components (4)
somatotyping omits the factor of size.

In considering the first objection he describes his
early attempts during the time of his Ph.D. thesis
to identify the primary factors in physical constitution: "Thurstone decided that 4 primary factors were

demonstrated and that one of these factors was size. When we expressed all the measurements as ratio to stature, thus eliminating size, three factors remained." (p. 844) These Sheldon took to be expressions of the three components he had discovered by his inspection of the somatotype photographs. If there were no relationship between the three, there should have been 343 somatotypes. If the correlations were highly negative there would not be three components, but only two, which, as we have seen, was a conclusion many of his critics arrived at. But Sheldon felt that this was not a good conclusion to come to when dealing with a three-dimensional organism. So he tried to steer a middle path. After a series of discussions with Thurstone he decided there was no way, a priori, to determine how many somatotypes there would be. It was going to be a process of "try it out and see". In his first book he identified 76 somatotypes. By 1954, in **The Atlas of Men**, there were 88, and the search still went on for those measurements which would more and more objectively determine the somatototype which Sheldon felt remained stubbornly constant through life. Finally, he discovered what he called the trunk index, which is the ratio of the thoracic trunk over the abdominal trunk. In other words, the trunk is divided at the waist into two sections and the area of each is measured by means of a planimeter on the standard somatotype photographs. Its discovery paved the way for solving three of the objections to somatotyping. It distinguished between endomorphy and mesomorphy; it remained constant from about the third year of life to old age, despite variations in fatness or leanness, and it opened the way for the complete objectification of somatotyping.

Sheldon had extensive opportunities to test out this new index. He examined the photographs of 400 subjects who were part of the Berkeley Growth Study, for whom somatotype photographs were taken

since they were children until they were fully grown.
The trunk index remained constant. He looked at the
somatotype photographs taken at the University of
Minnesota during a starvation experiment. Starvation
had not changed the trunk index. He also examined
West Pointers upon entering and leaving the Academy
after closely supervised body-conditioning programs,
Columbia University students who had been photographed as freshmen and then had been somatotyped
40 years later, a series of 46 identical twins, and
men and women in a weight-reduction clinic, which
included women who had lost as much as 150 pounds.
In all these series the trunk index remained unchanged from early childhood onwards.

   He finally had an objective way to distinguish
between endomorphy and mesomorphy. He had a
second parameter in the maximum weight the subject
had reached, and he found the third in stature. This
would allow him to measure the three-dimensional
organism: "First we have to have a measure of massiveness; then a separator for the two kinds of mass
(endomorphy and mesomorphy); finally a measure of
the degree of stretched-outness into space." (p. 848)
The Trunk Index has zero correlations with stature
and ectomorphy. The correlations between endomorphy
and mesomorphy approach zero in both sexes, and the
correlations between ectomorphy and endomorphy and
ectomorphy and mesomorphy average about -.40.
Sheldon realized that in his earlier more visually
oriented methods he had been doing the equivalent
of taking into account both stature and the trunk
index, but indirectly. Now he could simply measure
maximum weight, height and the trunk index and
calculate the somatotypes, and he could answer the
objections against his somatotyping:

   "1) The somatotype changes. It cannot change,
since maximal stature and maximal massiveness are
simply items of historical fact, and TI (Trunk Index)
is constant through life.

2) Is not objective. Now it is completely objective. Can be derived on a computer as a function of three parameters, thus providing an operational definition of the procedure.

3) There are only two, not three primary components. This difficulty no longer exists. It arose from the fact that the negative correlations among the primary components were too high. That condition has been corrected, thus permitting us to live and operate in three spatial dimensions again.

4) Omits the factor of size. Size has been restored by using stature as a determining parameter." (p. 848-9)

It gives one a strange feeling to read Sheldon's culminating contribution against the background of all the criticism his work provoked, and to realize it was met with a thundering silence. Here was a completely objective method that could be replicated by anyone, but virtually no one bothered. That this would happen is a good illustration of how much the scientific process is wrapped up in human nature with its passions and weaknesses. Sheldon resists objectification, antagonizes his critics, finally comes up with an objective method, and no one seems to have the time to examine it. But its implications are enormous. If this objective method is viable, and there is no reason to think that it is not, then it sheds an interesting light on Sheldon's less objective methods and on the question of the relationship between somatotype and temperament. If Sheldon was substantially correct in his choice of the three factors, was he also correct in finding a close relationship between somatotype and temperament? Let's look at two other studies, one which makes use of Sheldon's latest method, and another which studies the relationship between physique and temperament.

Richard Walker and James Tanner in their "Prediction of Adult Sheldon Somatotype I and II from Ratings and Measurements at Childhood Ages" (1980), examined the photographs of 82 boys at ages 5, 8, 11, 14 and 18, using both Sheldon's anthroposcopic method and his objective method. They found inter-judged correlations for the anthroposcopic ratings ranging from .79-.93, while the correlations for the Trunk Index method ranged from .94-.99. The mean somatotype changed little with age by either method, and the correlations between the two ratings were in the low .80s. In the case of the anthroposcopic ratings, nearly 40% of the ratings were identical, and nearly 80% within a half point. With the Trunk Index method, there was nearly complete agreement for ectomorphy, and 87-96% of the ratings for mesomor-phy and endomorphy fell within a half a point.

John Cortés and Florence Gatti in "Physique and Self-Description of Temperament" have given us one of the most positive evaluations of the relationship between somatotype and temperament using com-pletely objective methods. They created a simple questionnaire which emphasized the more psychologi-cal aspects of temperament, and they administered this questionnaire to three separate audiences, which they also somatotyped by Parnell's method.

Cortés and Gatti's
Self-Description of Temperament

Name   Age   Date

Below are some statements that we would like to have you complete about yourself. Fill in each blank with a word from the suggested list following each statement. For any blank, three in each state-ment, you may select any word from the list of twelve immediately below. An exact word to fit you may not be in the list, but select the words that seem to fit **most closely** the way you are.

1. I feel most of the time _____, _____, and
_____.

calm	relaxed	complacent
anxious	confident	reticent
cheerful	tense	energetic
contented	impetuous	self-conscious

2. When I study or work, I seem to be _____,
_____, and _____.

efficient	sluggish	precise
enthusiastic	competitive	determined
reflective	leisurely	thoughtful
placid	meticulous	cooperative

3. Socially, I am _____, _____ and _____.

outgoing	considerate	argumentative
affable	awkward	shy
tolerant	affected	talkative
gentle-tempered	soft-tempered	hot-tempered

4. I am rather _____, _____, and _____.

active	forgiving	sympathetic
warm	courageous	serious
domineering	suspicious	soft-hearted
introspective	cool	enterprising

5. Other people consider me rather _____,
_____, and _____.

generous	optimistic	sensitive
adventurous	affectionate	kind
withdrawn	reckless	cautious
dominant	detached	dependent

6. Underline **one** word out of the three in each of
the following lines which most closely describes the
way you are.

    a) assertive, relaxed, tense
    b) hot-tempered, cool, warm
    c) withdrawn, sociable, active
    d) confident, tactful, kind
    e) dependent, dominant, detached
    f) enterprising, affable, anxious

The first group consisted of 73 boys who were high school seniors, and clearly endomorphs, mesomorphs or ectomorphs, and the authors found a strong relationship between somatotype and the self-rating of temperament: endomorphy to viscerotonia +.51, mesomorphy to somatotonia +.69 and ectomorphy to cerebrotonia +.43, all of which were significant beyond the .01 level. And there were negative correlations between each physical component and the other two components of temperament. The correlations in their very extreme types were even higher: viscerotonia and endomorphy, +.66, somatotonia and mesomorphy +.74 and cerebrotonia and ectomorphy +.59.

In their second group of 100 college girls "there is perfect correspondence in all groups between the components of physique and the number of traits selected. In every instance, as the girls were higher or lower in each component of physique, they selected a higher or lower number of traits of the corresponding component of temperament." (p. 436) The correlations were: viscerotonia and endomorphy +.59, somatotonia and mesomorphy +. 57 and cerebrotonia and ectomorphy +.60. In their third group they tested 20 subjects who had committed serious crimes. All were high in mesomorphy, and they all selected more temperamental traits from the second group. The authors conclude: "All these findings are very positive. It has been shown that physique and self-description of. temperament are intimately associated." (p. 438) They also point out the diversity of the subjects they tested, the possibility of distortions by self-flattering as the subjects took the quiz, and the difficulty the subjects could have in understanding themselves as well as the meaning of the traits, all of which would have worked against positive correlations. Though they consider the possibility of various environmental factors at work, they state: "It seems reasonable to assume that physique, through the organs of the body, glandular secretions, and the particular chemotype, limits in individuals the range of temperamental traits and predisposes, together with other variables, towards some traits more than towards others." (p. 438)

It is safe to say, then, that while Sheldon has been neglected in recent years, he has not been discredited. There is something there and it is strongly there in Sheldon's somatotyping and its connection with temperament. Lindzey and Hall in an extensive review of Sheldon's constitutional psychology, pleasing in its sense of balance, state:

"One may quarrel over the degree of relation between physique and personality, or even over the factors that mediate this relation, but present evidence leaves little doubt, at least in the authors' minds, that something important is afoot here. Prior to Sheldon's forceful appearance on the scene, such a relationship was customarily dismissed in this country as representing little more than superstition or speculation." (Theories of Personality, p. 372)

Lindzey in a later article, "Behavior and Morphological Variation", perceptively adds:

"In his research and writing Sheldon is much more the sensitive naturalist, observer, and categorizer and much less the hard, quantitative, and objective scientist than would be optimal to assure a good press from our colleagues. Moreover, in his writings he has proven to be singularly adept at ridiculing or parodying just those aspects of the scientific posture of psychologists that are most sensitively, rigidly, and humorlessly maintained. One might argue convincingly that, if Sheldon had conducted the same research but had reported it in an appropriately dull, constricted, and affectless manner (consistent, let us say, with Journal of Experimental Psychology standards), its impact upon the discipline of psychology might have been much greater." (p. 228)

His comments on the high correlations Sheldon found between physique and temperament are equally well worth quoting. "If, as the climate of current opinion urges, the magnitude of association reported by Sheldon represents in large measure covariance attributable to experimental error, this fact remains to be demonstrated unequivocally. Moreover, in view of the extensive criticism of his study, it does seem odd that there has not been one single effort at a careful replication eliminating the major defects in Sheldon's study, while at the same time attempting to preserve other relevant conditions as exactly as possible. What we have witnessed, instead, has been the complacent dismissal of a potentially important set of results with no serious attempt at an empirical resolution." (p. 234)

In the 20 years since Lindzey wrote those words we still cannot point to any study that has tried to duplicate Sheldon's temperament work using the procedures that Sheldon advocated.

CHAPTER 6
THE WORLD OF SOMATOTYPES

It is time to look at some of the literature that has grown up around Sheldon's somatotypes. This will demonstrate further the basic validity of the positions he took and the valuable work he helped inspire.

Studies of Physique

Let's start with Sheldon's longtime colleagues C.W. Dupertuis and his wife and professional associate Helen Stimson Dupertuis, both physical anthropologists and both deeply interested in the anthropometric side of somatotyping. It was Dupertuis who had a role in introducing Sheldon to certain constitutional circles in the United States before World War II. In 1944 Draper, Dupertuis and Caughey published **Human Constitution in Clinical Medicine** based on their work at the Constitution Clinic at Columbia University founded in 1916. The Clinic had switched to Sheldon's somatotypes in 1940, and their book clearly illustrates how vital it is to analyze basic medical data like blood pressure and basal metabolism against a background of the whole human constitution:

"No one would have a high opinion of a veterinary who called a race horse sick and unable to run just because the animal weighed less than a draft horse of equal height." (p. 149)

They provide averages for the three components of physique and the andric and gynic ratings for duodenal ulcer, gall bladder, diabetes mellitus, diffuse toxic goiter and rheumatoid arthritis, and sound the prophetic note:

"It is fair to say that there is more virgin territory in this field (constitutional physiology) than in almost any other branch of clinical medicine." (p. 163)

In "Be Your Physical Self", the Dupertuises take on the thick accumulation of myths that surround the question of how much we ought to weigh. They dramatically show the inadequacy of the height-weight tables, even when divided into small, medium and large frames, by examining the Cleveland Brown's football team, many of whom, according to the charts, are 40 to 60 pounds overweight. Unless we can determine what size frame we have, we will be unable to determine our proper weight, and so they developed a method of determining frame size from actual skeletal measurements. By measuring 50,000 children and adults from different parts of the world, they have created tables that indicate the weight proportional to the individual's height and bone structure. Unfortunately, these tables have not been published.

Equally regrettable has been the lack of publication of their "Structural Profile", a kind of morphological fingerprint, based on height, weight and skeletal measurements which come from five different body regions. These measurements are plotted on a chart which already indicates the mean measurements of American men and women. When they are plotted a profile emerges that graphically portrays a wealth of information. It can indicate the dysplasias that might exist in a physique, and how this physique compares with others. With three additional measurements, a skeletal version of Sheldon's trunk index, called the Shape Index, can be determined which highly correlates with it and remains constant over time. The Structural Profile thus provides a way in determining the somatotype without the use of photography. It appears an ideal tool with which to do cross-cultural comparisons of physiques, and the Dupertuises have already employed it in various parts of the world. And why hasn't it been published? Perhaps it has suffered from the climate of criticism that surrounded Sheldon's work and prevented his own Trunk Index method from being recognized.

Let's stop and look at the methods that exist to determine somatotypes.

1. After Sheldon arranged his initial series of 4,000 somatotype pictures, he quantified this procedure by the use of 17 measurements plus height and weight, and showed it yielded comparable results. But this quantification was limited to college-age males and was laborious in practice. To facilitate its use S.S. Stevens created a machine that could and did handle most of the calculations, but in the days before computers it was a laborious task and was still limited to that narrow range of age.

2. Sheldon turned to structured observation, or his anthroposcopic method, which temperamentally suited him better. In it the height divided by the cube root of weight provided a clue to a number of possible somatotypes by means of the charts Sheldon provided in the **Atlas of Men**, and the final determination of which somatotype was to be preferred was done by the comparison of the somatotype photo with the pictures in the **Atlas.**

3. Still later, as we have seen, he developed the Trunk Index method based on height, maximum weight, and the determination of the Trunk Index. Sheldon provided detailed tables to convert this data into the somatotype number.

4. Now we can add the Dupertuis Structural Profile.

And while Dupertuis and Sheldon were on the long and difficult journey that would lead to a totally objective method, but zig-zagged back and forth between observation and objectification for many

years, others were following a somewhat similar
path.

5. In England R.W. Parnell, in 1954 and 1958,
produced two versions of an anthropometric method
which attempted to steer between the more observational techniques of Sheldon and the criticisms it was
being subjected to, and the factor analytic methods
which collapsed the three dimensions into two and
which he felt lost significant information. His M-4
method, which did not demand photographs, was based
on height over the cube root of weight, three measurements of the subcutaneous fat, two muscle girth
measurements and two bone measurements. Parnell
was aware that his final three factors were not
necessarily identical to Sheldon's, and so he called
them fat, muscularity and linearity.

6. In the U.S. Barbara Honeyman Heath who had
worked with Sheldon between 1948 and 1953, suggested in 1963 the broadening of Sheldon's observational
methods by employing the following modifications:
opening the 7-point rating scale, opening the limited
sums of the components that Sheldon had adhered to,
relating the height-weight ratio more linearly to the
somatotype, and eliminating the interpolations for
age. Later, in 1967, with J.E.L. Carter, she developed
a modified somatotype method which combined her
modifications of Sheldon's judgments of somatotype
photos with Parnell's M-4 techniques.

This method has been widely employed. Carter,
for example, has used it extensively in connection
with physical fitness and competitive athletics studying world class body-builders, Olympic competitors,
children in sports, and so forth. Carter and Heath
have a new book in press: **Somatotyping: Development
and Application,** which will hopefully illuminate many
of the byways in the development of the various
methods, as well as their applications.

The use of somatotypes in combination with exact
measurements reached a certain maturity in the work

of James Tanner, a noted English specialist on human growth. Tanner had come to the U.S. with a group of medical students at the beginning of WWII, and eventually worked with both Sheldon and Dupertuis. His work has included directing the Harpenden Growth Study, which ran from 1948 to 1971, and publishing an **Atlas of Children's Growth:** Normal Variation and Growth Disorders. The **Atlas** provides an excellent example of modern somatotyping in which the old quarrels are transcended. Here we can see how the various difficulties in somatotyping have been dealt with in practice. He provides photos that illustrate: both the difficulty and feasibility of somatotyping children, how well the somatotypes of children match their adult somatotypes (following Walker and Tanner, 1980), the issue of the relative constancy of size and shape during childhood, longitudinal series of monozygotic twins that tracks their development from childhood to maturity, and series of men somatotypes which show what kind of changes they undergo during adulthood. This **Atlas** not only carefully documents the many difficult problems in scientific somatotyping, but it also demonstrates, without any fanfare, the underlying continuity of somatotype that Sheldon was attempting to show for so long.

Earlier, in 1964, Tanner published a study of 137 track and field athletes at the Olympic games in Rome. This makes fascinating reading because the somatotype charts clearly indicate how certain kinds of physiques dominate certain sports. The physiques of the sprinters are different from those of the distance and marathon runners: 2.5-5.5-3 for the sprinters and 2.5-4-4 for the marathon runners. Similarly, competitors in the discus, javalin and shot and hammer have highly mesomorphic physiques: 3-6-2 or 3.5-6-2. The somatotype charts also clearly indicate that many of us do not have much Olympic potential. Half the somatotypes present in the general population are not found among the athletes. And though most of us have already become aware of the fact that we will not be Olympic champions, it is another matter for youthful competitors who might benefit from a more realistic evaluation of their potential based on the ever-growing literature on somatotypes and athletes, as well as a knowledge of their own somatotype and its dysplasias.

G. Petersen, a doctor from the Netherlands, produced an **Atlas for Somatotyping Children** in 1967. It follows closely Sheldon's **Atlas of Men,** though Petersen found some somatotypes not in the **Atlas.** And instead of using Sheldon's large format cameras he used a 35mm.

With all the different methods of somatotyping in existence, it was both natural and inevitable that they would be compared. We have already seen a comparison between Sheldon's anthroposcopic or observational method, and his Trunk Index method in the article by Walker and Tanner. In a follow-up study of the subjects in the **Varieties of Delinquent Youth,** the Trunk Index method was employed which allows us to compare it to Sheldon's initial somatotype ratings. We will see some of these differences in a later section. In 1965 Haronian and Sugarman did a comparison of Sheldon and Parnell's methods. In 1966 Heath and Carter compared Heath's modified method with Parnell's. In 1979 María Villanueva Sagrado in her short book, **Manual de Técnicas Somatotipológicas** presented and compared Sheldon's Trunk Index method with those of Parnell, Heath and Heath and Carter. She somatotyped 300 male subjects using the four methods, and concluded that the methods produced different results. She favored Sheldon's because of its biological grounding, so important in medical and psychiatric work. Conscious, too, of the expense of photographic somatotype work, she mentions a study by Stoute (1971) who used a "camera clara", instead of photographs, to determine the Trunk Index.

In 1980 Claessens and his associates at the two branches of the University of Leuven in Belgium were in search of a somatotyping technique. They somatotyped 132 young men using Sheldon's anthroposcopic method, his Trunk Index method, and the methods of Parnell, and Heath and Carter. They found a high agreement between the two Sheldon methods, and between the Parnell and Heath and Carter methods, but they also found differences between the two agreeing pairs on the question of the rating of mesomorphy. In a comparison between the ratings of mesomorphy and 24 motor ability tests, Sheldon's techniques related significantly to 16 of the tests, Parnell to 8, and Heath and Carter's to 4. The authors then developed a hybrid method using the methods of Parnell, and Heath and Carter to estimate endomorphy and ectomorphy, with a final evaluation of somatotypes dependent on the **Atlas of Men.**

Somatotypes have found a particularly durable employment in the field of delinquency and criminology. Perhaps the best known aspect of the **Varieties of Delinquent Youth** is that the young men on the whole are more mesomorphic and less ectomorphic than both the general population and their collegiate counterparts. This assertion caused a certain stir at the time of its publication, but subsequent studies have reaffirmed it time and again. For example, Sheldon Glueck and Eleanor Glueck in **Physique and Delinquency** (1956) compared almost 500 delinquents with 500 non-delinquents, and they found that roughly 60% of the delinquents were mesomorphic compared with 30% of the non-delinquents.

Cortés and Gatti in their **Delinquency and Crime: A Biopsychosocial Approach,** studied 100 delinquent boys, 100 non-delinquent boys, and 20 criminals. They used Parnell's method of somatotyping and found that 57 out of the 100 delinquents were mesomorphs compared to 19 out of the 100 non-delinquents. They made a determined effort both in method and in language to distance themselves from Sheldon, but their results were quite similar. For example, the mean somatotype of their delinquents were 3.5-4.4-3.1, whereas the mean somatotype of 150 of the delinquents of Sheldon was 3.5-4.5-2.8. And the more overt criminals were higher in mesomorphy. Cortés and Gatti also confirmed Sheldon's work when it was a question of the relationship between somatotype and temperament, as we have seen. More recently Wilson and Herrnstein have summed up the evidence favoring Sheldon in their **Crime and Human Nature.**

In two additional studies of male and female adolescents at the Anneewakee Treatment Center in Georgia, Horace Stewart used Sheldon's Trunk Index method to determine the somatotypes of 60 female and 194 male youth. In both cases the groups were highly mesomorphic. The therapeutic program at the Center made use of the relationship between physique and somatotype to develop a suitable program.

The evidence that can be construed in favor of Sheldon's basic formulations does not have to be restricted to comparisons of rating scales and physique, but can embrace factor analytic studies, as well. Burdick and Tess measured 159 photos in the **Atlas of Men** according to 36 different characteristics. Analysis of this data produced a number of factors, six of which they analyzed in their study. They felt that the first three major factors could be related to Parnell's fat, muscularity and linearity. And though there was an effect of age on somatotypes, they found a separate age factor, as well as one they called ideal, which indicated a "positive, aesthetic impact" (p. 513), which would make a student of Sheldon immediately think of his t index, but here, apparently represented something somewhat different. Their results shed some light on the question of whether it is reasonable to speak of three components rather than two, and the authors recognize the differences that exist between the various somatotyping systems and provide mathematical methods of converting their muscularity, linearity and fat to Sheldon's somatotypes.

Claessens and his associates (1985) studied 210 Belgian school boys from ages 13 to 18. They determined the somatotypes of these boys by the Heath-Carter method, and examined the physiques by factor analysis as well. They found 4 basic factors: "(1) a fat-massiveness factor; (2) a thoracical massiveness factor; (3) a limb width factor; and (4) a factor of length development of the trunk relative to the limbs." (p. 23)

Endomorphy was roughly equivalent to the fat-massiveness factor. Ectomorphy was the opposite pole of endomorphy and mesomorphy. And mesomorphy was highly related to the limb-width factor, and in a lesser degree, to the chest and fat factors. The boys, whether measured by factor analysis or somatotypes, revealed a considerable degree of stability during these teen-age years.

This issue of stability was examined at greater length in another paper (1986) in which the authors concluded: "Besides skeletal shape, total body shape, as expressed by the somatotype, can also be fairly well predicted from earlier ages, although there are some findings that the mesomorphic component is "difficult to spot"." (p. 242) These results are in good agreement with Walker and Tanner (1980) and the Tanner and Whitehouse findings in **Atlas of Children's Growth.**

It would be possible to pursue the use of somatotypes at the morphological level in much more detail, but this would take us too far afield into the technical details of somatotyping. What can we make of what we have already seen? If for a time Sheldon's work seemed to be buried under a growing wave of criticism, it should be clear by now that the basic methods of somatotyping are sound, and they are actually being employed. But clearly the trend has been towards the more objective methods, as might be expected, and their use at the physical more than the psychological level. For example, in a recent search in **Biological Abstracts** from 1984 and including part of 1987, the word "somatotype" appeared in 23 titles. Most of the items dealt with physical applications: J.E.L. Carter's "Somatotypes of Olympic Athletes from 1948-1976", a study by Claessens and his colleagues, "Body Structure, Somatotype and Motor Fitness of Top-Class Belgian Judoists", and so forth.

There was little, however, on the temperamental side of Sheldon's work, and what was done was usually of the order of somatotyping a group of subjects and administering a test like Cattell's 16-PF and seeing what results emerge, or analyzing culturally conditioned body type stereotypes. But let us examine a number of studies, new and old, that do focus on the question of the relationship between somatotype and temperament.

Studies of Physique and Temperament

One of the most detailed studies of the relationship in this area was carried out by Richard Walker and his associates on nursery school children. He began by making a valuable survey of previous work. This included a study of one hundred 6 and 7-year-olds by Davidson, McKinnes and Parnell who were somatotyped by Parnell's method, given standardized tests and had their mothers interviewed. Another was by Hanley, who took 12 to 14-year-old boys whose reputations at that time were compared to their somatotypes at age 18. A third was by Glueck and Glueck in which delinquent and non-delinquent boys were compared by physique, and with data coming from physical exams, Rorschach ratings and psychiatric evaluations. He also included the study of college sophomores, by Child, which we have seen before, as well as one by Cabot who used Kretschmer's typology. Walker combined these studies into one table, which makes interesting reading, for the portrait that emerges from these combined studies matches fairly well the descriptions given by Sheldon in the **Varieties of Temperament.** The endomorph communicates feelings easily, is confident, shows genital undevelopment, is described as sensuous and conventional, and so forth. The mesomorph has explosive rages, is a social leader, looks people right in the eye, withstands pain easily, etc., while the ectomorph is anxious and has nervous habits, is bashful, prefers few intimate friends to many, is sensitive and aesthetic, and so on.

In Walker's own study 125 children from 2 1/2 to almost 5 years old were rated for their somatotypes and on a specially devised 63-item scale. The somatotypes, done visually from standard photographs, were the average of ratings by three separate judges: Walker himself, who was acquainted with the children, and two other judges who worked solely from the photographs. The rating scale for each child was filled out by 4 or 5 teachers, of which at least 3 had no idea what the study was about. Out of all the 292 previously made predictions, "73% were confirmed in direction and 21% were confirmed beyond the .05 level, while 3% were disconfirmed beyond the .05 level. The mesomorphic boys and girls came out competitive, self-assertive, easily angered, etc." And it is interesting to note that the "girls combined this assertiveness with socialness, cheerfulness and warmth" (p. 87), which makes us think of our proposed distinction of the male mesomorphs being principally extraverted thinkers and the female mesomorphs being extraverted feelers. The ectomorphs showed aloofness, indirect problem-solving, daydreaming, etc. The picture of the endomorphs was more obscure, for it seemed influenced by endomorphy's relationship to mesomorphy, and the children in this category appeared aggressive, quarrelsome, easily angered, etc. Walker concludes, "that in this group of preschool children important associations do exist between individual's physiques and particular behavior characteristics. Further, these associations show considerable similarity to those described by Sheldon for college-aged men, though the strength of association is not as strong as he reports." (p. 79)

These same children plus an additional year's class were rated by their mothers by means of 68 descriptive adjectives and phrases. Much the same kind of results emerged, though weaker. What is amazing is not that Walker's study showed lower correlations than Sheldon's original work, but that it found the relationships it did considering the difficulties involved in such an approach. The somatotypes were evaluated by three judges anthroposcopically, but each judge had a highly distinctive method. And children are harder to somatotype, in any event. In addition, it is difficult enough to evaluate temperamental traits in fully formed personality. Imagine trying to pin down these qualities in a 2-year-old!

Considering the studies that Walker has summarized, and his own, he is well justified in citing Diamond's comments in **Personality and Temperament** that there is:

"...an overwhelming confirmation of the general validity of Sheldon's theories. Few propositions in the field of personality can claim to have stronger experimental support... Unfortunately, Sheldon's views have had so poor an audience among psychologists that some moral courage is required to confess to this degree of agreement with them". (p. 4)

In "Sheldon's Physical-psychical Typology Revisited" (1984) Janssen and Whiting took the first order factors underlying Cattell's extraversion-introversion, and had 100 Dutch university students assign these qualities to photographs of the extreme ectomorph, the extreme mesomorph and the extreme endomorph.

The qualities from Cattell's Q and E positive poles, that is, self-sufficient, resourceful, prefers own decisions, and assertive, aggressive, stubborn, were associated with the mesomorph, while the qualities of the A and F positive poles, warm-hearted, outgoing, easygoing, participating and enthusiastic, heedless, happygo-lucky, were related most strongly to the endomorph, while the characteristics of the H negative pole, shy, timid, restrained, threat-sensitive, were associated with the ectomorph. These relationships were graphically portrayed by a computer program that showed correlations as a function of distance so that the shorter distances represented higher correlations. What emerged is something similar to Sheldon's basic somatotype diagram.

Instead of there being simply a dichotomy of introversion and extraversion, we see extraversion breaking down, as the authors note, into an extraversion of action and an extraversion of affect. They also had the students choose what they considered the ideal body type, which turned out, as could be imagined, the mesomorph, and this confirmed the many studies of body stereotypes that have been conducted in which the mesomorph is most favored, and the endomorph least favored. It is also interesting to note that while approximately one quarter of the students thought there was a relationship between personality and body type, more than one half thought there wasn't.

In other somatotyping literature we find a wide variety of use being made of Sheldon's formulations. Robert Lenski, for example, reanalyzed the data on the 200 men in Sheldon's **Varieties of Temperament** in terms of the racial identifications, i.e., Nordic, Alpine, etc., that Sheldon gives for these cases but never makes use of. His results show that the different racial groupings have different characteristics, or put another way, the frequency of the different somatotypes appears to vary in different racial and national groups. While the vast majority of genetic variation is to be found within groups rather than between them, there are differences between groups, and one of the best ways to examine them would be the different frequencies of somatotypes and psychological types. Lenski does it anecdotally, as well, by analyzing the traditionally recognized differences between the English and the Italians, embodied in Emerson's "English Traits" and Barzini's **The Italians.**

Roberts and Bainbridge travelled to the southern Sudan in the Upper Nile province, and studied the somatotypes of the Shilluk and Dinka peoples who are among the most ectomorphic in the world. They found that Sheldon's 7 in ectomorphy seemed too moderate a way to describe some of the physiques they were seeing. Eventually they decided that it ought to be extended out to include such somatotypes as the 1-2-8 and the 1-1-9, whose extraordinary photographs they include in their article.

A fascinating sequel to this research would be a psychological study geared to discovering the temperament and psychological type of these world champion ectomorphs. The authors also compared the distribution of the Nilotic people, which is rather tightly grouped in the ectomorphic section of Sheldon's somatotype chart, with other research that has been carried on East Africans (more mesomorphic ectomorphs) and the Japanese of North Honshu (endomorphic mesomorphs).

Finally, among somatotyping literature R.W. Parnell's **Behavior and Physique:** An Introduction to Practical and Applied Somatometry should hold a special place because of its extensive coverage of a whole variety of topics based on Parnell's own research. In a fascinating collection of somatotype charts he summarizes his investigations in topics as diverse as "The Body Build of Mr. Universe Contestants", "What Type of Women have the Most Male Offspring?", "Who Gets Married at What Ages?", "The

Somatotypes of Physical Education Teachers", "Of
Boys Described as Anxious and Girls as Meticulous",
and the somatotypes of people suffering from different psychiatric disorders.

And if Sheldon's temperaments represent the clarification of a long tradition, then we would expect
them to appear in various ways in various places,
even when there is apparently no direct relationship
with his work. The enneagram whose origins are
reputedly in the distant past and which has become
popular today through the work of Oscar Ichazo,
describes nine kinds of personalities, three of which
are quite close to Sheldon's temperaments. Personality V includes the following qualities: "I need much
private time and space", "I often sit back and observe other people rather than get involved", "I seem
to be more silent than others", "People often ask me
what I am thinking", "I don't know how to engage
in small talk very well", and so forth, all of which
would, of course, fit Sheldon's ectotonic personality.

In contrast, we are told about Personality VIII:
"I enjoy the exercise of power", "I am very good at
standing up and fighting for what I want", "I know
how to get things done", "Generally I don't care
much for introspection or too much self-analysis",
which is roughly equivalent to Sheldon's mesotonic.

And Personality IX is said to agree with most of
the following statements: "I am an extremely easy-
going person", "I can't remember the last time I had
trouble sleeping", "Most people get too worked up
over things", "My attitude is: I don't let it bother
me", which is Sheldon's endotonic.

What conclusions are we led to after this somewhat laborious review of Sheldonian literature? The
substantial core of Sheldon's work has stood the test
of time and can be verified by practical experience
and observation, as well as by objective testing. What
caused the decline of interest in Sheldon's work cannot be laid to the work itself, but should be searched

for in the psychological climate of the 1940s and 1950s, and in Sheldon's own personality.

CHAPTER 7

WILLIAM H. SHELDON

It is Sheldon's life that holds the key to a better understanding of his work and why it has been fading from view. And it also provides a fascinating example of how both Jung's and Sheldon's typologies can throw light on behavior that would otherwise remain an enigma. The basic facts of Sheldon's life are easily told, but it will be harder, given Sheldon's autobiographical reticence, to understand his inner life, which holds the answer we seek.

William Herbert Sheldon was born in Pawtuxet, Rhode Island, on November 19, 1898. His parents, William Herbert and Mary Abby Greene, were related to old New England families like the Carders and Remingtons. And his father had been well off until a partner in the family firm ran off with the money. William and Mary had lost their first two daughters to diphtheria and then had three more children: Israel in 1889, Kate in 1891, and finally William seven years later. Sheldon's father had been able to keep the family homestead, which dated from around 1740, and supported his family by working as a jeweler in nearby Providence.

Sheldon had an archetypal rural American boyhood. The family was poor, but not poverty stricken. They grew a half acre garden of corn, tomatoes, carrots, peas, potatoes and onions. His father was an avid fisherman and hunter who supplemented his income by shooting game birds for market, and he was a man with a wide range of interests and talents. He raised Irish setters, bred fine poultry, and was a shooting champion of national stature, who was knicknamed Hawkeye. Sheldon later described him as a "lover of the wild and reader of books." Little William, whose father called him the last of the litter of Irish setters which had been born at the same time, went crabbing and clamming. He hunted rabbits and squirrels for the pot, and gathered hickory nuts, black walnuts and chestnuts. And he watched his father judge dog and poultry shows and preside over the gun club he founded. In those days they shot glass balls filled with feathers, which later gave way to clay pigeons, and William promised to become an exceptional shot himself - another Hawkeye.

Unfortunately, a boyhood accident, in which he fell on a knife, left a scar beneath his right eye and an inability to perfectly coordinate his eyes to track a moving target. Yet he maintained what must have been extraordinary vision. He could hit a small agate marble thrown 20 feet in the air with his .22 rifle, and once as a child he demonstrated this skill in front of Annie Oakley. He would hold his shot until the marble was just about to descend, and thus avoid a moving target.

Sheldon grew up on intimate terms with inhabitants of the woods and marshes. He would play with earthworms in the garden, and considered the great moths, who were a special love of his mother, as almost part of the family. He would watch sympathetically and protectively as the crabs molted and entered their vulnerable soft-shelled stage. It was life attuned to natural rhythms, but it did not lack for that reason a sense of refinement and culture.

As a child of five or six, during an excursion to the Boston marathon, he had been taken by his Aunt Mary to visit her old friend William James. And Sheldon believed it had been her intervention that had convinced James to allow himself to be called his godfather.

This idyllic and quintessentially rural childhood was to have two important consequences. First, Sheldon's visual gifts and powers of observation were encouraged and honed from his earliest years. He lived in a world where observation was not a form of idle curiosity, but the means of putting food on the table, or money in the pocket. It was a world where men prided themselves on their ability to shoot a duck flashing overhead, and to judge a fine hen or dog. And William took for granted that it was possible for different observers to come to virtually identical conclusions, for he saw this happen over and over again at dog, poultry and cattle shows.

By the time he was a teenager he was working for the state as a junior ornithologist, and he had a growing reputation as an appraiser of early American cents. On a more personal level, it was his childhood that remained the inviolate temenos of his feelings. He had only to think of the yellow-eyed beans his mother always baked, or the great moths, especially the Promethea which they called Prometheus, or the early American cents his father collected, to be back at the warm hearth at a turn of the century New England night:

"In the New England village where I was born, quite a few years ago, the long winter evenings about the open fire - or in colder weather around the kitchen stove - were filled with a number of pleasant occupations.

"First there was the general care and upkeep of guns, fishing tackle, and associated equipment. Chores done, there were chestnuts, apples, and sweet potatoes for roasting, popping corn and parching corn, checkerberries, walnuts and butternuts, cider. All these were part of the regular harvest of the countryside and so were taken for granted, like the logs in the fireplace and one's parents. There was one thing, however, which retained at all times such a halo of mystery and enchantment that it never came to be taken for granted.

"This was the cigar box of old copper cents which

my father kept locked up in the grandfather sea chest along with certain papers, some old spoons and jewelry, and other trinkets. On evenings when he was feeling especially well disposed, the kitchen lamp would be meticulously trimmed, the red kitchen tablecloth would be cleared of debris and brushed, then out would come the magnifying glass, four or five well-thumbed coin books, and the cigar box with the big cents." (**Early American Cents**, p. 3)

As a teenager William had been strongly encouraged to become a baseball player, for he had an uncanny knack of getting the bat on the ball. But his efforts never led to a career. In later years he realized a somatotyping knowledge would have spared him the disappointment, for he simply did not have enough mesomorphy to be a professional.

Sheldon graduated from Warwick High School in 1915 and entered Brown University. With the American entrance into World War I he was commissioned as a 2nd lieutenant in a machine gun company, and was demobilized in Europe. In 1919 he received a degree from Brown in absentia, and afterwards he wandered westward. He was an officer of the Round Rock Oil Company in Texas, and entered the University of Colorado where he earned an M.A. in English in 1923.

Obviously Sheldon had not yet settled on his career, but the role model of William James had to be in the back of his mind. He had gone with his father at James' invitation to hear the leaders of the new psychoanalytic movement speak at Clark University in 1909. This was the occasion of both Freud's and Jung's first trips to America. What a 10-year-old boy could make of it is entirely another matter. And he recounts how when he was about the same age he asked James about the meaning of the word God.

"He replied that some sixty years previously he had asked **his** godfather, Emerson, just about the same question; and had been told about the Oversoul

- a sort of personalized abstraction associated with all the constructive thinking and feeling of human and other creatures who have lived before us, or live now, or will live after us. This personified reality which has been called God, James said, seems to be the tie that binds us all to the common enterprise of life, and to the wisest purposes and the most rewarding appreciations of life. So at least God is real, he added, and wherever one good person remains alive, a part of God is alive." (**Prometheus Revisited,** p. 230-1)

These earlier impressions were reinforced by attending a seminar at Brown given by James' protege Martin Peck. James had sent Peck to Freud and Peck "considered Freud the foremost emancipator of mankind but emphasized that the job was still only half done; that somebody now must bring descriptive order to comprehending the constitutional patterns underlying the psychiatric patterns." ("Psychotic Patterns and Physical Constitution", p. 838)

When he was in Europe around 1919 he had visited both Freud and Kretschmer. (**Varieties of Delinquent Youth,** pp. 49, 832 and 834) Again, what he had to say to them at this point remains unknown, although Kretschmer must have been in the midst of the research that led to the publication of **Physique and Character** in 1921.

Somewhere these earlier experiences coalesced, and Sheldon discovered the joys of the old riddle of the connection between physique and temperament. We have seen him pursuing his psychological studies in Chicago where he received his Ph.D. in 1925. He taught psychology at Chicago and then at the University of Wisconsin. Sheldon felt that "James himself had gone through medical school not to practice but to become a better psychologist and religious philosopher." (**Prometheus Revisited,** p. 1) And so he entered the University of Chicago Medical School and received an M.D. in 1933.

Sheldon was now 35 years old and finally ready to embark on the last phase of the research that had been occupying him for at least a decade. He received a grant from what was then called the Council for Study of Religion in Higher Education, and he went off to Europe to renew his acquaintance with the master psychologists. He visited Kretschmer's clinic and he watched the master diagnostician at work. Kretschmer was classifying his patients according to his types: pyknic, athletic and asthenic, and one individual could possess a mixture of these types. Sheldon, watching Kretschmer work, intuited the next step: not types, but basic components exist in each person, and these components could be rated on a numerical scale.

He visited Freud and discussed the appropriateness of nach, gegen and ab (toward, against and away from) as fundamental patterns underlying the major classifications of psychopathology. By January of 1935 he had met with Jung in Zurich, a visit which was to be reflected in his **Psychology and the Promethean Will.** The relationship between Jung and Sheldon will occupy us in Chapter 8.

With his head filled with inspiration, Sheldon then retired to Dartington Hall in Devon, England. The Hall, which had been established by Leonard and Dorothy Whitney Elmhirst, was a refuge for writers and artists. There he drafted his Prometheus book and made a life-long friend and admirer in another writer in residence, Aldous Huxley. Huxley quickly grasped the basics of Sheldon's three-fold classification, for he realized he was an ectomorph and cerebrotonic. It became a source of not only personal insight, but instrumental in aiding his own writings. He wrote to a friend in 1945:

"...I remain sadly aware that I am not a born novelist, but some other kind of man of letters, possessing enough ingenuity to be able to simulate a novelist's behaviour not too unconvincingly. To put the matter physiologically, I am the wrong shape for a story teller and sympathetic delineator of character within a broad social canvas. The fertile inventors and narrators and genre painters have all been rather burly genial fellows. Scott looked like a farmer. Balzac and Dumas were florid to the point of fatness. Dickens was athletic and had a passion for amateur theatricals. Tolstoy was an intellectual moujik. Dostoevsky was physically tough enough to come through imprisonment in Siberia, Conan Doyle was a barrel, Wells is a tub. Dear old Arnold Bennett was a chamber pot on spindly legs and Marcel Proust was the wreck of congenital sleekness. So what chance has an emaciated fellow on stilts? And of course this is no joke. There is a real correlation between shape and mind." (as cited in Calcraft, p. 666)

Sheldon's influence on Huxley can be traced in his 1936 **Ends and Means** (a book which was read by a teenage James Tanner who went on to become an expert in human growth and somatotyping, as we have seen) and in **Time Must Have a Stop, The Genius and the Goddess,** and his utopia **Island,** where Sheldon's ideas become an integral part of the islanders' philosophy. Huxley also wrote an essay directly on Sheldon's work, which appeared in **Harper's Magazine** in 1944, illustrated by James Thurber's cartoons. But the affinity the two men felt extended deeper than the level of classification. Huxley was also striving to develop an integrated world view he would disseminate through his technical writings, and this allowed him to grasp readily Sheldon's psychology of religion, a science based religion that Sheldon hoped would be acceptable to thinking people and which he was just then setting down on paper. This fruit of Sheldon's book is the closest he came to autobiography. Between the lines of his Promethean program we can, now and again, get a vivid glimpse of Sheldon himself.

For Sheldon, too many human minds have become deadened by the age of 40. They have ceased to go forward and reach their full measure of development. They haven't heard the voice of Prometheus which continually whispers "no, this is not good enough. There is somewhere something better." (p. 5) Still less have they made this their predominant mood. But Sheldon had embarked on this journey to Europe and to his mature thought at the age of 35. He was on the threshold of his Promethean future, and it looked bright. He writes, "It seems to be a general principle that if the Promethean personality can hold out and remain true to itself past the 35th year, the second half of life is likely to be immensely happy." (p. 127) Fresh from Zurich Sheldon footnotes this passage: "In discussing this observation with Dr. Jung, I find that he too regards the middle thirties as a sort of critical threshold for emotional life. It is excessively rare for a person who has good emotional orientation at thirty-five, to lose it, and there is good reason to regard this period as the ideal one for analysis, or for psychological reëducation." (p. 127)

And what is the Promethean holding out against? He is less at home in a world which does not understand him, and which has gone by other values. For Sheldon the Promethean personalities are "more shy, less certain of themselves, and often seem young and undeveloped for their age." (p. 3) He fears that many of these gifted personalities will be harmed by being thrown in with more aggressive ones. "Put any sensitive adult into a company where there are one or two aggressive or loud personalities, and you cannot get a word out of him with a crowbar." (p. 161) He also fears that early marriage will deflect them from the time and energy they need for full maturation, or they will choose an inappropriate spouse. Most of the marital unhappiness that he has seen consists of one partner who has "dominantly sensitive tender-minded intuitional feeling qualities, while the other tended towards extraverted, objective, outwardly focused, waster identifications." (p. 176) The young Promethean can appear queer, shy, taciturn and immature and is prone to be misunderstood, but if he can maintain his active and questing intellect he will blossom in the second half of life. "For such individuals a year in the 50s or 60s is worth in intrinsic feeling value far more than a year of youth ..." (p. 4) Sheldon's Promethean foreshadows his description of the ectomorph and cerebrotonic, or ectotonic. But there is something more involved here. When Sheldon says, "Religion has to do primarily with the integration of feeling and intellect" (p. 29) we can understand it as his own program of individuation. This gives another meaning to his statements about religion when he says "the first function of education ought certainly to be that of carrying the feeling element of consciousness, along with intellectual growth, to the full maturing or ripening of a personality." (p. 28) And he poses the problem of the integration of thinking and feeling in a much less theoretical way in a passage that must be taken as autobiographical.

"Once a child lived near the seashore, and grew to love all the living things of the sea. Among them was the great blue claw crab, who dwelt in the deep pools where tidewater reached the salt marshes. He was a formidable creature in a small boy's order of things, greatly to be respected and even more wonderful and mysterious than his little cousins the fiddler crabs, who lived in holes in the sand. He was wary and slow to make friends, but if once you won his confidence he would come to you to be fed, and he would almost, but not quite, let you touch him. His great pincers would snap a heeded warning whenever you put your hand too close. He was the noble, powerful, independent, and self-sufficient lord of the pool.

"But when he shed his beautiful armored shell, he would lie very quietly for many days at the bottom of the pool, a soft, defenseless, tender creature. Then he was a soft-shelled crab. When in this defenseless condition, he was a delicacy greatly prized for the table, and this never sat well with a child's belief in the natural justice of things, but there came a shock to this child consciousness from which I believe he never fully recovered, when he grew aware of the manner in which many human beings customarily treat the blue claw when they catch him in this condition. **They boil him alive.**

"It is said that he tastes a little better that way. I do not know whether the child to whom I refer was unusually tender-minded, imaginative, or merely loyal to his friends; but the horror of this callous and un-imaginative thing sat upon his soul more poignantly that could in later years the burning of Bruno, the killing of men in war, or even the torturing and murdering of neurotic women by our own New England ancestors." **(Psychology and the Promethean Will, p. 30)**

What type was Sheldon himself? His somatotype was around a 3.5 - 3.5 - 5, and this makes him a mesomorphic ectomorph. And what was his psychological type? My own estimation is that he was an introverted thinking type with secondary intuition. It would be difficult to describe the introverted thinking type more appropriately or graphically than Sheldon has just done. From the outside he is formidable, armed with superb thinking powers and defenses. But periodically he is in his soft-shell stage, vulnerable and defenseless, and then he must beware, for they boil him alive! It is the introverted thinker who possesses amazingly tender yet volcanic feelings and who behind his armor is often easily hurt.

So when Sheldon describes the Promethean personality, he is describing himself. The Promethean is an introvert and cerebrotonic, but instead of Sheldon clearly distinguishing between the various personality types and their development or lack of it, he places the Promethean in opposition to more extraverted endomorphic and mesomorphic personalities and associates them with what he called the wasters. This sets the stage for a deep-rooted conflict that we will see emerge later in his life.

For Sheldon, feeling is intimately connected with nature and "...under no circumstances should a human child ever be born in a city, or allowed to spend any of the growing years within reach of the urban influence." (p. 205) Sheldon's feeling, or his inferior function, is filled with the numinosity of the unconscious and the self.

"Have you ever heard a migrating Bartramian sandpiper on a clear August night? Or the first Southward flying Canada geese in October? Did you only hear, or did you **feel** them?" (p. 224-5)

It is nature experienced in this feeling way that carries "the clearest reflection that we can see, of the **living** face of our God." (p. 225)

"In the insect world and in the world of night life, particularly in the romance of the great night moths, lie some of the soundest foundations for the human soul. Toads and frogs and snakes and turtles are among the best friends of human beings who would grow a soul. To learn to love these personalities, and to identify the necessarily more transitory **human** loves of a life with them, is to develop the fifth panel of consciousness, which is the soul." (p. 225)

The great night moth was rooted in Sheldon's childhood and the frogs and turtles become fitting symbols of the fourth function where earth meets water. And is it not a reflection of Sheldon's own feeling function to stress the more transitory character of human love?

By the beginning of 1936 Sheldon was back in the States, and whether as part of his commitment to

the grant he had received or as a first step in his
program of religious renewal from a psychological
point of view, he taught a course at the Chicago
Theological Seminary, a Congregational school affilia-
ted with the Divinity School of the University of
Chicago. This ran from January to June, 1937, and
was based on the human conflict and the ways to
handle it following the schema set down in the recently published **Psychology and the Promethean Will,**
which served as a text for the course. A young seminary student, Roland Elderkin, was struck by the
force and implications of Sheldon's thought, and the
rest of his life was to be interwoven with Sheldon's
and his extensive constitutional projects.

In April, 1938, Sheldon met C.W. Dupertuis at a
meeting of the American Association of Physical
Anthropologists, where they were both giving papers.
Sheldon spoke on what he was then calling anthrotyp-
ing, and called his components "pyknosomia, somato-
somia and leptosomia", reflecting Kretschmer's influence. Dupertuis had worked with Earnest Hooton at
Harvard, and had been involved in the measuring of
4,000 people at the Chicago's World Fair, and 10,000
men in a racial survey of Ireland for the Harvard
Department of Anthropology. At the time he met
Sheldon he was at George Draper's Constitution
Clinic at Columbia Presbyterian Medical Center. They
had reported on their work in 1944 in **Human Constitution in Clinical Medicine,** as we have seen. Sheldon
was introduced to Hooton through Dupertuis, who
invited him to work at Harvard. Now the stage was
set for Sheldon's most productive period, and it resulted in his **Varieties of Human Physique** in 1940 and
Varieties of Human Temperament in 1942.

Sheldon's project was building momentum. At
Harvard he collaborated with S.S. Stevens and in
Boston he found a receptive audience at Hayden
Goodwill Inn. The Inn had been set up during the
height of the Depression to deal with the many young

men from all over the country who had wandered to the Boston area. Under the direction of Emil Hartl the Inn developed a wide range of social services and vocational training. By 1938 there were boys in residence with all sorts of problems ranging from homelessness to lawlessness, as well as various kinds of mental and social maladjustments. And so there was a pressing need for more and more diagnostic and planning work. The Inn decided to set up its own Youth Guidance Clinic. Hartl, who had been working on a Ph.D. in psychology and pastoral counseling, had come across **Psychology and the Promethean Will** and was impressed with it. At the same time Roland Elderkin had come to work at the Inn, and they had discovered their mutual enthusiasm for Sheldon, and so Sheldon was invited to direct the Youth Guidance Clinic. Here was a good testing ground for Sheldon's ideas, and their integration into a practical setting with the collaboration of the rest of the Inn's staff. Both Elderkin and Hartl, as well as another of the staff members, Ashton Tenney, were to remain in close contact with Sheldon for the rest of his life. His work at the Inn began to coalesce into the idea of a book on constitution and human delinquency. In the summer of 1941 Elderkin, who was assisting him at the clinic, began gathering information about some of the Inn residents. It was probably during these years that Sheldon came closest to working out the practical implications of his constitutional psychology, and began to move in the direction of treatment. He leaves us some of his insights scattered throughout his works, especially **Varieties of Delinquent Youth.**

We can only surmise what would have happened if Sheldon had developed these ideas in the form of a therapeutic constitutional program. It might have made a great deal of difference both to him and his work. Unfortunately, the War intervened. In the spring of 1942 Sheldon was commissioned as a major in the Army. Stationed in Texas he eventually did

research on somatotypes and aviation medicine. Unfortunately, he was struck down by a severe lymphatic cancer and given a medical discharge with 100%
disability. Apparently he was not expected to live.
As late as 1946 Len Lye, a director for the newsreel
"March of Time" went to Boston to make a film on
Sheldon, lest the opportunity disappear forever. The
film was shot, but whether it was ever shown remains undetermined. About this same time work
resumed on **Varieties of Delinquent Youth,** which was
eventually published in 1949. In 1947 Sheldon became
the director of the Constitutional Clinic in New
York, where a series of studies was carried out on
the relationship between somatotype and peptic ulcer,
cancer, diabetes, etc.

Sheldon obviously had made a rather remarkable
recovery and was extremely busy, and furthermore,
his work was gaining wider and wider recognition. His
constitutional psychology entered its golden age in
the late 40s and early 50s. In 1948 C.W. Dupertuis
had set up a major somatotyping laboratory, later
called the McDermott Laboratory of Clinical Anthropology at the School of Medicine of Case Western
Reserve University. Eugene McDermott, cofounder of
Texas Instruments, had become deeply interested in
constitutional questions. He supported Dupertuis' later
work, and through Dupertuis had become acquainted
with Sheldon and eventually created a Foundation of
Biological Humanics to further his work. McDermott
as an engineer believed that if you can see it you
can measure it, and contributed to the final objective
method of somatotyping which used a planimeter, as
we have seen.

In 1950 Sheldon and his assistant, Barbara Honeyman, were invited to the Gesell Institute of Child
Development in New Haven, and worked with Louise
Ames, Janet Learned, Frances Ilg and Richard Walker
to establish a somatotyping clinic, which continued
for 20 years. In 1951 the University of Oregon Medi-

cal School invited Sheldon, with the help of a Rocke-
feller grant, to set up a constitutional clinic for
them, and it looked like Sheldon's gamble to explore
the human constitution by both measurement and
observation was paying off handsomely. Sheldon was
being lionized. In 1951, for example, when the American Medical Film Institute previewed Gesell Institute's "Embryology of Behavior", Drs. Gesell, Sheldon
and Ames were invited to the preview. Louise Ames
recalls:

"The chairman in his introduction said that after
the showing there would be a question period. He
commented that "With Drs. Gesell, Ames and Sheldon
available to answer questions there would in all prob-
ability be no questions about human behavior which
could not be answered.""

In June of the same year **Life** magazine came out
with a major article on Sheldon and his work entitled, "What Manner of Morph Are You?" (The illus-
trations by Michael Ramus that accompanied the
article were reprinted in our first volume.)

Sheldon's contacts at this time ranged from Walter C. Alvarez of the Mayo Clinic, to Ernst Kretschmer. Alvarez wrote of his interest in constitution
that went back to 1910, and his observations of the
mobile faces, bright eyes and quick movements he
had noticed among migraine patients. Indeed, he had
once diagnosed a case of migraine by the way a
woman started to leave his office, and had recognized schizoid girls by their dry, unpleasant smelling
skin.

And Kretschmer wrote in May of 1950 that he
tried repeatedly to contact Sheldon, but supposed the
postwar postal conditions had thwarted his efforts.
He was desirous of exchanging publications, for he
had only a small excerpt of Sheldon's work.

But there were really two different Sheldons
emerging. The first Sheldon was the major figure in
the study of the human constitution in the U.S., sur-

rounded by staff, students and admirers. Here was a man who had the natural ability to inspire loyalty to such a degree that some of the people who caught sight of the vision that animated him rearranged their lives completely to work with him. This was Sheldon the brilliant conversationalist, sharp, witty and perceptive, amused by the passing human show. His theme: "Watch this human scene, watch it with compassion, with courage, with discrimination. Record it, describe it, classify it. And strive to find within it the face of quality." (Maudsley Bequest Lecture, p. 4) This Sheldon was making major contributions to constitutional research in medical and psychological circles in the U.S., was an acknowledged and learned expert in the field with a large correspondence, and had any number of handsome opportunities to pursue his work.

But there was another Sheldon, a Sheldon on guard against the urban wasters and irked by human stupidity. He disliked: "the plush side of New York - concerts, the theater, fashionable dress, elegant stores, fine restaurants, and taxicabs. He preferred plain living, busses, and cafeterias. His Riverside Drive apartment was very starkly furnished. He detested man-made elegance. On the other hand he was vastly knowledgeable about and appreciative of Nature in its many forms. He was a keen observer, especially interested in birds.

"What he really liked was to work, and to have everyone around him working as well. He once described his ideal kind of life as one with everybody (or at least everybody with whom he came in contact) living in rather stark dormitories, and working. He especially resented the long holiday season from Christmas through New Years when so many places were closed and one could not get things done (film developed, manuscripts typed)." (Sheldon, by Ames, p. 3)

If Sheldon's wit had always been sharp and

inclined to both whimsy and vulgarity, now in the years after the War it got sharper. He had delighted in poking holes in the holy, but now he found a perverse joy in irritating people by exaggerated statements. The high temper that he had associated with the ectomorphic mesomorph became, in his own case, hardened into a certain brittleness and inflexibility.

Just as Sheldon was reaping the reward of his vast labors, a wave of neo-Freudian environmentalism was beginning to crest. No doubt it had, in turn, been a compensation for an earlier over-eagerness to believe in the all-pervasiveness of hereditary that had extended to eugenic laws in the U.S., and had been amalgamated with class consciousness and tinges of racism. Now, in the aftermath of the Nazis, the pendulum was swinging the other way. Sheldon's voice seemed more and more isolated, and became more strident. Criticism of his work began to mount, most of which was rooted in another concept of psychological science, as we have seen. But Sheldon had no real give in him. He took delight in noting how the somatotypes of psychoanalysts came from the same territory as those of the criminals, and beneath these surface jibes it is possible to sense his continuous battle against the wasters whom he too closely identified with the extraverted endomorphic mesomorphic personalities, and to see, as well, his own struggles for individuation. The feeling function was extremely difficult for him to come to terms with. He was married and divorced at least twice.

In 1949 he published the **Varieties of Delinquent Youth** based on the work with the young men at the Hayden Goodwill Inn, which is Sheldon's counterpart to his **Varieties of Temperament.** In contrast to the 200 young college men seen in the **VT**, here we have 200 young delinquents whom Sheldon studied between 1939 and 1942. These young men ranged all the way from serious delinquents setting out on a life of crime to psychotics, as well as fairly normal individuals who were suffering from problems of adolescent adjustment. It is not really a book about juvenile delinquency in the narrow sense of the term, but Sheldon uses his extensive contact with these young men as the springboard for reflections on psychiatry, medicine, and the state of our civilization. The book becomes a sequel to his **Psychology and the Promethean Will,** and the very scope of its subject matter tends to impare its unity. We meet, in turn, Sheldon the criminologist, Sheldon the constitutional psychologist, and Sheldon the philosopher and theologian. The overall result of almost 900 pages is somewhat overwhelming. But there is no need to agree with all these different Sheldons in order to find any number of significant ideas. He describes, in capsule biography, the mesomorphic nature of most of the young men at the Inn, and he makes a brilliant summary of his attempts to renew psychiatric language and classification, which we will look at later. But this book is not Sheldon at his best. He rails too loudly at the burgeoned massive mothers of his delinquent youth. He seems to be lamenting both the broken lives of the delinquents and the lost youth of the country which is being overloaded with indescriminate mongrelized breeding. He makes many points, which are either worth making, or at least worth debating, but his tone lacks the feeling qualities which he had extolled in the **Promethean Will.** Promethean hope seems to be giving way to disillusionment.

1949 marks a watershed. He expected to see his **Atlas of Men** ready by the end of the year. When it did appear in 1954, perhaps delayed by the labor and cost of preparing so many photographic plates, it was a worthy successor to the early volumes of the Human Constitution Series. But there comes a puzzling silence that stretched nearly unbroken to Sheldon's death in 1977.

What had become of William Sheldon, America's leading student of human differences? Had he run out of ideas? No. Sheldon told his friends he had six books left to write, and he gives hints of them in his published writings. He wanted to do an **Atlas of Women,** a project he devoted considerable energy to. There was to be an **Atlas of Children,** a study of constitution and clinical medicine, another of constitution and psychiatry, an examination of Spanish American war veterans, and a follow-up on the 200 subjects who appeared in the **Varieties of Delinquent Youth.** Bits and pieces of these projects appeared in various places. The **Varieties of Delinquent Youth** contained his psychiatric thoughts. As far back as 1938 he had traveled with Dupertuis, taking somatotype pictures of some 3,800 schizophrenic and manic-depressive patients in New York state, and had followed these men for years. The only part of this work that was ever published were the pages of his "Psychotic Patterns and Physical Constitution". The **Varieties of Delinquent Youth** had also contained some reflections on somatotype and the susceptibility to various diseases. In 1958 Sheldon had asked Elderkin to do follow-up work for the delinquent youth study, but he never got it written up. This work was finally completed by Hartl, Monnelly and Elderkin and published in 1982 entitled, **Physique and Delinquent Behavior: A 30-Year Follow-Up.** He even contemplated a book on the Oregon criminal, no doubt to be the fruit of his labors on the West Coast, and a handbook for somatotyping. What remains of this work in Sheldon's files, which are in the care of the Anthropological Archives at the Smithsonian Institute, are not even book skeletons, but mostly thousands of somatotype pictures.

Was he too ill to work? His health had been gravely impaired during the War, but his recovery, at least on the surface, was good. But he might have lacked part of his old energy, or even have suffered from some other illness that gradually weakened him.

At first glance his literary production in the years

between 1949 or 1954 and 1977 consisted of one article, "Psychotic Patterns..." He did publish **Prometheus
Revisited,** and a new version of his book on early
American cents, but both of these were substantially
rewrites of their earlier namesakes. What work Sheldon did during these years is best seen in two unpublished lectures. The first was given at Children's
Medical Center in Boston on March 13, 1961, and it
was entitled "History of the Constitution Research
Project and Objectification of the Somatotypes". In
it Sheldon describes the vicissitudes of his quest for
a complete objective method of establishing the
somatotypes, which had started with Thurstone in the
1920s and which had extended through the 1950s with
work in 1956 at Berkeley and later in the decade at
Dallas.

The second lecture, covering the same ground
though in a lighter style, was a Maudsley Bequest
Lecture on May 13, 1965, read for him by Emil
Hartl before the Royal Society of Medicine in London. Finally, "Psychotic Patterns and Physical Constitution, a thirty year follow up of thirty-eight hundred
patients in New York State", which summed up his
work of the 1950s and 1960s, was delivered at a
Symposium on Schizophrenia: Current Concepts on
Research" held in New York on November 14-16,
1968. Here the final objectifying of somatotyping was
unveiled to a world that was largely indifferent.

So part of the riddle of what happened to Sheldon
can be found in unpublicized and extensive labors
devoted to answering the objections that had been
raised against somatotyping. He also continued to
update his large collection of cases that were the
nuclei of the works he hoped to do in the future.

But this record of work achieved is not a total
answer to what had become of Sheldon. Where was
Sheldon the Promethean who had looked forward to
those years when he would be in his 50s and 60s?
The split between his thinking and feeling functions,

instead of being healed, or held in a fruitful tension, as he had imagined, fell into open conflict. And his feelings were moving away from his work. If he spent his intellectual time in the immensely difficult analyses that were to lead to the objectification of the somatotypes, his feelings which could not find purchase there strove for other channels - some positive and some negative.

Jung was very much the therapist. Sheldon was not, and so his feelings could not go out to his patients. After his marriages he finally found a measure of peaceful living with Dorothy Paschal, but he had no children to focus his feelings on. Nor could he turn to the many people, both professional and lay alike, who admired his work and wrote to him. Louise Ames tells the story of discovering:

"boxes and drawers full of letters which not only had not been answered, but which had not even been opened... So I offered to spend one Christmas vacation going through this mail, with him dictating to me answers to letters he thought perhaps should be answered. He ignored the fact that some of these letters were two or three years old by stating, "In response to your letter of December 10th", but not indicating **which** December. His position about mail was that if you didn't answer a letter, the person very likely would become discouraged and not write again. This would prevent the start of unnecessary correspondence." (Sheldon, by Ames, p. 6)

But Sheldon's neglect could only put at risk the future of his work. And somehow the future of his work seemed less and less important to him. He set up no enduring somatotyping laboratory, and while he considered somatotypes a professional task and thought little of self-diagnosis, he did not take the practical steps needed to insure there would be a trained body of experts to carry on his work when he was gone.

Here, again, he stands in contrast to Jung, even

the Jung who is supposed to have said, "Thank God
I am Jung and not a Jungian!" Although Jung was an
intensely private man, his practice kept him in close
touch with people's actual problems, and it is out of
this practice that came the first Jungian analysts
who, in turn, analyzed others, setting off the still
spreading circles of Jung's influence.

Sheldon could have done the same, but there was
something in him that resisted it. He could have
continued to publish and counter the growing attacks
on his work and weathered the long period of American environmentalism in the hopes that the pendulum
would again begin to swing and more of a balance
reassert itself. His failure was not a failure of his
ideas, but a more personal one of a man whose
energy had given out after an extremely productive
career, and could not, or would not, fight on in the
published word until the end.

Unfortunately, Sheldon's behavior went beyond
benign neglect. He seemed compelled to antagonize
precisely those people upon whom the future success
of his work depended. He had an unerring knack of
finding people's sore points, or we might say their
particular inferior function, and he would do so just
when one of his projects was going particularly well,
and thus putting its future in jeopardy, or just when
the efforts of his friends had put within his reach
a research plum of the first magnitude in the form
of an invitation to establish himself at a university
or medical center. He had become his own worst
enemy. These bursts of inferior feeling extended to
his colleagues, as well, who had to bear them with
a patience which had heroic qualities, or in other
cases caused them to become permanently estranged
from him. Thus, it was Sheldon, himself, who caused
his work to fade from view, rather than any inherent
flaws in that work itself.

In 1949 he published **Early American Cents 1793-
1814:** An Exercise in Descriptive Classification with

Tables of Rarity and Value. It would be a mistake to ignore this book as simply an indication of one of Sheldon's hobbies. He sat in his office at the Constitution Clinic in New York working on it, and wrote of it, "...now that I have achieved a neighborly acquaintance with old age, and meantime have written other, less soul-satisfying books, I am no longer able to summon up a good reason for **not** requisitioning the necessary time and materials to write a book aimed at helping a younger generation of kitchen-table-scientists-on-Friday-nights to "make out the big cents."" (p. 4)

But what were these "less soul-satisfying books" but his Human Constitution Series! His interest in these large pennies can be understood on two levels, just like his **Prometheus** book. On the professional level Sheldon was, indeed, an expert numismatist. He had graded the American cents professionally from the time he was a teenager, and had associated with the noted early cent collectors of the century. And more importantly, this was another example where trained observation spelled the difference between success and failure, and so illustrated the role this kind of observation could have in psychology. What Sheldon did in his early American cents book paralleled what he had done before with Kretschmer's typology. He took an adjectival system of coarse, fine, very fine, etc., and quantified it on a 70-point scale, after clarifying the basic principles which governed the coin's value.

Let's look for a moment at the techniques used by professional coin graders today. **Professional Coin Grading Service**, for example, which graded over a quarter of a million coins for the rare coin industry in one yearly period, has an elaborate set of procedures to arrive at the most exact evaluation which, of course, is of great interest to the coin owner because the values of the coins vary greatly according to grade. They have a special dark grading room which is lit only by the light of the grading lamps. Each coin is held over a soft black velvet pad, and is evaluated independently by three professional graders. Then it goes to the finalizer who grades the coin himself, and then compares his grade with the other three. If his evaluation agrees with two of the other evaluations, that grade will be maintained. But if there is disagreement there are other, more elaborate procedures to arrive at the final decision. This company would be horrified by the suggestion that they let just anybody into their coin grading room, armed with a simple checklist. Their final judgment depends on observation, which they have made as objective as possible, depending on highly trained observers.

But the cents played a central role in Sheldon's psyche and feelings, as well. In fact, they were one of the prime carriers of his feelings, for old pennies were "intimately associated with family tradition and with the memories of grandparents and the like." (p. xi)

"For generations American schoolboys bought, sold, swapped, or swiped old coppers. Some of these boys, especially in old age, have returned to the early enchantment, there to forget or condone the singular incompatibility between human dreams and fulfillments." (p. 5) What is this but a description of Sheldon, himself, who fulfilled his professional dreams but not himself?

These pennies are imprinted with "the bright hopes of yesterday morning". (p. 339) "They are an intriguing family and they never die, fade, or get broken... The early cents carry the memory, and an indelible impress, of a little stretch of human time that was fragrant with high hope. It was the flowering period for what might have become a great people in a land of unmatched beauty. We always live in a valley lying between the nostalgic past and an unknown future. To own a family of the early cents is in some measure to command a causeway between what for Americans is becoming a dearly remembered island of the past, and the grim urban mainland of the future." (p. 335)

And we must remember his words quoted before about his boyhood and the occasions when his father took out the box of old cents. "There was one thing, however, which retained at all times such a halo of mystery and enchantment that it never came to be taken for granted." (p. 5) It is the large copper cents with their different colors and knicks and scars of time that were symbols of Sheldon's childhood and a vanishing American way of life. And his feelings were bound to this New England past and rebelled against the life he saw in New York and the other large cities. It was not an entirely conscious rebellion, either. His feelings, bruised and tormented without a proper channel to emerge, would burst forth in an involuntary and often offensive manner.

The cents were his symbols of the self, the final goal of the individuation process, that he had dimly divined at the time of writing the Prometheus book. They were the symbols of the wholeness of his childhood that eluded him in later life. He lashed out in the diatribes which found their ways into the pages of the **Varieties of Delinquent Youth,** and vented his feelings in derogatory comments he muttered about various ethnic groups, that in some way seemed to be tarnishing the purity of the American life represented by his New England boyhood.

Sheldon the Promethean in these moments of enantiodromia becomes Sheldon Epimetheus, the man of the right. He railed against cigarettes, alcoholism, Freudianism, and the Federal Reserve Bank, and he collected the ravings of extreme right wing fanatics which were so much in opposition to the thrust of his conscious objective scientific spirit. And significantly, when he sold his own substantial collection of early American cents, he gave the money to his nieces and nephews and made no provision for his work.

In 1971 he moved from New York to Cambridge, Massachusetts and died there on September 16, 1977. He once commented to Louise Ames that "almost nobody knew him as he really was - that almost everybody thought he was better or worse than the actual fact of the matter." (Sheldon, p. 10)

There are, then, two Sheldons: the Sheldon who found that something deeper down and laid the firm foundation for a scientific study of physique and temperment, and then the Sheldon who in the grip of his feelings, which often opposed his thinking, worked unconsciously to obscure the magnificent work he had created. He once wrote some lines of verse about the author of **The Forest of Arden** that we should take as our guide in judging Sheldon and his work:

> "And found in mar and flaw
> A kind significance
> And in the broken part
> An image of a whole"

In summary, Sheldon's life illustrates both genius and one of the most common and least diagnosed personality disorders: the emergence of the inferior function in opposition to the conscious personality. A deeper understanding of Jung's psychology could have helped him, and it provides one of the best frameworks for realizing the full potential of his work.

PART III
CHAPTER 8
AN INTEGRATED TYPOLOGY

The year 1921 saw the modern beginning of typology with the publication of Jung's **Psychological Types** and Kretschmer's **Physique and Character**. C.A. Meier in his paper on psychological types comments about Kretschmer's book: "...it is a shame that this most genial contribution to psychiatry has never been decently evaluated in respect to its relation to Jungian psychology." (p. 278) And this is even truer in regards to Sheldon's somatotype and temperament index. I can think of no better way to rescue Sheldon's work from the obscurity in which it has fallen than to integrate it into Jungian typology where it can be brought into relation to the process of individuation, and a full complement of therapeutic techniques. And Jung's psychology would gain from this integration as well, by becoming more conscious of the biological foundation implicit in psychological types, finding in somatotypes a gateway by which to bring psychological types in contact with the exciting advances taking place in neurobiology and genetics, and by mounting an attack on the difficult problem of type diagnosis.

Jung makes it clear in the beginning of Chapter X of **Psychological Types** that his typology has a biological foundation, and this is a position he never changed. More than 25 years later he wrote, "My typology is based exclusively on biological data." (**Letters**, Vol. I, p. 453) These foundations were the two ways that organisms adapted: "The one consists

in a high rate of fertility, with low powers of defense and short duration of life for the single individual; the other consists in equipping the individual
with numerous means of self-preservation plus a low
fertility rate. This biological difference, it seems to
me, is not merely analogous to, but the actual foundation of, our two psychological modes of adaptation." (p. 331-2) He goes on to describe how two
children in the same home situation can show very
different attitudes, and if they deviate from this
disposition they can land in neurosis. As to the basis
of this disposition, he states, "Physiological causes
of which we have no knowledge play a role in this."
(p. 333)

But this was a path that Jung was destined not
to follow. He had his hands full upholding the
sovereignty of the psyche against the materialism of
the 19th century, and its view of the mind as the
epiphenomenon of the brain. He wanted to explore
the nature of the psyche as psyche, and he was wary
of anything that hinted of reductionism. These difficult inner explorations of the psyche were his particular gift and absorbed all his energy. But we should
not turn this predisposition into some kind of separation of mind and body on Jung's part. He was keenly
aware of the profound unity between the two. "In
fact so intimate is the intermingling of body and
psychic traits that not only can we draw far-reaching
inferences as to the constitution of the psyche from
the constitution of the body, but we can also infer
from psychic peculiarities the corresponding bodily
characteristics." (Vol. 6, p. 524) For Jung the individual disposition "is innate and not acquired in the
course of life". (Vol. 6, p. 529) Therefore we have
to look at it as a given, something of the same
order as the physical constitution. But Jung realized
it was going to be an extremely difficult problem to
bring his psychological types in line with a constitutional psychology. What made it difficult, in his

mind, was the diagnostic problem that exists in psychological types. And why should he go on and try to resolve this issue when his inclinations ran elsewhere and his own psychological types were not being understood?

He writes in 1929:

"I personally have the impression that some of Kretschmer's main types are not so far removed from certain of the basic psychological types I have enumerated. It is conceivable that at these points a bridge might be established between the physiological constitution and the psychological attitude. That this has not been done already may be due to the fact that the physiological findings are still very recent while, on the other hand, investigation from the psychological side is very much more difficult, and therefore less easy to understand." (1929, p. 108)

During C.A. Meier's long association with Jung he can't remember either Kretschmer or Sheldon being mentioned. (1983) Nor did the meeting of Jung and Sheldon leave more than minor traces on their respective typologies.

Fresh from Kretschmer's clinic Sheldon was preoccupied with the vision of taking Kretschmer's types, reducing them to basic components, and quantifying them. The conversations he had with Jung in Zurich colored his **Psychology and the Promethean Will**, but he never grasped the full meaning of psychological types. Later he was to imagine that Jung's concept of extraversion was inadequate because he had discovered an extraversion of affect in his viscerotonia or endotonia, and an extraversion of action in his somatotonia or mesotonia. He never really understood the nature of the functions as qualifying the different kinds of introversion and extraversion. It was after the publication of his **Atlas of Men** in 1954, which had completed the foundations of his constitutional typology, that he thought of Jung. Humphrey Osmond, the noted orthomolecular psychiatrist, was going to visit Jung to discuss Jung's early toxin theory of schizophrenia.

"Before I left for Zurich Bill Sheldon gave me a copy of his **Atlas of Men** inscribed to Jung from his former pupil. He told me that he was apologizing to Jung for not having paid sufficient attention to Jung's teachings but explained that he was preoccupied with what was to become somatotyping. When I reached Jung's villa in Kusnacht (the date was November 1955) I carried the **Atlas of Men.** Jung was delighted and said, '"Why we must always give the body its due - did not your Shakespeare say 'Let me have men around me that are fat, sleek headed men and such as sleep o'nights. Your Cassius has a lean and hungry look, he thinks too much, such men are dangerous."'

So Jung certainly knew of Sheldon's work and expressed his explicit approval to me and told me to thank Sheldon and give him his congratulation and warm regards." (1983) This volume is still in Jung's library at Kusnacht.

Even in 1935 the formative stage of Jung's typology was over, but it is just possible that his talks with Sheldon left some outward sign. In February, 1936, Jung's article "Psychological Typology" appeared in Süddeutsche Monatshefte. Had they requested it, or had Jung been somehow inspired to write his last extensive essay in the field of typology? Perhaps we can find an echo of his meeting with Sheldon when he writes, "The whole makeup of the body, its constitution in its broadest sense, has, in fact, a very great deal to do with the psychological temperament, so much that we cannot blame the doctors if they regard psychic phenomena as largely dependent on the body. Somewhere the psyche is living body, and the living body is animated matter." (p. 543) But Jung's basic attitude remains unchanged. More than 20 years later, replying to a letter of Ernst Hanhart who had asked about the types of Freud and Adler and the relationship between Jung's typology and that of Kretschmer, Jung, using Freud as an example, emphasizes how difficult the diagnosis of psychological types can be, and this still remains his principle reason for considering the question of the relationship between body and psychological types an unresolved one. And neither were the followers of Jung, who favored both introversion and intuition, inclined to follow the road that led from psychological types to the realm of the body. One exception, however, was the American analytical psychologist, James Oppenheim, who in 1931 in his **American Types:** A Preface to Analytical Psychology added an appendix called "The Physiognomy of the Types":

"As if to furnish a convincing proof that Jung's theory of the types, with my American elaborations, was true, I stumbled, about two years ago, upon the discovery that the types were differentiated physically." (p. 189)

He considers that the diagnosis of types is extremely difficult for a variety of developmental reasons, and he hopes that the physical makeup of the patient will be a clue to the type, but it, too, has its problems and so, "What is really necessary to determination is a co-ordination of both methods, the one helping to confirm the other." (p. 190-1) So he sets forth his preliminary findings adding "so far as I know (or as the Zurich analysts seem to know) ...mine is the only beginning that has been made in the work on the physiognomy of the types." (p. 191) If alchemy preceded chemistry, now Oppenheim considers that phrenology proceeded "my mite of a discovery", and he goes on to try to describe the facial characteristics of the different types. He is aware that it would be better to use the whole body, a view that Sheldon would concur with, but his descriptions still make intriguing reading. They are hard to follow, but this does not mean that they are wrong. How closely have we ever examined the faces of people of different types? We have a reflexive rejection of things like phrenology like we once had for alchemy before we saw the use that Jung put it to. Who is to say that someone could not carry the same process out among the old treatises of phrenology that Jung carried out in alchemy? Oppenheim describes the difference between the nose of intuition and the nose of sensation. "Preposterous" is our instinctive reaction, but this is precisely what people have said about Jung's typology and Sheldon's. Oppenheim described the face of the intuitive thinking type, and considered the writer Count Herman von Keyserling an example of it. And this is an assertion we can evaluate, for Keyserling was the recipient of a number of Jung's letters in which Jung discussed Keyserling's type and gave advice to him accordingly. These letters, incidentally, provide yet another example of Jung's continued use of his typology, and he did, indeed, consider the Count an extraverted intuitive type. Unfortunately, these intriguing leads were never followed up. Oppenheim died soon after writing the book. Louis Corman also drew some parallels between facial features and Jung's typology in his "Manual de Morphopsychologie" (Gille, p. 14).

If James Oppenheim was building the bridge that could join body and psychological types from scratch, we do not have to undertake such a laborious and difficult endeavor. There is a common ground, a series of commonly accepted relationships, between these two areas that is embraced in various ways by Jung, Kretschmer, Sheldon and the factor analytic school. This common ground finds a basic equation between ectomorphy and introversion, and endomorphy and mesomorphy with extraversion. This is an insight that can be traced long before Jung and Kretschmer, and is embedded in a commonsense understanding of body types. The importance of this common ground should not be underestimated. It could serve as the starting point of an increased dialogue among students of individual differences, and it is a giant step towards the goal of establishing a more detailed correlation between somatotype and psychological type. Once we admit the introversion of ectomorphs, and the extraversion of endomorphs and mesomorphs, we are already within a context that admits the possibility of finer differentiations and correlations. The next step is admittedly a big one to make, for it is a question of the complete Jungian typology in relation to somatotypes. We have already indicated the struggle Jung underwent to move from a consideration of introversion and extraversion to one of the various kinds of the attitudes. Once these nuances are appreciated, and we have gone from Kretschmer's type descriptions to Sheldon's emphasis on the components of physique and temperament, the way is open to try to go beyond the initial relationship of introversion, extraversion and somatotype.

We explained in **Volume I** how a natural process of observation had led us to a growing awareness that there was a close correspondence between psychological types and Sheldon's somatotypes and temperament, or to the conclusion, put in Jung's terms that somewhere, indeed, the psyche is living body. Now this kind of seeing, which was a matter of learning to see in the footsteps of Jung and Sheldon, and then using both ways at once, remains the foundation of our conviction about this relationship, and it is a similar seeing by others that will be the most effective way to gauge the accuracy of what we are proposing.

This brings us right back to the question of method that has interwoven itself throughout the course of the book. If we assert that the only way to prove something is by means of the so-called objective method, then we must demand an "objective" proof for the psychological type - somatotype relationship. This is to put the cart before the horse. Jung never objectively proved his psychological types,

and Sheldon spent a lifetime trying to satisfy his
critics in this regard, with scant success. After Jung
wrote **Psychological Types,** then the efforts at objectification could and did take place. The same was
true of Sheldon's work. And the same is true about
the relationship between them. Once we see in
actual life an extraverted thinking type and his inferior feeling who now, because we are schooled to see
it, exhibits the square jaw and head of mesomorphy,
the thick-boned heavy-muscled physique, etc., of the
mesomorph, then we have somewhere to begin our
attempt at objectification, fully aware of the limits
of these techniques. The condensation of our observation thus far looks like this:

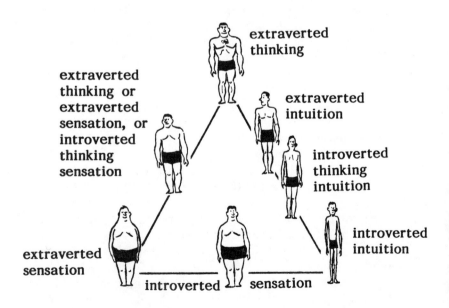

Fig. 1
Somatotype - Psychological Type Relationship

Imposed on Sheldon's somatotype chart it looks like this:

E=Extraversion
I=Introversion
T=Thinking
F=Feeling
U=Intuition
S=Sensation

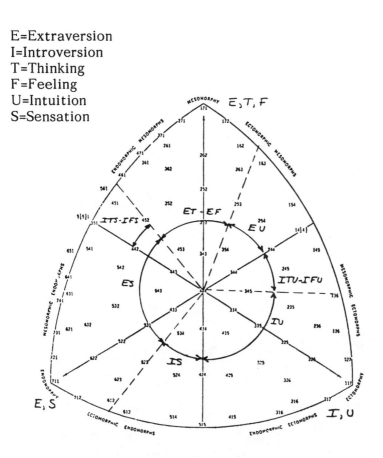

Fig. 2. Psychological Types of Male Somatotypes

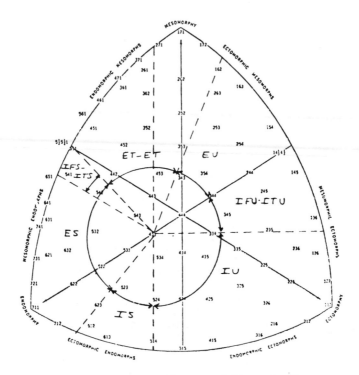

Fig. 3. Psychological Types of Female Somatotypes

Keeping in mind that each psychological type covers a whole somatotype area, the following pictures from the **Atlas of Men** illustrate just one possible somatotype for each psychological type.

126

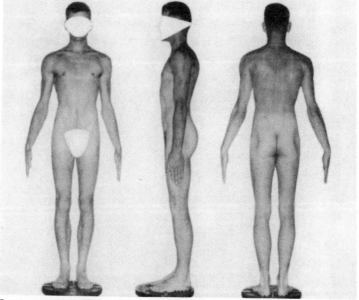

Introverted Intuition Type

244

Introverted Thinking Intuition Type

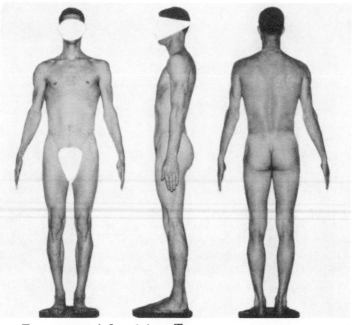

254

Extraverted Intuition Type

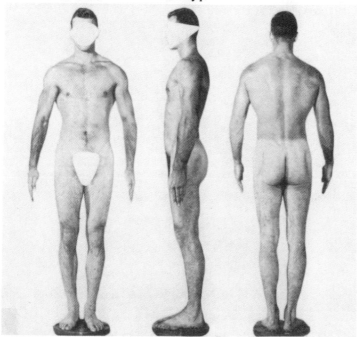

163

Extraverted Thinking Type

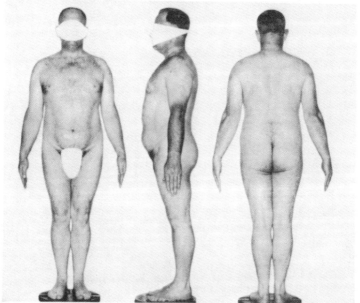

452

The extraverted sensation thinking type, extraverted thinking sensation type or introverted thinking sensation type are all in this general area.

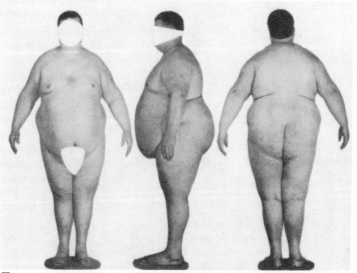

721

Extraverted Sensation Type

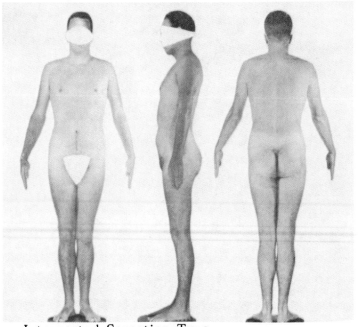

534

Introverted Sensation Type

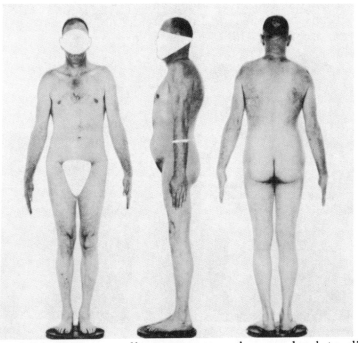

444

Midrange - small somatotype changes lead to different psychological types

Psyches are not disconnected from bodies, or randomly placed in them, but rather we are body and psyche, and they are intimately united and interacting. Let's take a few steps on the road to objectification by looking at data that already exists. Sheldon provides in the **Atlas of Men** a breakdown of three populations by somatotypes: 4,000 college men, 4,000 college women and 46,000 American males. We can convert these sample to psychological types by applying our somatotype-psychological type relationship, and then compare the results of the various MBTI samples.

The samples for 4,000 college men and 4,000 college women are summarized in the form of two somatotype charts in the **Atlas of Men.** After superimposing the somatotype-psychological type relationship on the charts, we counted the dots that fell in each area, and then arrived at the percentage figure for each psychological type. Because of the difference in men and women somatotypes, we have used Parnell's method (1958) of shifting the center of gravity of the women's somatotype chart to the southwest, to the 4-3-3.

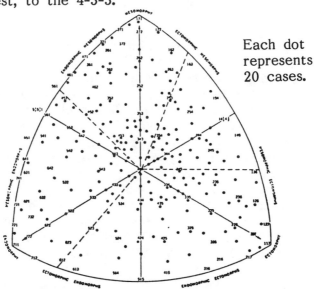

Each dot represents 20 cases.

Fig. 4. 4,000 College Men and Psychological Types

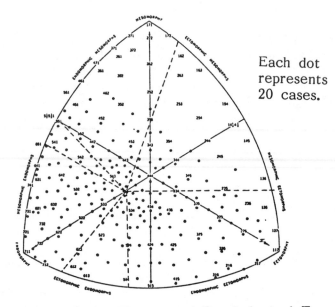

Each dot
represents
20 cases.

Fig. 5. 4,000 College Women and Psychological Types

For the sample of 46,000 American men which is tabulated by incidence per thousand by somatotypes, we superimposed the somatotype-psychological type relationship on Sheldon's somatotype chart (Figure 10, **Varieties of Human Physique**) that shows the area that each somatotype occupied, based on the incidence of the somatotype. On this basis we assigned each somatotype to a psychological type. Where the psychological type line cut through a somatotype area, we assigned half value of that somatotype to each of the adjoining psychological types with the following exceptions: 4-4-3 and 4-4-2 divided 2/3 ES vs. 1/3 ITS and IFS; 5-4-1 and 5-4-2 divided 2/3 ES vs. 1/3 ITS and IFS; while the 4-4-4 was split into 8 parts.

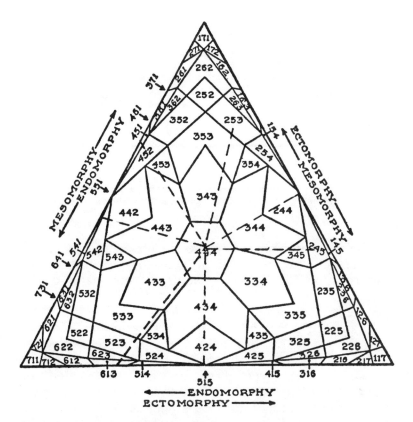

Fig. 6. Somatotype Territory and Psychological Type Territory

The MBTI data comes from Myers (1962) and Myers and Myers (1980). We chose the 3,503 high school students, college prep, a common basic sample used in MBTI comparisons, and two other samples to form a rough match with Sheldon's college men and women.

Sample	Introversion	Extraversion
46,000 American males (Sheldon)	38.7	63.0
3,503 high school college prep males (MBTI)	38.5	61.5
4,000 college men (Sheldon)	41.5	57.0
3,676 liberal arts college males (MBTI)	45.7	54.3
4,000 college women (Sheldon)	50.1	50.1
240 Pembroke college women (MBTI)	42.3	58.0

Table 1. Percentage of Introversion and Extraversion by MBTI and Somatotype

The convergence of these results can be viewed as evidence in favor of a somatotype-psychological type relationship. It also could be seen as a confirmation of the reliability of the MBTI extraversion-introversion scores on large samples.

There are a number of points to consider:

1. The samples are only a rough match. It would be better to have a sample for American women from the somatotype direction, and adult men and women from the MBTI, as well as matching samples of the same kinds of college students.

2. Both sets of samples share a trend towards introversion in the college sample.

3. From a theoretical point of view the introversion-extraversion scores of the MBTI probably possess a higher degree of accuracy than the other scores. This is simply because introversion-extraversion is easier to measure. The introversion-extraversion scores by somatotype will also tend to be more accurate because they involve only a few divisions of the whole sample.

4. The problems of whether to somatotype women in the same fashion as men, and where the division lines between the types should fall, make more detailed comparisons difficult. Further, the MBTI scor-

ing of women and men in thinking and feeling could probably be refined.

A further analysis of the 3,503 males from MBTI and Sheldon's 46,000 males by specific type, though premature, is nonetheless interesting. The most prevalent type in each case is the ET-EF type (32.3 MBTI and 27.7 Sheldon). Table 2 shows the eight types compared by percentage of type in the MBTI sample and the Sheldon sample.

Type	Sheldon (46,000 males)	MBTI (3,503 males)
ET-EF	27.8	32.3
ES	20.2	14.2
IU	19.1	6.8
EU	15.1	15.0
IT-IF	14.5	19.7
IS	5.1	12.1

Table 2. Percentage of Type by MBTI and Somatotype

The greatest discrepancy exists between the IS and the IU types. This problem will reappear later when we examine the psychological type of schizophrenics both from the point of view of the MBTI and from somatotypes. One possibility is that the IS territory should be expanded to embrace part of the IU territory and part of the ES territory. This would lower the figures for the ES and IU Sheldon figures and bring them more in line with the MBTI data. The other possibility is that the MBTI figures are weighted in favor of the IS, or finally, a combination of both reasons is at the bottom of these discrepancies.

If we make the assumption that the MBTI results, while being more accurate in determining the predominant components, will be less accurate in determining which function is the primary function and which is the auxiliary, we can group the MBTI results according to the following categories: ETS (EFS) and EST (ESF); ETU (EFU) and EUT (EUF); IST (ISF) and ITS (IFS); IUT (IUF) and ITU (IFU), thus combining the functions into groups most likely to be mistaken for each other. These groupings can be compared by MBTI and somatotype.

Type	Sheldon (46,000 males)	MBTI (3,503 males)
ETS-EST	36.3	36.3
EUT-ETU	26.8	25.2
IST-ITS	13.0	21.6
IUT-ITU	25.7	16.9

Table 3. Combination of Type MBTI and Somatotype

Again the major discrepancy exists in the IS-IU area.

A Temperament-Psychological Type Experiment

There is one study that deserves our careful attention because it comes the closest to being the forerunner of the objective tests that may be undertaken in the future. In it Ralph Metzner administered the Eysenck Personality Inventory, the Gray-Wheelwright and the Cortés-Gatti Self-Description Temperament Quiz to a group of 60 men and 96 women who were attending a conference of the Association for Research and Enlightenment at Virginia Beach, Virginia. Though it is not a direct test of Sheldon's somatotypes, we have already seen the good correlations found by Cortés and Gatti between temperament and somatotype when employing their quiz. There was a strong correlation between the extraversion as measured by the Eysenck test and by the Gray-Wheelwright, and when the results between Eysenck's test and the temperament quiz were compared, Metzner found for both men and women "strong positive correlations between extraversion and somatotonia and negative ones between extraversion and cerebrotonia." (p. 345) Although this appears as part of the common ground long observed, it says something more. Eysenck's notion of mesomorphs was a statistical one halfway between the ectomorphs and endomorphs. Here the extraversion of the mesomorphs is clearly brought out, while at the same time the extraversion of the viscerotonics does not appear. Perhaps this is an indication of the two different kinds of extraversion that Sheldon described.

More interesting are the correlations that he found that have a bearing on the relationship between the Jungian functions and the Sheldonian components of temperament. In the male sample, he found a positive correlation between intuition and extraversion, and a negative one between sensation and extraversion. When he compared the functions tested by the Gray-Wheelwright with the three components of temperament, he found in the male sample a positive correlation between intuition and mesotonia and a negative correlation between intuition and ectotonia. He also found a negative correlation between sensation and mesotonia, and a positive one between sensation and ectotonia. There are two groupings: extraversion, intuition, mesotonia and a negative correlation to ectotonia forming the first, and introversion, sensation, ectotonia and a negative correlation to mesotonia forming the second.

What can we make of this? Since the Gray-Wheelwright has a forced choice format, the results can be viewed as two sides of the one type being measured at significant levels. The most logical choice is the extraverted intuition type, for it would not be surprising to find them in considerable numbers at the Association for Research and Enlightenment which deals with the work of the psychic Edgar Cayce. In the extraverted intuition type intuition will appear extraverted, as well as mesotonic, and opposed to the ectotonic introverted pole. The sensation of the extraverted intuition type will come out introverted, negatively related to the extraverted pole of mesotonia, but positively related to the introverted pole of ectotonia. If the author had plotted the results of the Gray-Wheelwright and the Cortés-Gatti quiz on Sheldon's somatotype chart, then we might pictorially begin to get a sense of what these underlying correlations mean. As it is, if you have trouble visualizing what these correlations mean, you should not feel bad. There was virtually no way in which an examination of the data analyzed in this way could provide any number of significant clues to the relationship between somatotypes and psychological types. It's not that the clues are not there, but it is critical to have some sense of what we are looking for in order to evaluate them properly. This is the dilemma that we have already seen in the many objective tests done of Sheldon's and Jung's work, and it will, no doubt, be the dilemma that will exist if anyone undertakes to determine the relationship between body and temperament and psychological type by purely objective means. I am not saying that this objective testing is not worth doing. It is very much worth doing. Someday if the proper circumstances present themselves we can already see an interesting way to do it. This would be to somatotype people by one of the objective methods, preferably Sheldon's Trunk Index method, then administer the Cortés-Gatti quiz, and a battery of psychological type tests. At the same time, on the observational level, these individuals should be tested using Sheldon's long method of determininging temperament and the more laborious observational ways to determine psychological type. The analysis of the data from all these different directions will go, we believe, a long way into showing how closely these three levels of personality are related.

Gray, in a study we examined before, administered the Gray-Wheelwright test to 13 markedly obese people and 25 markedly lean ones. Among the obese he found that 85% were more extraverted than introverted, 69% were sensation types vs. intuitive types, and 68% feeling types more than thinking types. Thus, the predominant type was extraverted sensation, making a nice, independent, confirmation of our hypothesis that extraverted sensation predominates among endomorphs. Gray does not indicate whether the obese were women or men, and so it's hard to evaluate his findings of more feeling than thinking. Among the lean people he found 72% introversion, 71% sensation and 76% thinking, where we would have expected more intuitive types.

Finally, in a book entitled **Types de Jung et Tempéraments Psychobiologiques** Jean-Charles Gille-Maisani describes the temperaments discovered by the French psychologist Léone Bourdel. By studying the reactions of people to different kinds of music, she distinguished four kinds of temperament: the harmonic, the melodic, the rhythmic and the complex, all of which she found had ramifications far beyond the musical field. The melodic is characterized by social adaptability. He or she is an extravert, active and open, a person whose life is deeply affected by the circumstances of the moment. They love to live in large cities and are oriented to the rooms in their houses that have to do with social interaction. They love well-being, and can adapt themselves to all kinds of other people. Here we begin to recognize the face of our old friend, Sheldon's viscerotonic or endotonic temperament. The rhythmic temperament, in contrast, is more independent, less emotional, loves movement, has an objective judgment, and can tolerate a monotonous cuisine. If the melodic is drawn to the social professions and business, the rhythmic is found among military officers, police, executives and so forth. Here we find a temperament that closely resembles Sheldon's somatotonic or mesotonic. The third temperament, the harmonic, is an introvert, habitually reserved and even inhibited. "The harmonic is, more than the other temperaments, vulnerable to the environment, with which he would love to be in harmony but to which, in fact, he is rarely well adapted. Criticisms inhibit him, especially if he feels himself misunderstood, not loved." (p. 86) The harmonics have a tendency to prefer jobs in research. This, of course, matches Sheldon's cerebrotonic or ectotonic. The fourth temperament is a mixture of the three previous ones.

What is interesting about these temperamental descriptions, which were experimentally derived, are not only their confirmation of Sheldon's, but how Gille goes on to explore their relationship with the different blood groups and with different kinds of handwriting. And most importantly, in the process of doing so makes some comments about the relationship between these temperaments and Jung's types which he had examined in the first part of the book. Will these comments coincide with the relationship we are proposing between Sheldon's temperaments and Jung's types? The melodic is characterized as an extravert whose sentiment in the terms of Janet is not inferior, making us think of Sheldon's extraversion of affect. The melodic-rhythmic, that is, the melodic with secondary rhythmic development, is characterized by Gille as having sensation well developed. (p. 107) And this is the area we described as extraverted sensation thinking and extraverted sensation feeling. When it is a question of the rhythmic, Gille had stressed his

well-developed action, but also his relative independence from his milieu and does not characterize him
as either an introvert or an extravert, making us
think of the independence that Gray subscribed to
the thinking type and, sure enough, Gille relates this
type to Jung's thinking type. When it is a question
of the harmonic he says he finds all the Jungian
types there, but the introverted intuition type is the
most frequent. We will return to this interesting work
in connection with blood types later on, but here it
is important to note we have some more independent
evidence that tends to anchor the three poles of
Sheldon's somatotype chart in relationship to Jung's
psychological types in the way we have proposed.

Indirect Comparisons

While it is true that direct comparisons between
somatotype, temperament and psychological type will
shed the most light on the relationships between
them, indirect comparisons, created by comparing
somatotype and psychological type to a common third
thing, would also be interesting and worth doing.
Indirect comparisons of this kind are difficult to do
because of the difference in the samples that are
available, and in the procedures used to gather them.
In the following comparisons we have simply selected
some highlights that agree with our overall relationship between somatotypes and psychological types.
We have done this in order to encourage careful
comparisons between these two areas.

1. Myers (1960) compared the MBTI and Strong
Vocational Interest Blank scores of 727 male freshmen, while Parnell (1958) examined the somatotype
and the choice of faculty of 2,866 male freshmen
upon entering Birmingham University (Great Britain).
In the case of mathematics the MBTI results indicated a preference for introversion, intuition and thinking, while Parnell found the highest concentration of

somatotypes in the endomorphic-ectomorphic range, which is the equivalent to our IU type. In the same way, in the interest of physics, Myers found the same type elements predominated, while Parnell found the highest concentration of somatotypes among the mesomorphic ectomorphs, which we are taking to be equivalent to the IU and IT types.

2. Deabler, Hartl and Willis (1975) somatotyped and gave the Strong Vocational Interest Blank to 300 male subjects. They found, for example, a significant correlation between psychology and ectomorphy. Myers, in the previously cited study, found a strong preference for the intuitive function among psychologists. Under the category of purchasing agent, Myers found the elements of extraversion, sensation and thinking predominating, while the Deabler study found a positive correlation with endomorphy.

3. In a comparison of MBTI scores with the All-port-Vernon-Lindzey Value Scores, Myers (1962) found a correlation between aesthetic interests and introversion and intuition. This fits very well with Sheldon's (1942) correlation of ectotonia and aesthetic intelligence. In the same way, Myers found a correlation between political interests and extraversion, sensation and thinking, while Sheldon in various places indicated the endomorphic mesomorphic build of political figures. The same type preferences, E, S, T, were found by Myers for economic interests, and these, too, fit Sheldon's comments about the endomorphic mesomorphic build of many businessmen.

4. Myers (1962) compared MBTI results with the Personality Research Inventory. She found that **gregariousness** was correlated with E, S, as was **social know-how.** Both traits are similar to qualities ascribed by Sheldon to the endotonic, which we have related to the ES personality. She also found a relationship between **self-sufficiency** and I, U, T, and between **liking to use the mind** and U, T. These findings are in line with Sheldon's traits of the ectotonic

and our equation with the IU personality.

5. Myers (1962) compared the MBTI results with faculty ratings of student characteristics. She found traits like **solitary** related to introversion and intuition, and **deep, shows originality, imaginative,** all related to intuition, as well as **good grasp of the abstract** and **independent.** All these ectotonic traits could be applied to the range of psychological types running from the IU through the IT to the EU. The trait **pleasant** was related to extraversion, sensation and feeling, while the traits **cooperative, poor at analyzing** and **willing to take directions** were all correlated to sensation. These are all close to Sheldon's endotonic traits which we have related to the ES personality.

6. Myers (1962) found that the IU type had the highest mean I.Q.s and the highest mean grade point averages. This matches Sheldon's (1942) correlation of ectotonia and I.Q.. Parnell (1958) also found a relationship between academic performance and ectomorphy, which also fits in with our correlation between ectomorphy-ectotonia-IU. Both Sheldon and Parnell found that the 2-2-5 somatotype was the somatotype that most distinguished itself academically, and the 2-2-5 falls right in the middle of the territory we have delineated as that of the IU type.

Following the 2-2-5 somatotype in academic performance was the 5-2-3. If we look at the somatotype chart, this falls right near the IS, ES boundary. Myers found that the IST, along with the EUT, have the highest grade point averages after the IU types. Myers felt that the superior performance of the IU type could not be attributed to their higher I.Q. or application, but could be a habit of mind which produces a certain interest in academic kinds of activities. Sheldon, looking at the same issue from the perspective of somatotypes, felt that somatotypes like the 2-2-5 and the 5-2-3 did not have the distraction from academic pursuits because of their low meso-

morphy. Both of these considerations seem roughly
equivalent, and could form the starting point of a
consideration of I.Q. differences among groups in
virtue of the relative frequency of the different
types within the groups.

7. Myers (1962) reported on a four-year study of
employee turn-over by Laney where the turn-over
rate of intuitive workers was much higher than that
of sensing workers, especially in mechanical jobs.
This can be compared with Parnell's report of a
study of Bullen where among female factory workers
who were engaged in piece-work stitching, the meso-
morphic-endomorphic women lasted the longest.
Linear women had a higher turn-over rate. These
results are also consistent with our conversions of
somatotype to psychological type.

These are not the only areas where comparisons
might be fruitful. Sheldon describes a number of
three-way traits which distinguish the three components of temperament. For example, in reaction to
trouble, the endotonic needs and seeks out people,
the mesotonic needs action, and the ectotonic soli-
tude. Or in the case of alcohol, the endotonic becomes more relaxed and sociophilic, the mesotonic
becomes more aggressive and assertive, and the ectotonic becomes more resistant to alcohol and depressed by it. Attitude towards death and privacy
preferences can also be viewed as three-way temperamental traits. All of these traits could serve as
common points of comparison for somatotype, temperament and psychological type evaluations.

Sheldon also made observations about the somatotype and temperament type of delinquent boys, temperamental susceptibility to hypnosis, and to heat and
cold sensitivity, sleeping styles, space and housing
preferences, and many other things. These could be
compared to psychological type evaluations of the
same traits. These kinds of comparisons will serve
not only as further evidence for a relationship be-

tween the three levels of type, but also serve to clarify and delineate the interrelationships between these levels and help knit them together into one typological instrument with many possible applications.

Continuity and Discontinuity

Sheldon's somatotypes are described as an ever-varying continuum while Jung's psychological types are distinct entities set off rather sharply from each other. These two modes of descriptions seem on the surface to be strongly opposed to each other and an obstacle to the integration of somatotypes, temperament and psychological types.

If discontinuity can be demonstrated underlying Sheldon's somatotypes, the problem will begin to resolve itself, and incidentally serve as another kind of evidence in favor of the relationship between the two typologies. The young men who were the subjects of Sheldon's **Varieties of Delinquent Youth** were strongly clustered in the endomorphic-mesomorphic northwest of the somatotype chart. If we study the capsule biographies of the majority of the men who were somatotyped 4-5-1 and 4-5.5-1 or 4-5-2 and 4-5.5-2, two distinct patterns emerge.

The first is a series of cases where mesomorphy has been rated at 5 and endomorphy at 4 or 4.5. The descriptions seem more appropriate for the ES than for the ET. For example, case 18, a 4.5-5-1.5, evokes the comments, "Although powerfully built, he can neither fight nor run, but he swims fairly well. He is emotionally extraverted, relaxed, gluttonous, also stubborn and surly. The youth has held a job for nearly a year, is fatter, seems more dull and bleary." Case 192, a 4-5-1.5, is described as: "sociable, happiest where the crowd is thickest and noisiest, enormous energy combined with a total absence of physical combativeness."

In the other series mesomorphy advances to a 5.5, while endomorphy remains at 4. These young men are described in quite a different way. Case 164, a 4-5.5-1.5, is seen as: "of tremendous energy, he seems to have a constant need for letting off steam in dangerous actions, his unlimited courage, directness, psychological callousness, and lack of restraint define extreme somatotonia (mesotonia)". And case 200, a 4-5.5-2, "a picture of relaxed, resourceful and aggressive somatotonia (mesotonia) without a smile. Behind the menace lies both physical power and a violent, destructive temper. He looks upon life through the eyes of a predator." Table 4 gives the somatotypes of these two series, and Figure 7 shows them represented on the somatotype chart.

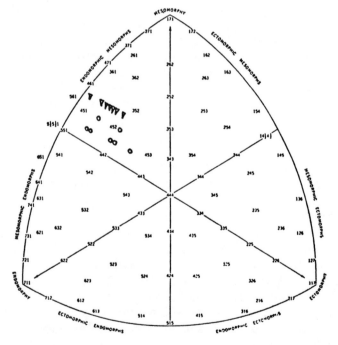

Fig. 7. VDY Cases

EST			ETS		
Case	VDY	VDY 30	Case	VDY	VDY 30
12	4½51½	451½	13	45½1½	45½1½
18	4½51½	55½1	90	45½1½	35½1½
23	452	64½2	118	45½1½	451
47	4½52	4½53	164	45½1½	45½2
120	4½52½	55½2½	193	45½1½	35½1½
172	4½52	44½3½	195	45½1	3½5½1½
192	451½	452½	200	45½2	2½62½

Table 4. Selected EST and ETS cases in VDY and VDY 30

If we avert simply to somatotype we would conclude that the underlying temperaments and psychological types would be quite close. The half point in
mesomorphy should not have such an impact as to
strongly differentiate these young men, yet a reading of the cases indicates that there are two distinct
types involved. With the publication of **Physique and
Delinquent Behavior:** A Thirty-Year Follow-Up of
William H. Sheldon's Varieties of Delinquent Youth
by Emil M. Hartl, Edward P. Monnelly and Roland
D. Elderkin (1982) we were able to pursue this question further. The men were re-somatotyped by using
Sheldon's Trunk Index method. If our original assumption was correct, the re-somatotyping to the degree
it corrected the original somatotypes should show the
cases we labeled ES moving towards the endomorphic
pole, while the cases we labelled ET should move
towards the mesomorphic pole. (See Figure 8)

This kind of discontinuity, which can also be seen
in the Gabriel and Eugene cases in the **Varieties of
Temperament,** cannot be explained adequately within
the framework of somatotype alone. If we imagine
a psychological type boundary running through the
4-5-1 - 4-5-2 area, then the divergence on either side
becomes comprehensible.

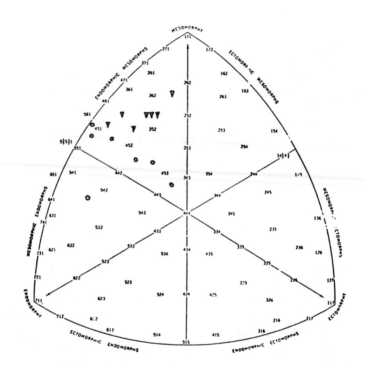

Fig. 8. VDY 30 Cases

An integrated typology could have a great effect on both Jung's and Sheldon's psychology. First let's look at its potential for effecting how we see psychological types.

1. It allows us to make a new attack on the intractible problem of diagnosis without being compelled to try to reformulate Jung's typology. Typological diagnosis, integrally considered at the three levels of type, instead of becoming a more complex procedure, is actually easier once the initial skills have been gained. What makes it easier is that a wider range of empirical material is available for observation. What is striking in one case may be absent in another, making set rules often difficult to follow.

For example, an extreme ectomorphic physique is naturally more suggestive than when it is a question of a midrange somatotype. In other cases, temperamental traits might be in the forefront, like the booming voice of mesotonia or the special kind of amiability of the endotonic. At the level of psychological type, the inferior function might catch a person's attention, or the degree of introversion and extraversion, or even something subtler like the distinctive quality of thinking as a third function. Characteristics from all three levels give rise to particular lines of inquiry, and since there are more roads leading to the final diagnosis, it is often easier. The multiple directions of approach tend to check and confirm each other, yielding a greater certitude.

2. It makes us face the question of intratype variation at the level of the psychological type. If we look at the extent of the somatotype territory that each psychological type covers, we see graphically depicted the possibility that two people of the same type can differ considerably. This is something we may have instinctively realized before, but now we have a way to characterize it.

Is the 6-3-2 ES, for example, really the same as the 4-5-1 ES? And does this variation have something to do with the actual structuring of the functions with one another? Are people different, not only in attitude and function, but also in the internal configuration of the functions in terms of the distance of one function from another, that is, in terms of psychological accessibility? Is integration harder for some people than for others because of this kind of articulation? When seen in this light, Sheldon's remarks on the 4-4-4 temperament are potentially significant. These people exhibit a greater ability to develop in different directions, but do they also exhibit a higher degree of susceptibility to neurosis, i.e., the unwanted intrusion of unconscious material into consciousness? In the same way, does the extreme polar physique have more difficulty in integrating the auxiliary functions? Are some people naturally closer to their inferior function? Such questions, if they become answerable, could have an important effect on actual therapeutic practice and provide a way to differentiate what kinds of techniques to use in different cases.

3. The third possibility that this integration opens up for Jungian psychology is that Sheldon's constitutional psychology can form a bridge which allows Jung's work to be brought to bear in new areas. This is our task in Part IV.

Typing the Typologists

We have already seen that Sheldon was around 3 1/2 - 3 1/2 - 5 in somatotype and an introverted thinking intuition type. These evaluations agree with our determination of the somatotype area of the introverted thinking intuition type. Incidentally, for each somatotype in the **Atlas of Men** Sheldon named an animal totem, and for the 3-4-5 it was an Irish setter, which calls to mind his father's joke of William being the last of the litter. Sheldon remarks about this somatotype totem, "Bird dogs who are more ectomorphic than pointers. More fragile, more delicate boned. Higher spirited, keener nosed and more temperamental. Longer haired and less sturdy, they stand rough country poorly." (p. 159)

Sheldon left us approximate somatotype ratings for both Kretschmer and Jung. Kretschmer, who gives the impression in his writings of being a genial and sociable man, he rated 4.5-4-2.5, which would make him an extraverted sensation thinking type or an extraverted thinking sensation type.

But what of Jung? Jung thought of himself as an introverted thinking intuition type, and ever since the creation of psychological types many people have tried their hand at reevaluating Jung's type. Usually they want to stress his intuition or are impressed by the large measure of extraversion he seemed to possess. This is, of course, a somewhat speculative pastime, but as long as we don't take it too seriously, it can be fun. Jung had to be aware, at least from the publication of Kretschmer's **Physique and Character,** that the schizophrenic had been identified with Kretschmer's asthenic physique (or in Sheldon's terminology, the ectomorph), while he, himself, had previously associated schizophrenia with regressive introversion. It would have been natural, therefore, for him to see the connection between introversion and the ectomorphic physique. But Jung was highly introverted and not at all the typical ectomorph. He had been knicknamed by his school friends "the barrel", and the Indians at the Taos pueblo in New Mexico had thought that the bear was his appropriate totem. He impressed many of his visitors not only with his height, but with his burliness. Jung, himself, was aware of the apparent incongruity between his psychological type and his body type. Writing in 1929 to a woman who was attempting a portrait of him he says, "My exterior is in estranged contrast to my spirit. When I am dead no one will think that this is the corpse of one with spiritual aspirations. I am the clash of opposites." (**Letters,** Vol. I, p. 51) Sheldon gave him the approximate somatotype of 4-6-2.5. Interestingly, Sheldon's totem for the 4-6-2 was the Great Alaska brown bear. This would make him either an extraverted thinking type (which I don't believe he was), or put him near the range we have described as belonging to those paradoxical introverted thinking sensation types who are more outwardly forceful than the usual run of introverts, but are introverted nonetheless. It would also make us wonder if the ITS territory goes closer to the mesomorphic pole than we had realized.

Van der Hoop in his **Conscious Orientation** does, indeed, suggest that Jung was an introverted thinker with sensation rather than intuition as his secondary function. He finds evidence in the fact that Jung "lives out of doors, travels a great deal, and welcomes all the pleasures of existence. In his scientific work, this factor leads to the exposition of much concrete detail." (p. 327)

He contrasts Jung with Kant as a typical introverted thinking type with intuition as the auxiliary function, and he recognizes that Jung diverges from what he feels is the "very practical and solid intellectuality" of the typical introverted thinking sensation type. Jung concerns himself with ultimate issues and van der Hoop surmises this represents the working of the polar aspects of his mind, that is, his compensating intuition and feeling.

Not only was Kant selected as an example of an introverted thinking type by Jung, but Kretschmer saw him as a schizothyme, and so we could say that he was a representative of the slim muscularity that we have come to recognize as one of the hallmarks of the introverted thinking intuition type, which does, indeed, contrast with Jung's body type.

After this chapter was completed I received some data through the good offices of Emil Hartl and Edward Monnelly that confirmed my instincts that proof of the somatotype - psychological type relationship by paper and pencil "objective" methods is not going to be a straightforward task. It consisted of 16 men and 6 women who had been somatotyped by Sheldon's objective method and who had taken, as well, the MBTI. In some of these cases we could perhaps find some support for our somatotype - psychological type relationship. For example, a man who was somatotype 4.5-3-5 predominated in introversion, sensation and thinking, making it conceivable he was an introverted sensation type. But in general no easily analyzable pattern emerged. What is happening? We could conclude that psychological types are more or less randomly connected to body types, but I don't think this is correct. The most probable source of error is in the establishment of the psychological type solely by means of a type test. Perhaps if this kind of somatotype - psychological type experiment were done on a large enough scale, some hint of these relationships would emerge through statistical analysis, but I would still like to see the kind of experiment described above in which more laborious, but I think more accurate methods would be used to determine the psychological type.

PART IV
THE FUTURE OF TYPOLOGY

CHAPTER 9
IN SEARCH OF A
BIOCHEMICAL TYPOLOGY

Our integrated instrument composed of psychological type and somatotypes can be employed in two different directions. One looks upward to the questions that arise when we try to relate typology, and the psychology they embody, to philosophy and theology. I have traced some of these issues in **St. John of the Cross and Dr. C.G. Jung.** The other direction is to see somatotypes as the outer sign of a biochemical typology that is just beginning to dawn on the far horizon. The idea of a biochemical typology goes back to the four humors of the Greeks and has influenced the study of human differences ever since then, but it is only recently that the advances in the natural sciences are beginning to make it a real possibility.

In our search for a biochemical typology we are like someone who wants to put together a jigsaw puzzle but who first must find the scattered pieces and has no guarantee that the ones he finds even belong to the same picture. First of all, let's look at some attempts to create a biochemical typology.

In 1965 a California physician, Henry Bieler, wrote a book entitled **Food is Your Best Medicine** summing up a long career in which he successfully treated many patients by a program of detoxification and a typology that divided them into three basic types: the adrenal, the thyroid and the pituitary. Some of the characteristics of the adrenal type are already quite familiar to us. The lower jaw is heavy, solid and often protruding, the chest is broad and thick, containing a large heart and lungs. And Bieler comments: "the skeletal muscles are well-developed and have splendid tone. Fatigue is practically unknown to the adrenal type. His muscular endurance is spectacular." (p. 85) But this is not quite our old friend the mesomorph. "A member of the adrenal-type group has a phlegmatic disposition - easy-going, jolly, slow to anger, never bothered with insomnia, fear or 'cold feet'. He will often go out of his way to avoid a quarrel." (p. 85) Clearly this particular kind of mesomorph has moved considerably towards Sheldon's endomorphic pole.

Bieler describes the thyroid type as having delicate and finely molded features, a long, thin chest, graceful hands with beautiful fingers, and if the adrenal person is a draft horse, the thyroid person is a race horse. Again, we discover Sheldon's ectomorph, but in the form of a mesomorphic ectomorph. "Usually several streams of thought actually whirl through his brain at once, making concentration most difficult. He is frequently fatigued..." (p. 87)

Bieler's description of the third type, the pituitary, was left undeveloped. He has a large head and long arms and legs, but we don't learn a great deal else about him. In his practice, which was apparently very effective, Dr. Bieler would estimate the degree of functioning of each of these particular types in the individual, and he would rely heavily on detoxification and proper diet, and an awareness that people overindulged in foods "that are most toxic to them because of their stimulation value." (p. 153)

These suggestive ideas have been recently taken

up by Elliott Abravanel who amplifies the description
of Bieler's basic types, fills out the picture of the
pituitary type, and adds for women a gonadal type.
Abravanel's early work was directed towards obesity:
"I studied carefully the relationships between foods
and the glands, and on this basis was able to develop, for each type, the precise diet to enable
people with that body type to lose weight most effectively." (Dr. **Abravanel's Body Type Diet and Lifetime Nutrition Plan,** p. 5) The adrenal type is Sheldon's endomorphic-mesomoprh, or Kretschmer's pyknic
type. "They are solidly built, have square or round
faces, strong, squarish hands and feet, broad shoul-
ders and thick waists - body shaped for power rather
than speed." (p. 24-5) Dr. Abravanel describes one
of his adrenal type patients, a high-powered sales-
man:

"I heard his booming voice in the waiting room
before I saw him, and he had all the other patients
laughing. He is a good-looking man, with great
energy, verve and an infectiously charming personality
- and eighty extra pounds. I knew at once he was
an adrenal type, for this body type has its own typical fat distribution. Where thyroid types balloon
around the middle and remain slim in their arms and
legs, A-types thicken all over, though they do put
a great deal of their excess weight in front, in a pot
belly." (p. 25)

It is the adrenal gland, in his estimation, that
orchestrates the metabolism of this kind of personality, and with the thyroid type, which is Sheldon's
mesomorphic ectomorph, it is naturally the thyroid
that plays this role and creates a distinctive metabolism.

The pituitary type is described as having a head
slightly too big for their body, a fat distribution
which is spread all over, a childlike face and a
stomach rounded like a child. The gonadal type has
a larger, lower half of the body than upper. The

pituitary type is described as intellectual, cool and detached, while the gonadal type is sensuous, warm and comfortable. But neither one of them are easy to visualize in terms of Sheldon's body types.

Each type has its own particular craving, its way of overstimulating its metabolism. The pituitary type wants dairy products, the thyroid type sweets and starches, the adrenal type meat and salty foods, and the gonadal type fats and spices. Dr. Abravanel's treatment of obesity has been to recognize the different body types, their particular food weaknesses, and to create a diet crafted to their own needs. Later Abravanel extended his insights about obesity to the more general field of health and fitness, and he recognized the importance of the gland that is next strongest, or has a secondary predominance in the physical makeup, for this accounted for the variations found among the various body types, and he even describes people who have gone beyond their original body type, not that it is no longer recognizable, "but their physiology appears to have a more general and more organized structure about it". (**Dr. Abravanel's Body Type Program for Health, Fitness, and Nutrition,** p. 345) This is curiously reminiscent of Jung's wholeness seen at the level of the metabolism.

Another modern pioneer in biochemical or metabolic typology is William Kelley. Kelley's earlier interests in nutrition came into sharp focus when he was diagnosed as having a metastasized liver and pancreatic cancer, and given only a short time to live. He developed a nutruitional therapy that cured him, and which he describes in his book **One Answer to Cancer.** Later, when his wife was ill, he put her on his diet with disasterous results, and came face to face with the problem of biochemical individuality. Out of these experiences he formulated two basic principles that have governed his nutritional work: non-specific metabolic therapy, which is building up the whole body so that it can fight off the disease, and metabolic typing in which he describes a variety of different metabolisms. The metabolic types are divided into three broad categories based on the two divisions of the autonomic nervous system: the sympathetic or activating nervous system and the parasympathetic or inhibiting nervous system. According to the relative predominance of these aspects of the autonomic nervous system, Kelley describes sympathetic types, parasympathetic types and balanced metabolisms. Again, we can see strong traces in Kelley's descriptions of the familiar body and psychological types. For example, he says of the sympathetic types, "Their muscles are usually quite well developed and show good muscle tone" (**Metabolic Typing,** p. 3). They are also prone to high blood pressure and arteriosclerosis. He describes them as liking to make decisions, having explosive actions, being extremely active and angering easily. But Kelley pays little attention to the overall body type, and his lists of characteristics of the sympathetic type goes well beyond what could be attributed to the mesomorph or the endomorphic mesomorph, as for example, when he characterizes them as suffering from the cold, gagging easily and having poor circulation.

The parasympathetic types "have poor muscle tone. They are in general lethargic, slow, fall asleep easily. They usually have a good reserve of strength." (p. 6) They also have a desire to be cautious and are slow to make decisions and have slow breathing rates, and are inclined to obesity. They have very enlarged round chests, good fat metabolism and often feel sad or dejected. Here we can see the endomorph, but, again, the total picture is not clear. Kelley's balanced group falls roughly in between. He divides each of these three groups further and ends with a total of ten types that reflect not only sympathetic or parasympathetic dominance, but the level of metabolic efficiency. But even these ten types he found inadequate, and so he refined his classifications to describe the percentage of each type that exists in a particular individual. He also tried to come to grips with the question of the original genetic metabolic dominant type changing due to various stresses.

Kelley has apparently employed his two basic principles of non-specific metabolic therapy and metabolic typing to good effect in dealing with intractible degenerative diseases like cancer. Recently a book on his work by Tom and Carol Valentine has appeared entitled, **Metabolic Typing:** Medicine's Missing Link.

In each of these three biochemical typologies we see the difficulties that arise when the authors try to talk of types instead of basic elements or components that make up the various types, and their type descriptions could be clarified against the background of the more developed typologies of Jung and Sheldon. But their works represent a wealth of practical experience and therapeutic expertise that should not be neglected.

These individual efforts parallel, in part, the recent development of orthomolecular medicine. The word orthomolecular, meaning the right molecules in the right proportion, was coined by Linus Pauling in a 1968 article, "Orthomolecular Psychiatry", whose basic tenet was that individual biochemical needs vary greatly, and if the natural nutrients that the brain needs can be supplied, then many serious mental disorders can be more effectively treated. The modern roots of orthomolecular medicine can be found in the work of Abram Hoffer, Humphrey Osmond, and John Smythies, the insights of Roger J. Williams and the research of Irwin Stone and Fred Klenner, and many others.

Roger J. Williams, for example, was a biochemist, nutritionist and the discoverer of pantothenic acid. He had developed a keen interest in biochemical individuality, for he had once received a shot of morphine after a surgical operation, and instead of it putting him to sleep, it made his mind race from one thought to the next all night. Another time, working in his laboratory on the alcoholic consumption of rats, he found that it:

"(1) was highly individual (as were also their excretion patterns), and (2) was genetically controlled (as evidenced by the distinctive behavior of each inbred strain and the relatively small variation **within** inbred strains), and (3) could be increased by deficient diets and abolished by fortified ones..." (**Biochemical Individuality**, p. 173-4)

But he found that the idea of biochemical individuality had been largely ignored. He combed through the literature and culled what references he could find, and in 1956 produced his masterful **Biochemical Individuality**: The Basis for the Genetotrophic Concept. Here he shows in great detail the variations that exist between people in anatomy, endocrine activities, reactions to drugs, and in almost any kind of measurement of the body. In anatomy, for example, "the observed variations encompass all structures, brain, nerves, muscles, tendons, bones, blood, organ weights, endocrine gland weights, etc." (p. 45) People differ in endocrine activities. They differ, for example, in the size of the thyroid gland and the amounts of protein-bound iodine in the serum, and the retention of radioactive iodine. (p. 82) Even babies who have been fed largely on a milk diet exhibit distinctive excretion patterns. People differ in the way they react to alcohol, much like Williams' mice:

"An interesting way in which individuals differ in their response to alcohol is the reaction when a small amount (0.03 cc.) of 60 per cent alcohol is injected into the skin. In all individuals there is produced a localized wheal about 1 cm. in diameter, but the reaction in the surrounding area varies greatly from individual to individual. In about 18 per cent of the cases tested, the surrounding area was unaffected; in the others the inflammation graded from a small very slightly pink corona to a highly inflamed area 4 cm. in diameter." (p. 109)

And not everyone has the same ability to adapt to changed climatic conditions. "One study indicates what might be expected, namely, that there is variation in ability to adapt metabolism to changed climatic conditions. Of 21 women examined, 13 showed a 6 to 11 per cent drop in basal metabolism when they moved from a temperate climate into the tropics; 8 on the other hand showed little or no change." (p. 120)

Williams amassed data in many fields, and it led him to his genetotropic principle. "Every individual organism that has a distinctive genetic background has distinctive nutritional needs which must be met for optimal well-being." (p. 167) And far from this being a hereditarian point of view, he feels it allows him to overcome the old breach between nature and nurture. "Understanding and appreciating what heredity distinctively does for an individual may make it possible to cope environmentally with his difficulties." (p. 169) And he is well aware of the important implications this genetotropic principle has for psychiatry. We vary in brain morphology and brain metabolism, and if we could understand our individual needs, we could try to meet them.

Men like Bieler and Abravanel had a nodding acquaintance with Sheldon's work, but that was all. Their attention was focused on the biochemical types. In orthomolecular medicine the early insights of Hoffer, Osmond and Williams, and others, have grown and coalesced into a penetrating understanding of the biochemical nature of many diseases and their treatment in a nutritional and ecological way. This is one of the most promising developments in modern medicine, but the whole field of orthomolecular medicine, like its counterpart in genetics, is so new and so involved in specifics, that it has yet to have the leisure to think in terms of biochemical typology.

But the creation of a biochemical typology and its coordination with Sheldon's somatotypes and through them to Jung's psychological types is not a project that defies the imagination. We have met Humphrey Osmond before, both in the field of Jungian typology and, somewhat symbolically, playing the role of intermediary between Sheldon and Jung, and Roger Williams had this to say about Sheldon's work:

"Sheldon's extensive classification of body types constitutes an important contribution to the understanding of the human differences which make for susceptibility to numerous diseases. What he has done with body form is just a beginning; anatomical features such as those mentioned in Chapter III and VI need to be brought into the picture. Classifications need to be worked out at the physiological and biochemical levels." (p. 171)

Imagine if someone were to take ectomorphs, endomorphs and mesomorphs and administer Williams' alcohol injection test. Sheldon made reaction to alcohol one of his three-way traits that distinguished between the three temperaments. Would the ectomorphs react more strongly than the other somatotypes? Or is it really fanciful to talk about an ectomorphic thyroid type? Williams indicated human variation in the retention of a radioactive iodine. Would the ectomorph differ from the endomorph and mesomorph? G.P.S. Dubey and his associates administered 131 Iodine to 86 men of different constitutions, and measured the whole body retention of the radioactive iodine at the end of 24 hours. The ectomorph showed maximum retention, the endomorph minimum retention, and the mesomorph fell in between.

E. Arthur Robertson and his colleagues profiled 10 volunteers for 22 different substances during a 6-week period, and then examined the same subjects two years later.

"Using linear discriminant functions derived from

the first five (or first 10) specimens from each subject, we were able correctly to identify 96% (or 100%) of the specimens collected during the remainder of the six-week testing period. Ninety percent of the two-year follow-up specimens were correctly identified when we used all the original profiles to calculate the discriminant functions. Deliberately mislabeled specimens were also correctly identified by discriminant analysis." (p. 30)

In essence, each person had a distinctive biochemical profile that remained relatively stable, and deviations from it could be indications of the beginning of disease. The authors, realizing how difficult it was to portray this wealth of information in numerical form, used various graphic techniques, the most interesting of which was the computer generation of faces. Each one of the substances measured created the shape of the upper head, or the width of the mouth, or the separation of the eyes, and so forth. From the point of view of a biochemical typology the results were intriguing. Each of the 10 subjects had his distinctive face. But between the 10 subjects there were also similarities. For example, the shape of the upper head was controlled by the dopamine-ß-hydroxylase and the sample could be broken down into the narrow or pointy heads, and the wide heads. Would it be possible to see biochemical introversion and extraversion graphically portrayed in these faces? If groups of ectomorphs, mesomorphs and endomorphs and groups of introverted intuition types, extraverted thinking types and extraverted sensation types were profiled by these methods, would the corresponding groups have similar biochemical faces?

Sheldon once estimated 1,000 individuals could be somatotyped by 2 men working together for 90 working days, and this time could be reduced to 30 days using the somatotyping machine. What would be possible today in the age of video cameras, computers, and advanced techniques for aerial mapping? Could

somatotype poses be recorded by video and automatically analyzed by computer using, for example, Sheldon's trunk index method? The technical problems
involved in such an undertaking could be resolved.
What is lacking is the will to do it, and that could
be generated by an understanding of somatotypes as
a way to integrate information coming from various
disciplines. Such an automatic determination of somatotype, if linked with the data generated by the
automatic testing for various biochemical markers,
would go a long way towards the creation of a biochemical typology. What I am suggesting is that a
biochemical typology is not unthinkable. In fact, once
we have begun to see in terms of an integrated
typology of psychological types and somatotypes, we
will read the news of scientific advances in neuroscience and genetics from a new perspective.

But do these rapidly expanding fields have any
need of Sheldon and Jung? Don't they have the force
of hard science on their side and therefore are replacing these earlier, more subjective, methods? Not
at all. There is a tremendous need to integrate the
bewildering variety of new information that is continually being produced by laboratories all over the
world. And that's what typology can provide in terms
of a framework that can bring this data together so
it can interact and can be used effectively. The
developments in these fields are so new that the
question of typology has not begun to be asked. But
let's go ahead and, working from both directions,
attempt to make some small steps in building our
bridge further. It has gone from Jung to Sheldon, and
now we can trace what a biochemical typology would
be like.

In a 1983 interview David Baltimore, the Nobel
prize-winning geneticist, clearly indicated how difficult it is going to be to avoid the question of human
differences:

"Scientists will discover many subtle genetic factors in the makeup of human beings, and those discoveries will challenge the basic concepts of equality on which our society is based. Once we can say that there are differences between people that are easily demonstrable at the genetic level, then society will have to come to grips with understanding diversity - and we are not prepared for that. Until now we have said, "We will assume there is no diversity because we can't measure it; we will assume equality."...But we're going to find very quickly that a true genetic analysis leads us to differences." (U.S. News & World Report, March 28, 1983, pp. 52-3)

Translated into our present context, we can say that previously it was possible to ignore men like Jung and Sheldon and pretend their work was subjectively inspired, but we are rapidly approaching a time when we are going to see the biological foundations of the differences that they described, and see them with a force and impact on our society that there will be no escaping. The psychological ramifications of this genetic revolution will be issues that are going to be vital and then the work of someone like Jung in dealing with human differences on the psychological plane will come into its own in a new way.

Once we are in the possession of the rudiments of an integrated typology we have a framework in which to look at the explosion of information that fills the popular media, and even the sports page, with news of scientific breakthroughs and the results of psychological studies. Let's look at some examples.

In 1983 the Pan American games in Caracas, Venezuela were marred when drug tests revealed steroid use, which led to the return of almost two dozen medals. But this was, and is, only the tip of the iceberg. William Taylor, a specialist in sport medicine, suggests that there are more than

a million steroid users in the United States alone.
And the anabolic steroids which are versions of the
male sex hormone testosterone will soon be joined
with other substances like human growth hormone in
the athlete's black market pharmacopeia. Taylor has
already received dozens of phone calls from fathers
willing to fly their children to his Florida office and
pay thousands of dollars to have them hormonally
manipulated with the chance they will grow an extra
few inches. Many athletes are convinced that steroids
offer them physical and psychological advantages:
increased muscle mass, reduction in body fat, quicker
healing, a desire to train and concentrate, and a
general psychological high. But steroids have been
connected with liver damage and heart disease, and
of particular interest to our study of types is that
these steroids seem to be a kind of artificial mesomorphy, not only physically, but psychologically. What
would Sheldon have made of the following qualities
that Taylor lists under the heading of potential psychological alterations induced in anabolic steroid-using
men: increased aggressiveness, increased tolerance to
pain, increased tendency towards one-track-minded-
ness, increased tendency towards "explosive" aggressive behavior. If many professional athletes are already physically and temperamentally extreme mesomorphs, the use of steroids will just make them more
so, and make maintaining physical and mental balance
an even greater chore. In women the use of steroids
is complicated by the fact that some of the effects
appear irreversible: increased facial hair, deepening
of the voice, and various other physical and psychological alterations, which would put the woman athlete
more at odds with the society she has to live in and
with herself.

Steroid abuse and the potential for abuse of the
other hormones that genetic engineering is making
available will be all the harder to control because
of the temperamental imbalances in our society. We

worship mesomorphy and reward it excessively. We tempt our athletes to these dangerous and illegal procedures because we dangle in front of them large amounts of money and fame which depend on a fraction of a second more speed, or an inch or two in better performance. We pay no attention to the psychological imbalance that this can create in them, even without steroid use. We can't expect to feed our children a steady diet of masters of the universe and then turn around and imagine they will not take the chemical means that seem to promise that they, too, can become extreme mesomorphs. What is lacking is an overall sense of temperamental and psychological balance. Mesomorphy is just one of the basic temperamental components and it is inextricably linked with certain psychological disadvantages - as every aspect of temperament taken by itself is - which must be compensated for by a program of individuation.

We are going to have an increasing ability to alter our physiques and personalities by artificial means. In the 1960s intuition and introversion came in vogue, no doubt in compensation to the placid and complacent extraversion of American culture, and it was induced by LSD and mescaline. But whether we are promoting introversion or extraversion by artificial means, they won't work, for there are no substitutes or shortcuts for the long and difficult process of personal development. Let's look at another example.

"At Duke University Medical Center, Susan Schiffman has been conducting blind taste tests in which more than 60 percent of her obese patients show an acute ability to recognize different tastes. "I'm sure there is a connection," Schiffman says, "between a keen sense of taste and a craving for flavorful food. Many overweight people need more variety and intensity of taste, smell and texture than thinner people do. If you deprive them, they'll keep eating. They're not satisfied."" (Reader's Digest, July 86, p. 34)

What immediately springs to the mind of the Jung-Sheldon typologist is the supposition that here it is a question of the endomorph who is a sensation type, a thought we can pursue in the work of Stanley Schachter. Schachter describes a variety of experiments, his own and others, under the title, "Some Extraordinary Facts About Obese Humans and Rats". If we make the assumption that the obese humans are primarily endomorphs, and therefore have an endotonic temperament and a personality type dominated by extraverted sensation, we can read these experiments from our own distinctive point of view. Schachter performed an experiment in which the subjects were fed roast beef sandwiches or nothing, and then sat in front of five bowls of crackers with the impression that they were conducting a taste test, when the experimenters were really going to determine how many crackers they ate. The subjects with normal body weight ate considerably fewer crackers if they had already eaten the roast beef sandwiches, as we would expect. But the obese subjects ate "as much as - in fact, slightly more - when their stomachs were full as when they were empty". (p. 130) Schachter and his colleagues came to the conclusion that for the obese the internal state was irrelevant to how much they ate, which was determined by the sight, smell, and taste of food.

This interesting result led to the review, as well as creation, of a variety of experiments that examined the conduct of obese humans and rats. The results indicated that the obese will eat more than the subjects of normal weight if the food is right in front of them, but less if they have to go look for it. And they will eat more if it tastes good but less if it tastes bad. They will eat more when the food is easy to get and eat less when the food is hard to get. And so Schachter concluded that they seem stimulus-bound.

His next step was to consider whether this state of being stimulus-bound was restricted only to food, or was a more general state of affairs. He found that the obese subjects could recall more objects that had been seen quickly, and were better in tests of complex reaction time in which there were two lights and two telegraph keys, and the subject had to lift his or her left finger when the right light came on, and vice versa. They were also more prone to distracting stimuli, "presumably, the impinging stimulus is more likely to grip the attention of the stimulus-bound obese subject". (p. 138)

The picture that develops is that these stimulus-bound people appear to have a higher threshold of stimulation. When the stimulus is present they react to it, and when it is absent they are much less active. This is similar to Sheldon calling the endomorphs biologically introverted organisms who need a certain level of stimulation to keep them going and bring them to a normal level of social interaction. Without it they tend to fall into inactivity. From the point of view of psychological type we would expect the extraverted sensation type to be keenly aware of his surroundings and highly responsive to what is happening to them. But he lacks intuition. He is oriented to the here and now, but finds it hard to motivate himself to work for what could be. And if he is stimulus-bound or geared to extraverted sensation, then he is highly distractible, for he has a hard time turning off extraneous stimuli and concentrating on the one task that he has set for himself. One of the facts about obese rats that bothered Schachter was that these highly reactive creatures were hyposexual, but this hyposexuality is one of the traits that Sheldon ascribed to the more extreme endomorphs.

In another study a team of Danish and U.S. scientists studied 540 adopted children:

"The evidence, as reported in the New England Journal of Medicine, was unequivocal: the size of the children consistently reflected the size of the natural parents. There was absolutely no correlation between the body builds of the adoptees and their surrogate mothers and fathers. And these parallels held true in all weight classes, from skinny to grossly fat." (Newsweek, Feb. 3, 1986, p. 61)

There is no need to read this in the context of the old nature-nurture arguments. It's better to see obesity having a strong genetic component or dimension of endomorphy which predisposes the person to a difficult struggle to preserve a reasonable weight in a society that exercises too little and eats too many refined foods.

Another example. In an interview with U.S. News & World Report, psychologist Jonathan Cheek discussed his studies on shyness. He found it afflicted as many as 40% of American adults who have "a general tendency to be tense, inhibited and awkward in social situations, particularly in face-to-face interactions with strangers and especially with those of the opposite sex." (Oct. 31, 1983, p. 71)

The percentage among the Japanese runs about 60%, and what is the reason for this?

"We feel that there is a genetic component to shyness for about 40 percent of the adults who suffer from the problem. In a study of high-school students I did with Alan Zonderman of Johns Hopkins University, we found that genetically identical twins are much more similar in their degree of shyness than are fraternal twins, who average only 50 percent of their genes in common...Arnold Buss of the University of Texas has proposed a distinction between early-developing and late-developing shyness. The early-developing type is very much a physiological symptom. For example, a Harvard study found that infants who are shy and fearful when encountering strangers often have unusually high heart rates when confronting any unfamiliar situation. This indicates that the physiological component of shyness involves having a particularly sensitive nervous system." (p. 72)

In addition to heart rate this higher level of physiological arousal embraces upset stomachs and blushing, as well. This physiological shyness appears to be our old friend the introvert-ectotonic, and the 40% estimate in the U.S. population which Cheek presents elsewhere in the article as being between 33 and 40% fits well the MBTI and somatotype introversion percentage of 38%. The twin study brings to mind Sheldon's examination of 46 pairs of identical twins whose trunk indexes were identical within each pair.

In still another study Jack Block spent 20 years studying several hundred subjects followed from the 1930s by Berkeley's Institute of Human Development. He analyzed some of the extensive archives of material including attitude checklists and interviews which had accumulated on these people in order to try to determine whether their personalities changed with time. To accomplish this usually three clinical psychologists were assigned to rate portions of each person's record independently.

"Using this painstaking methodology, Block found a striking pattern of stability. In his most recent report, published earlier this year, he reported that on virtually every one of the 90 rating scales employed, there was a statistically significant correlation between subjects' ratings when they were in junior high school and their ratings 30 to 35 years later, when they were in their 40s." (Psychology Today, May 1981, p. 20)

Hints of this coming biochemical typology have appeared in Jungian literature, as well. Ernest Rossi in "The Cerebral Hemispheres in Analytical Psychology" reviews the left-brain research in which the left brain is connected with verbal and logical thought, while the right brain is more synthetic and spatially oriented, and tries to relate this brain laterality to various Jungian ideas, including psychological types. He associates extraversion, thinking and feeling with the left hemisphere, and introversion, intuition and sensation with the right, and he proposes the suggestive view that individuation or "the integration of hemispheric functioning may turn out to be one of the neuro-psychological foundations of the transcendent function". (p. 45)

In a comment on this paper J.P. Henry suggests broadening the framework to include the subcortical brain systems. Then it is a question not only of left and right hemispheres, but the affects that have to do with the lymbic system and the drives associated with the hypothalmus and the brain stem. Introversion and extraversion would be explained by the relative development of different vertical pathways and one hemisphere over the other. Under the heading of possible neurological basis for Jung's concepts Anthony Stevens in his **Archetypes: A Natural History of the Self** reviews these ideas in the context of an extensive study of the relationship between Jungian psychology and ethology.

Attempts to relate introversion and extraversion to brain biochemistry are not new. In 1929, for example, William McDougall in an article entitled, "The Chemical Theory of Temperament Applied to Introversion and Extraversion" suggests that extraversion is a positive state which has a certain substance X while introversion is the lack of that substance. "The marked introvert is the man in whom the inhibition normally exerted by activity of the cerebral cortex on all lower nervous functions is manifested in high degree." (p. 22) This introversion is a result of the development of the cortex in man and so poses a danger that men will become excessively introverted and rendered unfit "for the life of action and unfit for social intercourse, for maintaining that sympathetic rapport with their fellows..." (p. 23) The substance X, then, becomes the antidote to this excessive introversion, and McDougall likens it to the effect of alcohol, which he describes as an extraverting drug.

In 1986 Ernest Rossi in **The Psychobiology of Mind-Body Healing** gives an account of recent developments in neuroscience in the course of forging an intriguing argument on how the cortex through the midbrain effects the rest of the body. His intention is to provide an explanation for the power of mind over body, whether in the placebo effect or in therapeutic hypnosis. He carefully traces the potential routes by which the electrical impulses of the neurons of the cerebrum reach the hypothalmus and limbic areas of the brain, and are converted then into various neurotransmitters that effect every part of the body via the endocrine, immune, and neuropeptide systems. Changes in the mind directly effect the body down to the level of the cell. Rossi calls this the mind-gene connection, for some neurotransmitters apparently actually enter within the individual cell and induce its genes to produce messenger RNA which creates various proteins. When we start thinking in terms of these kinds of mind-body systems, it becomes unthinkable that the body and temperament would not be intimately linked.

"What happens is that collaterals from the ascending sensory pathways produce activity in the ARAS (ascending reticulating activated system), which subsequently relays the excitation to numerous sites in the cerebral cortex." (p. 197) Then introversion and extraversion become "identified largely with differences in levels of activity in the corticoreticular loop."

Eysenck has proposed two theories of introversion and extraversion. The more developed 1967 theory indicated that the higher cortical arousal of the introverts was connected to the mid-brain and the ascending reticulating activated system. The common ground we saw between Jung, Sheldon and the factor

analytic school can be described in an even more
detailed way by examining the conclusions that the
Eysenckian school of individual differences has arrived
at. Here the introvert is considered to have a higher
cortical arousal, while the extravert has more cortical inhibition. This higher arousal of the introvert is
manifested and demonstrated in many ways. In EEG
comparisons the introvert has lower amplitude and
higher frequency of alpha waves than the extravert.
The sedation level between them differs, as well. The
introvert has a higher threshold and needs a higher
dosage of sedation than the extravert. The extravert,
on the other hand, has a higher preferred level of
stimulation. The introvert, at least in certain experiments, has the longest tolerance of sensory depriva-
tion, but he also has a lower tolerance of pain and
a lower pain threshold. His sensory threshold, that
is, the level he becomes aware of sensory inputs, is
also lower, and his critical flicker fusion level, which
is the degree he can maintain an awareness of the
discreteness of the flickers of a light, is higher.
What kind of picture do we get of the introvert and
the meaning of this cortical arousal? He or she
seems to be amplifying the sensory stimulation, but
if the sensory stimulation gets too great, a process
which Eysenck calls "transmarginal inhibition" sets
in. The introvert seems to shut down and shut out
the overstimulation.

These various laboratory measures of introversion
and extraversion can be complemented by observations of introverts and extraverts in social situations.
The extravert appears underaroused and therefore
seeks greater personal intimacy and engages in more
overt sexual behavior. He wants more social and
physical stimulation, but since the introvert is already
aroused, crowded and stressful situations like dealing
with criticism or authority figures can overwhelm
him. Introverts show higher levels of academic
achievement and an interest in scientific and theore-

tical subjects, while extraverts show a desire for more social contact. Extraverts are less easily conditioned and apparently commit more crimes, though other factors like Eysenck's neuroticism and psychoticism enter in here.

All these assertions are carefully qualified and discussed in various works like Eysenck and Eysenck's **Personality and Individual Differences,** but the assiduous reader of Sheldon can't help a feeling of dejá vu. Isn't the introvert with higher cortical arousal the same as Sheldon's hyperattentional cerebrotonic who resists sedation, has a low pain threshold, and must devise continual strategies against overstimulation, or what Eysenck is calling "transmarginal inhibition"? There can be little doubt that what the factor analytic school is describing from an experimental point of view is the same personality differences that Sheldon described in terms of somatotype and temperament. What Eysenck and his colleagues do from a statistical and factor analytic point of view, Sheldon and Jung were doing at the level of the individual.

We may also note parenthetically that recent challenges to Eysenck's cortical theory of arousal based on the various circadian rhythms between introverts and extraverts show just how complicated Eysenck's theories must become to account for all the data. From the Jungian point of view this difficulty could possibly be explained by the existence of both introversion and extraversion in the one personality. Another factor could be the different functions which will be somehow entering into these experimental situations and complicating the interpretation of their results solely in terms of introversion and extraversion.

We have seen that Sheldon's indications that the three basic components appear to be derived from the three layers of the embryo met with various objections on the part of Hunt and others. For exam-

ple, Hunt suggested that the lungs, which derive from
the endoderm, are equally or more developed in the
mesomorphs. But most of his remarks are rather
general. On the whole embryologists do not seem to
have invested any substantial amount of energy in
trying to verify or disprove Sheldon's thesis. Cortés,
who looked into the question in some detail, under-
took to summarize the present state of knowledge
in an appendix to his book on delinquency entitled,
"Embryological Foundations to Constitutional Types".
Here he answers the hesitations of Hunt and Eysenck, and provides a chart of the three embryological layers. From the endoderm comes the digestive
system, respiratory system, metabolic system and
para-sympathetic system, and this metabolic system
includes thyroid, thymus and para-thyroid. From the
mesoderm comes the circulatory system, the muscular
and skeletal systems, the sympathetic system and the
genital system, which includes the sexual and adrenal
glands. From the ectoderm there is the sensorial
system, the central nervous system, the integumen-
tary system of skin, hair, teeth, mammary glands,
etc., and the central glandular system of the pituitary and pineal gland.

In addition to the early studies on intestine length
and internal organs that Sheldon made use of and to
which he added his own observations, Cortés adds the
work of Reynolds and Asakawa who, with the use of
X-rays, found that endomorphs had the most fat,
ectomorphs the smallest amount of bone, muscles and
fat, and mesomorphs the largest amounts of bone and
muscle. And then Cortés raises two potential objections: if the thyroid comes from the endoderm, why
do a lot of endomorphs appear to show a low degree
of functioning? And the other objection is Hunt's
question about the lungs: why do mesomorphs appear
to have larger lungs than endomorphs?

And to answer these questions he turns to the
work of Martiny who probably should rank as the

person who has given the most developed view of the relationship between the embryological layers and body types. Martiny suggests that while diiodothyroxine in the thyroid is present in large quantities in the endomorph, its transformation, which activates the metabolism, is dependent on outside factors originating in the mesoderm and ectoderm which are deficient. In the case of the lungs, while they are derived from the endoderm, they are related to the circulatory system, and in this way have a mesodermal element. Martiny sets forth these views in considerable detail in his **Essai de biotypologie humaine.** This book was the fruit of 20 years of work pursuing body types from the point of view of the basic layers of the embryo, and what makes it even more interesting is that it was written independently of Sheldon's work, but shows a remarkable convergence with it. Martiny describes in detail 4 types: the entoblastique, the mesoblastique, the chordoblastique and the ectoblastique, with the chordoblastique representing the midrange physique. His basic descriptions of these types are so similar to Sheldon's as to dispense us from recounting them.

But Martiny goes beyond Sheldon and lays the foundation for what we are calling a biochemical typology. Let's assemble, then, some of his more suggestive remarks. The endomorph has an excess of qualities derived from the endoderm, but his mesodermal qualities are normal or deficient, and his ectodermal qualities always very deficient. The mesomorph has an excess of the qualities of the mesoderm, his endodermal qualities are normal, and ectodermal ones deficient. The ectomorph abounds in the qualities of the ectoderm, but those derived from the other two layers are deficient. These remarks fit well with the close relationship Sheldon found between endomorphy and mesomorphy, which, on a psychological plane is reflected in their common extraversion, and the distance between them and the ectomorph. Martiny relates this to the fact that the mesoblast derives not from the ectoblast, but from the endoblast. (p. 99)

While Martiny's anatomical descriptions match in detail Sheldon's they go beyond them in probing the physiology of each type. He suggests, for example, that the endomorph is the lymphatic type described in earlier literature. Not only does the lymph circulate slowly, but the cells of the endomorph exhibit a certain hydrophilia. Martiny finds a high incidence of hyperinsulinism and excessive functioning of the pancreas, together with a low level of metabolic functioning, despite the origin of the thyroid from the endoderm.

He notes that the steroid hormones are derived from the mesoderm, which explains the virility of this type (p. 117) as well as the development of their muscles and bone. He feels that among mesomorphs there is often a dysfunction of the pancreas and an elevation of uric acid in the blood. He writes, "The mesomorph is a hyperpituitary in whom the somatic hormone of horizontal enlargement of the metaphysis of the bone predominates over the hormone of growth of the pineal for vertical elongation." (p. 118) And he describes an experiment in which he injected small amounts of pineal extract in young rabbits, and in some cases saw them become gawky and long-legged. (p. 121)

In his description of the ectomorph he indicates that it is the excess of pineal function that explains his morphology, and notes how certain pineal tumors are connected with a long, thin body. He cites Chiray who insisted that ectomorphs have a blackish bile, which, if true, would be an interesting confirmation of the early typology of humors of Galen and Hippocrates. Martiny develops an explanation of the hypothyroidism of young ectomorphs leading to exhaustion, and suggests the special need that ectomorphs have for the B vitamins, enumerating B-1, B-2 and

B-6, and perhaps in some prescient way anticipating the work of Osmond and Hoffer using B-3 in the treatment of schizophrenics. He suggests that the lack of vitamin B-6 is related to the muscular weakness, fatigue and insomnia found so often in ectomorphs. The ectomorph, while resistant to acute infections, suffers from chronic malaise, and a constitutional myopia that appears at puberty. Martiny also makes some tentative suggestions about blood types and body types: endomorphs B and some AB, mesomorphs B and some O, ectomorphs O and A, and a little AB.

As far as we know, these highly suggestive remarks of Martiny have not been evaluated in the light of modern advances in embryology and biochemistry. However, the founding of the elements that make up the body types on the embryonic layers not only has a high degree of intuitive appeal, but the evidence that can be adduced for it seems at this point to far outweigh that which has been brought against it. And it is a promising road that should be explored in the future.

When faced with material as diverse as that which has appeared in this chapter, we might well become a bit bewildered and wonder if the time is ripe for a biochemical typology after all! But let's pursue the search for this biochemical typology under the more specific headings of type and psychopathology, type and heart disease, gender and I.Q., type and neuroscience, and type and genetics.

CHAPTER 10

TYPE AND PSYCHOPATHOLOGY

The typologies of both Jung and Kretschmer are rooted in their psychiatric work. Jung, for example, in his 1913 paper that announced his interest in types identifies the schizophrenic as an introvert, albeit a regressed introvert, and the hysteric as a regressed extravert. Kretschmer, in his turn, described the manic depressive as a pyknic, and his schizophrenics as predominately asthenic or leptosomatic. And their work helped establish a psychiatric common ground, which has been tested many times, and in which the schizophrenic is introverted and ectomorphic, and the manic-depressive extraverted and endomorphic and mesomorphic. But despite the strong psychiatric origins of Jung's typology it would probably be fair to say that the application of his typology to psychopathology has been neglected, with some notable exceptions.

J.H. van der Hoop, who attempted to blend both Jungian and Freudian interpretations in his book on psychological types, **Conscious Orientation** (1937), makes some remarks on the relationship between Jung's types and Kretschmer's descriptions. The obvious starting place is a comparison of introverts and extraverts with schizothymes and cyclothymes, but he goes further and makes some other interesting suggestions. For example, "we should most likely expect to find severe manic-depressive states developing in extraverted instinctives (sensation types) and in extraverted intuitives." (p. 227) He notes in Kretschmer's descriptions of the manic-depressive both their materialistic disposition with their enjoyment of the good things of life which leads him to the conclusion that they are extraverted sensation types, and he interprets their wealth of ideas and an eye for opportunity as an indication of the presence of extraverted intuition types. Then he makes an interesting connection between the introverted intuitive type and Kretschmer's schizoids. "From a clinical point of view, the strongly introverted intuitive seems to offer the closest comparison with the manifestations of schizophrenia, and when there are strong influences derived from complexes in persons of this type, they sometimes resemble very closely Kretschmer's schizoids." (p. 246)

Let's look more closely at van der Hoop's suggestion that the manic-depressives are both extraverted sensation types and extraverted intuition types. He refers to Kretschmer's descriptions which point of their enjoyment of life, their zestful eating and drinking, and so forth, as signs of their extraverted sensation, whereas their wealth of ideas, daring and overestimation of the self seem to indicate the extraverted intuition type. We can pursue this matter a little further by looking at the portrait that Kretschmer paints of Quick, the cheery hypomanic type. Quick is 40 years old and with him no one can get in a word edgewise. He wanders from the subject and comes back again, and as "he is closing the door there are always one or two things that occur to him and which he must quickly get off his chest." (p. 141) Van der Hoop's estimation that this is an extraverted sensation type is supported by comments like this: "With one glance round he has taken in all the decoration of a room, down to a small nail up on the ceiling, and has figured out the price of every object." (p. 141-2) He has a knack for making money. He came under Kretschmer's care for his increasingly outrageous conduct which culminated in having a brass band celebrate the birthday of his mother-in-law starting a 6 o'clock in the morning. When he was hospitalized he soon knew the regime of the whole hospital and filled his room with knick-knacks, including a toilet paper dispenser, which, whenever a piece of paper was torn off, gave forth with "Make Hay While the Sun Shines". He is consistently and solidly people-oriented and wins their tolerance even for his outrageous conduct, all of which are not traits of the extraverted intuiter. He simulates the extraverted intuiter in terms of his constant flow of ideas, but these ideas are very concrete and executed with a sureness of worldly touch that is often lacking in the extraverted intuiter.

K.W. Bash (1961), while not relating the specific psychological type to the various kinds of psychopathology, does examine the psychological function in relation to psychiatric illnesses. Delusion and illusion, for example, are related to the function of intuition.

Bisbee, Mullaly and Osmond (1982) gave the MBTI to 372 psychiatric patients close to the time of their admission and found that schizophrenic patients tended to be more introverted with the introverted sensation thinking type, the introverted sensation feeling type and the introverted feeling sensation type predominating, while the manic-depressives were more extraverted with the extraverted feeling sensation type, the extraverted intuition thinking type and the introverted feeling intuition type overrepresented. Part of the paucity of the studies in this area can be attributed to the diagnostic problem which returns with a vengeance when it is a case of people with serious psychiatric illnesses. Jung made it clear that the schizophrenic who shows an introverted character during the incubation of his illness can reach a stage of morbid compensation where "he seems constrained to draw attention to himself by his extravagant, insupportable, or directly aggressive behavior." (1913) He could then easily be typed at variance to his natural disposition.

This difficulty of typological diagnosis makes it

hard to assess studies on the pre-morbid characteristics of schizophrenic children. Type is often difficult to discern in the fluid and unformed personalities of the children, and this problem is compounded by the possibility that the sub-clinical onset of schizophrenia may express itself, as Jung stated, in an acting out coming from the other side of the personality. Thus, shy, withdrawn children might be found rarely to become schizophrenic, while unsocialized aggression could be a prominant characteristic without either finding necessarily contradicting the affinity for schizophrenia to express itself in the introverted personalities.

But the difficulty encountered in trying to estimate type is far outweighed by the potential benefits. Just who is the person who is ill? What were they like before their illness, if there was ever a time before? And to what kind of personality are they meant to return? There is a certain ambiguity in psychiatric terminology when we fail to distinguish between the description of normal differences and their exaggeration in the diseased process. What are we to make out of a description of the schizoid personality described by Seymour Kety as follows:

"He is withdrawn, he has few friends, he is very strongly religious and he reads a great deal of philosophy which is something schizophrenics often do. He has an inappropriate grin when he talks. He flunked out of school, although he is obviously intelligent. He never married. He doesn't go out often and his room is very messy. He looks unkempt. He has a lower level job than his social class or intelligence would warrant." (Rosenthal, **The Transmission of Schizophrenia,** p. 73)

Are we seeing society's view of the introvert or some mild phase of schizophrenia? We will not find the answer until we can subtract normalcy from the equation. But how can we make this subtraction when it is so difficult to diagnose psychological types? The answer lies in our project of creating an integrated typology that would consider not only psychological type but somatotype and eventually a biochemical typology as well.

What can help us in this endeavor is the important psychiatric work that Sheldon did to reformulate the basic three psychiatric categories which stemmed from Kraepelin, and relate them to his work in somatotyptes and temperament.

In 1949 with the publication of his **Varieties of Delinquent Youth** Sheldon was like a prophet peering in the mists trying to catch a glimpse of a biologically founded criminology and psychiatry. Sheldon thought that what the psychoanalyst called the unconscious just might be the body itself, and the body "is really an objectification, a tangible record, of the most long-standing and most deeply established habits that have been laid down during a long succession of generations." (p. 4) And so he started with an objective record of the body with his somatotype photos. And when he studied the young men at the Inn he saw what he called the asthenic and burgeoned estates. Asthenia was a failure to flower, a retreat of the organism from its proper line of development, while burgeoning was an overexuberance, an overaccumulation of mass that becomes a debilitating burden. And what is true at the level of somatotype Sheldon felt would be seen at the cellular level, as well. When he writes, "A cell is a living thing with a personality. Whatever the asthenic estate is at bottom and the burgeoned estate, these are without doubt expressions of the personality of the cells of the individual..." (p. 800), he is trying to read behind and through the somatotype and divine the biological foundations of personality and behavior that we are only beginning to unravel today.

Even the uneven development or dysplasias he found in the somatotype he felt could be found at the cellular level, as well. When he came across individuals who had mesomorphic skin and hair in some parts of their bodies, and ectomorphic skin and hair in others, he reasoned, because of the connection between skin and the nervous system, that "it is not improbable that similar dysplastic variations in nervous and brain structure exist..." (p. 808)

How more comfortable would he have felt if instead of being confronted with a thoroughly environmental view of crime he could have drawn on the modern studies such as the following:

William Walsh compared the trace elements in the hair of 24 matched pairs of violent and non-violent siblings, and 96 extremely violent men, and 96 controls. The violent people showed increased levels of lead, cadmium and calcium, and excessively low levels of lithium, zinc and cobalt. Even the violent could be broken down into two classes: those subject to sudden fits of rage, and those who are anti-social, and these groups could be distinguished by the trace elements in their hair. The impulsively violent men showed high levels of sodium and low levels of copper, while the anti-social men showed high levels of copper and low levels of sodium. Walsh also felt that the trace element profiles of the hair of normal people tended to divide them into six types.

Michael McGuire found that the dominant males in 45 different monkey colonies had twice as much serotonin in their blood as the other males, and the serotonin fluctuated according to their social status. When a monkey was acknowledged as the leader, his serotonin level rose. When he was deposed, it fell. There has also been some evidence of high serotonin levels in human leaders and Type A personalities. Paradoxically, low levels of serotonin have shown up in violent people, and has been detected by means of their 5-HIAA levels, which is a result of serotonin breakdown. In a study of 38 violent servicemen Gerald Brown and Frederick Goodwin discovered that the level of serotonin matched the level of violence.

The lower the serotonin level the higher the violence. There is also a connection between low
5-HIAA and suicide. Markku Linnoila and Matti Virku-
nen compared the 5-HIAA levels of psychopaths who
had committed apparently senseless and random
murders and what they called paranoid murderers who
had acted with premeditation, and found that the
psychopaths had lower 5-HIAA levels. Mass murderers
have also been found to have unusually low levels of
5-HIAA. (cf. Hooper and Teresi)

Serotonin has been connected with inhibition and
we are probably looking at something similar to asthenia that Sheldon had begun to discern at the level
of somatotype. It is inevitable that these discoveries
would pose the question of biochemical treatment of
violence, and one aspect is the orthomolecular treatment of delinquent and criminal behavior. If there
is a possibility to alter behavior by chemical means,
the safest way to do this would be to do it by
changing the proportions of the natural substances
that already exist in our diet. Even when prisons
offer a halfway decent diet, the prisons eat selec-
tively or reject meals entirely in favor of junk food.

In **Ecologic-Biochemical Approaches to Treatment
of Delinquents and Criminals** we have a collection
of articles that are beginning to spell out an orthomolecular approach to the very problems Sheldon
confronted in his 200 young men, but without the
tools to make a biological attack on their difficulties. He would have been happy to read Allan Cott's
"The Etiology of Learning Disabilities, Drug Abuse
and Juvenile Delinquency" or William Philpott's "Ecological Aspects of Antisocial Behavior".

Sheldon's earlier autopsy work which was instrumental in his describing the basic components of
somatotype in terms of the various embryonic layers
had been augmented by the work of Nolan D.C.
Lewis. Lewis "in a series of more than 2,000 autopsies of psychotic patients had shown that whenever

the diagnosis hebephrenic dementia praecox (schizophrenia) occurred, vascular hypoplasia, especially in the terminal vessels, was a constant finding". ("Psychotic Patterns and Physical Constitution", p. 840) And it was inevitable that Sheldon would evaluate Lewis' finding in terms of the basic components of physique. Were the hebephrenics actually deficient in mesomorphy, or mesopenic? Gradually Sheldon anchored the old psychiatric terminology on a firm biological foundation by seeing that each one of three major psychiatric classifications could be looked at as the deficiency of one of the basic elements of physique. The hebephrenic schizophrenic lacked mesomorphy, the manic-depressive lacked ectomorphy, and the paranoid lacked endomorphy. Therefore, these newly created psychiatric poles would fall on the somatotype chart opposite the somatotype and temperamental poles.

With this hypothesis in hand, Sheldon noticed as he poured through hundreds of psychiatric records that the greatest variability in diagnosis centered on certain kinds of patients. The midrange somatotypes, as would be expected, were described in a variety of ways, but intriguingly the patients that fell at morphological poles, that is, midway between the psychiatric poles, were also given a greater variety of diagnoses than those that fell near the psychiatric poles.

Sheldon set out to test this insight in a more scientific manner. In 1945 he initiated an experiment with Phyllis Wittman at Elgin State Hospital in Illinois. Wittman created a checklist of psychotic behavior reactions, somewhat similar to Sheldon's checklist of temperament, but only this time the main components were affective-connative exaggeration, paranoid projection and schizoid regression. Each of these basic components was described by ten traits, and each of the traits was to be evaluated on a scale ranging from 1 to 7. With this checklist

in hand it was soon demonstrated that two psychiatrists could reach a large measure of agreement in
evaluating patients. In the meantime Sheldon had independently photographed and somatotyped 155 psychotic male patients. Then the psychiatric evaluations
that Wittman had made from the psychiatric records
and Sheldon's somatotype ratings were turned in independently for statistical analysis. The correlations
were sufficiently high to lend good support to Sheldon's attempts at creating an integrated way of
viewing psychiatric illness. The manic-depressive
psychiatric component correlated +.54 with endomorphy, +.41 with mesomorphy and -.59 with ectomorphy. The paranoid component correlated -.04 with
endomorphy, +.57 with mesomorphy and -.34 with
ectomorphy, while the third or hebephrenic compon-
ente correlated -.25 with endomorphy, -.68 with
mesomorphy and +.64 with ectomorphy. These correlations would have even been higher if allowance had
been made for the fact that the psychiatric poles
were 60° away from the morphological poles.

In another experiment Sheldon correlated his psychiatric evaluation of the 155 patients by means of
the somatotype performance test with Wittman's ratings taken from the psychiatric records. The performance task was simply how well the patient could
hold the standard somatotype pose while the picture
was being taken. If the hebephrenic component predominated, for example, the patient could not hold
his arms in full extension, that is, as if he were
standing at attention. Again, Sheldon was reading in
the somatotype the psychiatric condition of the patient. The two evaluations correlated +.71 for the
first component, +.76 for the second component and
+.82 for the third component.

If we look at the somatotype charts on which
Sheldon plotted the three major psychiatric divisions
of these Elgin Hospital patients, we see that the
cluster of manic depressive patients is much like

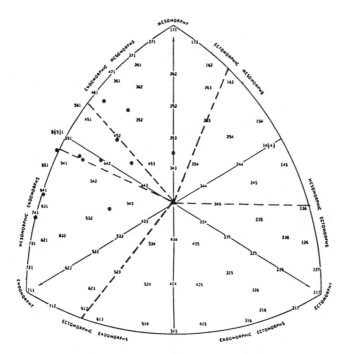

Fig. 9. Manic-Depressive Somatotypes

Sheldon anticipated, for they are well grouped in opposition to the pole of ectomorphy. From the point of view of the relationship between psychological type and somatotype we would expect them to be extraverted with predominant sensation and thinking and sensation and feeling. This agrees fairly well with Van der Hoop's evaluation that the manic-depressive is an extraverted sensation type, but not with his impression that they are extraverted intuition types. It is also close to the extraverted feeling sensation type that Bisbee, Mullaly and Osmond found, but not to their extraverted intuition thinking type and the introverted feeling intuition type. It may well be that the extraverted sensation thinking type in a manic phase of behavior simulates well the quick changeability and innovative character of the extraverted intuition type. Jung was once questioned about the variability of the superior function and responded, "If you consider the case of manic depressive insanity, you occasionally find that in the manic phase one function prevails, and in the depressive phase another function prevails." (**Collected Works,** V. 18, p. 31) Keirsey and Bates state, "Sensation seems equivalent to Kretschmer's cyclothymic temperament." (p. 30)

There is a certain amount of evidence that the extraverted and cyclothymic personality traits are related to bipolar disorder, while introversion is related to primary non-polar depressions. (cf. Akiskal,

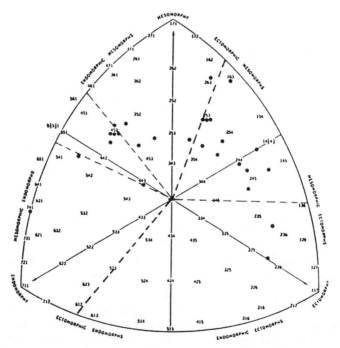

Fig. 10. Paranoid Schizophrenic Somatotypes

"The Relationship of Personality to Affective Disorder") Unfortunately, attempts to distinguish the various kinds of affective diseases often do not take somatotype into account.

Sheldon's somatotype chart of the paranoid schizophrenics show the majority of patients clustered in the area opposite the pole of endomorphy, as he anticipated. The paranoid component showed a positive correlation with mesomorphy, but was virtually neutral in regards to endomorphy, and instead of a positive correlation with ectomorphy it showed a negative correlation (-.34). What could explain these unexpected correlations? If we are correct in our evaluations of the psychological types connected with the somatotypes, then the paranoid personalities cover the extraverted intuitive range. It is a fairly well-established fact that the paranoid schizophrenics are more mesomorphic than the hebephrenic schizophrenics, and they have a better prognosis. This has been demonstrated from the point of view of Sheldon's somatotypes by Kline and Tenney, and the difference in body build between the two groups has also been demonstrated by means of the Rees-Eysenck body index. From the psychological point of view it could well be that the more extraverted paranoid schizophrenics share the same saving grace of many of the manic-depressives in that their extraversion keeps them in touch with the outer world, while the introverted hebephrenic schizophrenics lose contact. Does the extraversion of many of the paranoid personalities mute the opposition that would be expected to the pole of endomorphy because of the common extraversion involved? And at the same time, does this extraversion accentuate the difference between the paranoid component and the pole of ectomorphy which we are taking as an introverted pole?

The final chart shows the hebephrenic schizophrenics grouped predominantly near the ectomorphic pole. Sheldon found that the third psychiatric com-

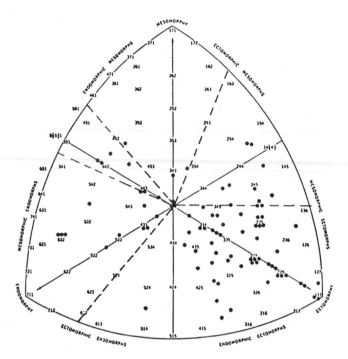

Fig. 11. Hebephrenic Schizophrenic Somatotypes

ponent showed the expected correlation with ectomorphy (+.64) and the expected negative correlation
with mesomorphy (-.68), but instead of a positive
correlation with endomorphy there was a negative one
(-.25). If the schizophrenics are lacking in mesomorphy, why do they cluster about the pole of ectomorphy rather than opposite the pole of mesomorphy?
Sheldon suggests that in the particular sample he was
working with the more mesopenic personalities could
have already collapsed and literally could not stand
up and have their picture taken. This would help
explain the failure to find a positive correlation with
the pole of endomorphy. Bisbee and her colleagues
found a high number of introverted sensation types

among the schizophrenic patients. This may be due to the fact that these patients were actually introverted sensation types which had already disappeared from Sheldon's sample, but here were caught at the beginning of their hospital stay, or it may be that the introverted intuitive types are more highly represented among schizophrenics and only appear like introverted sensation types and this would explain their clustering around the ectomorphic pole and their opposition to the pole of endomorphy. For Keirsey and Bates "what Jung called intuition appears to be equivalent to Kretschmer's schizothymic temperament". (p. 30) Once again, there are a number of cases in the 4-4-2 and 4-5-2 area that are found in the paranoid schizophrenic samples, and it is possible that these represent the introverted thinking sensing or introverted feeling sensing people who are classified as either schizophrenics or paranoids instead of manic-depressives.

Various aspects of Sheldon's psychiatric work have found independent confirmation. Parnell, for example, made extensive studies of the somatotypes and ages of the various categories of mental patients. He found that earliest admissions started around the ectomorphic pole of the somatotype chart, and then seemed to proceed counter-clockwise. The mesopenic ectomorphs broke down first, but at later ages, the more mesomorphic and endomorphic somatotypes ran into psychiatric difficulties. Parnell's somatotype chart of 22 consecutively admitted male schizophrenics shows roughly the same distribution as Sheldon's, with the highest incidence in what we have called the introverted intuitive territory. He also shows the paranoid schizophrenics as more mesomorphic than the other forms of schizophrenics, again with roughly the same kind of distribution as Sheldon's.

Sheldon's insights about the lack of mesodermal development in schizophrenics must be seen against the background of the various studies on the cardio-

vascular apparatus of schizophrenics. Some of them
have been summarized by Arieti and show that the
blood pressure of schizophrenics is lower than that
of the general population with the highest values
found in the paranoids and the lowest in the catato-
nics. The volume of circulating blood in schizophrenics has been found to be smaller than in manic
depressives, and there is a tendency toward vaso-con-
striction, when schizophrenics are exposed to cold
temperatures. Arieti summarizes the alterations under
the headings of a "(1) decrease in the size of the
heart; (2) decrease in the volume of the blood flow;
(3) decrease in systematic blood pressure; (4) exaggerated tendency to vasoconstriction and resulting
diminished blood supply." (**Interpretation of Schizophrenia,** p. 465) Additional studies have focused on
the immature capillary structure of schizophrenics
and the particular capillary pattern in their nail
folds. It's easy to see here the dilemma that psychiatrists face when they attempt to interpret these
findings without any awareness of the underlying
normal variations of personality. What would happen
if the blood pressure of the schizophrenics was compared not to the normal population, but to the introverted intuitive personality? Arieti also mentions that
these kinds of studies tapered off after 1955. Why?
The search for an answer can be informative, for it
will allow us to breach the question of a biochemcial
typology from another direction.

We saw Sheldon, beset from within and without,
losing heart with the 1949 publication of the **Varieties of Delinquent Youth.** This is especially regrettable because if he would have only used his Promethean foresight he might have sensed the first signs
of a shift of psychological climate away from the
prevailing environmentalism in psychiatry.

Off in Australia in obscurity that same year John
Cade had begun experimenting with lithium, which
was to lead to a new treatment of manic-depres-

sives. In St. Louis in the 1950s men like Eli Robins, Samuel Guze and George Winokur were initiating a neo-Kraepelinian revival which wanted to strengthen the ties between psychiatry, medicine and neuroscience. In Paris, 1952, two French psychiatrists, Jean Delay and Pierre Deniker, were experimenting with chlorpromazine, which was going to have such a dramatic effect on the treatment of mental disease all over the world. In 1950 John Smythies and Humphrey Osmond had noticed that the molecular structure of mescaline was close to that of adrenaline, and they reasoned that a faulty metabolism in schizophrenics might alter the adrenaline and give it a psychedelic function. This led to the work of Hoffer and Osmond with niacin, and vitamin C in the treatment of schizophrenia, and became one of the sources of orthomolecular medicine, and it had another unexpected side-effect. Osmond, in the course of his experimentation, took mescaline in order to experience something similar to what his patients were undergoing. His first paper on the subject brought a letter from Aldous Huxley, and it was Osmond who helped send Huxley on his first mescaline trip which was to lead to Huxley's **The Doors of Perception.** In turn Huxley introduced him to Sheldon and his work in a novel way: "On one of our shopping expeditions in Orbachs, Los Angeles, Aldous introduced me to the art of escalator somatotyping. People on escalators are unselfconscious, unaware of scrutiny and at their ease. As we were wafted by them passing in the opposite direction, Aldous would call out, "Humphrey, did you see that marvellously somatotonic woman with the Aztec features?" Further, it was Huxley and Osmond who met and encouraged Timothy Leary to undertake serious psychotropic drug research in 1960, and thus, somewhat inadvertently, helped spark the psychedelic revolution in the United States.

In addition, one of Sheldon's former students, Nathan Kline, played an important role in the transition from a psychoanalytically oriented psychiatry to a more biological one. Almost accidentally he became involved in testing reserpine, a drug extracted from a plant that grows in the hill country of India and which had been used for ages in Indian folk medicine, and achieved good results by calming disturbed schizophrenics. Then he reasoned that if there was a chemical compound that would calm people, there should be another one that would excite them, and he found it in iproniazid, and it had a remarkable effect on people suffering from severe depression. This work had coincided with the discovery in Switzerland of imipramine, the first of the important tri-cyclic anti-depressants.

In his 1957 review of Sheldon and Eleanor Glueck's **Physique and Delinquency** Sheldon amplifies some of his remarks that appeared in **Varieties of Delinquent Youth** on how to view somatotypes: "They are aware that the somatotypic description of an individual, far from supplying an explanation of all his conduct, is actually no more than a necessary starting point, or organizing principle, from which to initiate a study of conduct and behavior." (p. 125) Then he quotes Kline and Tenney whom the Gluecks had quoted, as well:

"The ultimate answers probably lie in the biochemical and biophysical fields. Direct approach to the problem through biochemistry and biophysics has, however, resulted in a welter of data that are consistent only in the fact that they are extremely variable. We have already obtained considerable information...which leads us to believe that many physiological responses - and ultimately the biochemical and biophysical relations upon which they rest - vary in direct relationship with somatotype. The introduction of somatotyping as an 'organizing principle' may quite possibly make order out of what is now chaos because of individual differences." (N.S. Kline and A.M. Tenney, "Constitutional Factors in the Prognosis of Schizophrenia", p. 441.)

But like a biologically oriented Moses Sheldon saw the promised land, but never entered it. And this new psychiatry has been so preoccupied with its fascinating discoveries it has not yet had time to remember the work of the typologists, although they inevitably have to face typological issues. Rosenthal and his colleagues, for example, in an evaluation of the children of schizophrenics reared in adoptive homes, found data that suggests: "that the inherited core diathesis is the same for both schizophrenia and manic-depressive psychosis, but that manic-depressives may have other modifying genes or life experiences which direct the clinical manifestations of the diathesis in a different way." (1968, p. 387) The same causative agent might very well appear differently and show itself as hebephrenic schizophrenia in one instance, paranoid schizophrenia in another, or even manic-depression in a third.

There really is no normal or average personality. The evidence seems clear that certain kinds of individuals are more prone to schizophrenia or one of the other major illnesses than others. But we have really yet to fully utilize this kind of information. We are faced with an embarrassment of riches. We have ennumerable studies which are tremendously hard to bring together within a common framework, and one of the elements of that common framework is a common way of describing the normal personality at the level of somatotype, temperament and psychological type. If we could understand the biochemistry and genetics of the normal personality we could take this knowledge into account when we study the psychiatric patient. Instead, we are studying both the illness and the distinctive structure of the normal personality at the same time. Whatever the particular metabolic dysfunction schizophrenia turns out to be, it is a dysfunction that is going to effect each particular type in a particular way. We differ in our susceptibility, in symptomotology, and prognosis because we differ normally in the very chemistry of our brains.

CHAPTER 11
TYPE AND HEART DISEASE,
I.Q. AND GENDER

Type and Heart Disease

"If you're trying to avoid cardiovascular disease, a pear-shaped figure is better than a beach-ball body, according to research from the University of Göteborg, Sweden.", read a recent news article. (Reader's Digest, June 85, p. 169) It reported the work of Ulf Smith and his colleagues who made hip and waist measurements on 3,000 people, and found that the distribution of fat predicted heart attacks more precisely than weight alone. The pear-shaped figure is our old friend the endomorph, while the beach ball figure is the endomorphic mesomorph.

This study can be compared with others dealing with android or deep body obesity vs. gynoid obesity in which scientists propose that fat cells in the abdominal area are more active in releasing fatty acids, and therefore in posing a risk of heart disease. Their observations are another link in a long chain of evidence that stretches back to Hippocrates and his apoplectic type.

James Mitchner recounts a conversation he had with the famous cardiologist Paul Dudley White who had supervised Eisenhower's 1955 heart attack. White had listed eight factors predictive of heart disease. They had included heredity, blood pressure, cigarette smoking, etc., but also body build. He was leary about excessive claims in this area, but asserted, "...if you classify a thousand deaths from heart failure, you find that very few strike ectomorphs, not too many hit endomorphs, but a heavy predominance knock down mesomorphs." (New York Time Magazine, Aug. 19, 1984, p. 77) He described Mitchner as an archetypal mesomorph who was barrel-chested and heavy across the heart and rump.

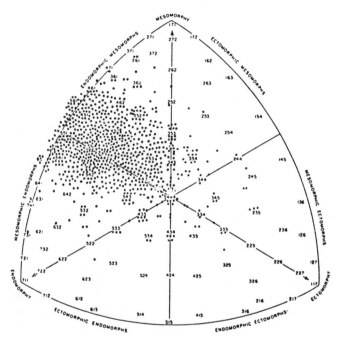

Fig. 12. Coronary Heart Disease Somatotypes. Dupertuis and Dupertuis.

Sheldon had remarked on the endomorphic-mesomorphic qualities of victims of heart disease, but it was his colleagues C. Wesley Dupertuis and Helen S. Dupertuis who made an extensive examination of this whole issue in a study that focused on who survived longer among cardiac patients in **The Role of Somatotype in Survivorship Among Cardiac Patients.** The Dupertuises eventually examined almost 2,000 indivi-

duals, and it was a portion of this larger group who
became the subjects for their study on the length of
survival. Using Sheldon's trunk index method of somatotyping, they compared somatotype photos of 118
deceased patients who had survived more than five
years with 82 patients who had died 5 years or less,
and then examined another 319 people who had also
survived 5 or more years. They found that the long
term and short term survivors did not differ in socio-
economic background, height, weight, heart disease
patterns, and blood pressures. But what they did differ on was physique. The heart disease patients in
general differed from the normal American population
in somatotype. Their mean somatotype was
4.1-4.5-2.1, while the normal American somatotype
was 3.3-4.1-3.4. But somatotype also distinguished
between the long term and the short term survivors.
There were more mesomorphs among the short term
survivors and more endomorphs and balanced endo-
morphs-mesomorphs among the long term survivors.
The short term survivors also showed larger dysplasias. There is, then, consistent evidence about the
somatotypes of heart attack victims, but what about
their personalities?

In 1974 Meyer Friedman and Ray Rosenman inaugurated a new era of interest in the personalities
of heart attack victims with their **Type A Behavior
and Your Heart.** Earlier an upholsterer, repairing the
chairs in their office, had remarked that the chairs
were in great shape except for their front edges, but
the import of this comment had escaped them. Gradually, though, they began to compile a portrait of
the Type A personality, starting with the traits of
excessive competitive drive and a chronic sense of
time urgency. Their portrait of the coronary prone
personality grew until it included competitiveness,
aggressiveness, love of action, explosive accentuation
of speech and laughter, excessive energy for action,
rapid eating, guilt about relaxation, limited introver-

sion, leadership in a competitive situation, a total commitment to the job at hand, a chronic sense of time urgency, haste, impatience, hyperalertness, the doing of multiple jobs simultaneously, and the inability to relate to things or people not job-related. They found that serum cholesterol levels could vary directly with the intensity of Type A behavior, and in a study of over 3,500 men it was the presence of Type A behavior that was the most powerful predicter of who was to come down with coronary heart disease. They saw the Type A personality engaged in a chronic struggle which triggered the hypothalmus to signal the sympathetic nervous system to secrete large amounts of epinephrine and norepinephrine.

By now we have become too familiar with Sheldon's mesomorph not to recognize him in the Type A personality, especially since we have already been alerted by the somatotype studies of coronary patients. What Friedman and Rosenman are doing is rediscovering part of Sheldon's temperament descriptions from the point of view of cardiologists, but they are not aware that they are doing it, which, in some ways, makes it all the more interesting. They had an inevitable but passing knowledge of somatotypes: "If you were to sit in the reception room of a busy cardiologist for several afternoons and observe his patients, you would not be struck by their obesity. While it is possible that one or two out of thirty to fifty persons were a bit roly-poly, few of them would appear to be downright fat. Well-nourished, yes; perhaps a bit on the burly side; but not grossly overweight. You also would probably not see a single, quite tall (over six feet), very lean or almost gaunt individual." (p. 159) But it never occurred to them that these different body types had been carefully related to their corresponding temperaments. This is both good and bad. It's good because it allows us to compare their independent descriptions of the endomorphic mesomorph to Sheldon's in which we read:

assertiveness of posture and movement, competitive aggressiveness, physical courage for combat, the unrestrained voice, horizontal mental cleavage, and so forth. There can be no real doubt that Friedman and Rosenman are describing the mesomorphic temperament when it becomes excessive and overdeveloped, and so these two sets of descriptions confirm each other.

But on the negative side, the proponents of Type A personality are creating a specialized fragment of a typology without realizing that it could gain in strength by being integrated into a larger framework. They are finding, for example, Type A behavior among children, which brings to mind the many studies on the temperament of children like Walker's, or the classification of babies as suckers, kickers, and watchers. Recently there has been a disturbing trend in Type A research in which a number of research studies have failed to find a relationship between the Type A personality and heart disease. Ray Rosenman is quoted as saying that Type A behavior "may not necessarily be bad for any given individual at all", and other researchers have found that fast-paced speech and eating, and a sense of time urgency did not appear to increase the risk of heart disease. What is happening? It seems reasonable to suppose that the initial Type A description was an amalgam of normal temperamental traits, and their excessive development. It is entirely normal to be a mesomorph, and so many of the mesomorphic traits will not only not be found to be directly predictive of heart disease, but they will be connected with high achievement. But this should not be taken to mean there is no Type A personality in the sense of a particular kind of imbalanced mesomorphic personality that is at risk for heart disease. Type A description has to become more refined by being able to separate the underlying temperament from its distorted development.

In **Treating Type A Behavior - and Your Heart,** Meyer Friedman and Diane Ulmer describe a study of 800 men who had already suffered heart attacks and were divided into two groups. The first received normal cardiological counseling and the second received Type A behavior counseling. The second group suffered only one third of the number of subsequent heart attacks of the first group. Friedman and Ulmer go on to describe a program by which the Type A personality can modify his behavior, and their advice is not simply medical, but humanistic in the best sense of the term. They want the Type A personality to broaden his range of interests, to take a deeper interest in the lives of other people, to interest himself more in art, literature and religion, and to be more demonstrative in showing affection. And again, our typological point of view allows us to read these recommendations from a special perspective. If the coronary prone personality is an endomorphic mesomorph with a predominantly mesomorphic temperament, then the extraverted thinking psychological type should predominate, and therefore, the question of the modification of the Type A personality can be seen against the larger backdrop of the process of individuation that the extraverted thinking personality is called to. Is it outlandish to imagine that Jungian analysts or Jungian-oriented counselors could work with coronary prone people? They would be aware both of the extraverted thinking drive of these personalities, as well as their undeveloped feeling function. If they were to read a case study of a Type A personality in conflict with his family in which "he often blurts out cutting, hurtful remarks", (p. 93) this would not be strange to them at all. Or if they hear of the Type A's attraction to "affectionate puppies and nondesigning children" (p. 219), or the difficulty they have in "the verbal expression of love - or at least of human love, for he can love and freely receive the love of various animal pets. A strange paradox." (p. 36) they will see those traits as reflections of the state of the feeling function. If the Type A personality were to be brought into the Jungian perspective, then the whole range of analytic techniques could be brought to bear on the problem.

Sparacino reviews a variety of studies on the effectiveness of various ways of measuring Type A behavior. And it is interesting to note in light of our discussions of the ways to measure temperament that the standard interview technique has become the norm against which the other instruments are evaluated.

In the Dupertuis study of the survival of cardiac patients, the short term survivors were described as being "more apprehensive about their illness, more reluctant to accept any limitations in their physical expression or their role as head of the household and breadwinner, and more opposed to any show of sympathy or protectiveness by other members of the family. It appeared also that the short-term survivors as a group exhibited a persona that was more outgoing, aggressive, energetic and restless than was true for the long-term survivors. The latter group seemed more able to accept their 'fate' and appeared to be more relaxed and willing to adapt to the situation in which they found themselves." (1968, p. 96)

What is emerging, then, is the description of the coronary-prone patient at the level of somatotype and temperament, and the possibility that it could be extended to psychological type. What we would need to complete our program of an integrated typology in this area would be a biochemical profile of the victim of heart disease. And in the last few years this, too, has begun to emerge. Michael Brown and Joseph Goldstein, for example, have identified mutations in a gene involved in the premature onset of arterial sclerosis which causes a defect in the person's ability to remove low density lipoproteins.

Other gene defects have been found which hinder the body's ability to create high density lipoproteins. But what are the normal levels of high density and low density lipoproteins among the endomorphic meso-morphs from which most heart attack victims come?

The parallelism between the somatotype based description and that of the coronary prone personality which, as far as we know, developed independently of each other, is too striking to be ignored. It illus-trates the possibility of using typological language as a basic framework within which to place biochem-ical, genetic, social factors, etc. It also suggests the possibility of using Jung's model of the individuation process to find ways to modify the behavior of Type A personalities. The differentiation between long and short term survivors in what first appears to be a rather homogenous group of cardiac patients is strik-ingly similar to the differentiation we have noted in the Delinquent Youth series, and could be interpreted in the same fashion, i.e., that underlying the somato-type distribution are two distinct psychological type territories.

Type and I.Q.

"In 1858, 20-year-old Paul Morphy of Louisiana toured England and France, routed every known chess giant of the day and then returned home to live the rest of his life in seclusion." ("Introverts at Play", p. 72) This is how Ralph Olmo and George Stevens begin their report on the psychological type of chess masters, which they determined by giving the MBTI. They found that 17 of the 19 high-level players were introverted, and intuitives outnumbered the sensation types by 2 to 1. Surprisingly, they found no differ-ence between thinking and feeling, though this result might be an artifact of the test itself.

I.Q. is a lot like mesomorphy, in fact, it's treated often like a mental mesomorphy, a quality we never can get enough of, and should have more of than other people. But if mesomorphy is a more or less unitary notion, it's hard to say the same about I.Q. From a typological perspective we would expect that each type would have a particular kind of intelligence, and if we were to administer the same test to different types, some types would excel more than others. Far from this meaning that they are more intelligent, it simply means the test is measuring a kind of intelligence that is closer to the kind they possess. We have already seen how the 2-2-5 somatotype and the introverted intuitive psychological type excel in academic performance. Part of the reason resides in their particular kind of intellectual gift, and part, as Sheldon suggested, lies in environmental factors such as the fact that they are not distracted by social life or tempted to devote their energy to athletics.

In the Myers-Briggs Manual we find this following salutary caution as a preface to their reporting of the results of type and I.Q.: "In examining the data that follow, it is important to keep in mind that academic aptitude tests are designed primarily to measure knowledge and aptitude in the IN (introversion, intuition) domain; there are many other interests and capabilities that aptitude tests are not designed to measure. It is unfortunate that aptitude tests are often interpreted as being equivalent to measures of intelligence. Their scope is more limited." (1985, p. 96)

We are far from getting a clear picture of what these different kinds of intelligence mean, and how to weigh the components of innate ability and environment. There is an element of natural ability. The psychological types of the chess champions are no more surprising than the fact that the somatotypes of the marathon runners are different than that of the discus throwers or the shot putters. The real danger is that we will exalt one particular kind of intelligence, just like we have idealized mesomorphy. The fact that I.Q. appears typologically conditioned gives us a particular way in which we can read about the I.Q. controversies. For example, much has been made over the difference in I.Q.s between blacks and whites, and more recently over the fact that orientals have I.Q. scores that are about as much above the Americans as the American whites are above the American blacks. Does this mean that the Japanese are smarter than the Americans, or the American whites are smarter than the American blacks? The usual response has been to point out the vastly different environmental conditions for each group, and this should be the primary answer. But it's also possible to look at this issue typologically. If different types perform differently on I.Q. tests, then if there are different frequencies of types in different populations, the I.Q.s of the groups would tend to differ slightly. The Japanese are probably more introverted as a whole than Americans, and they could easily possess more people of those types that do well on I.Q. tests. The same could easily be true between American blacks and whites. If we factored out the differences due to environment, the small differences remaining might easily be explained by the differences in typological frequencies. But we really should go further. If I.Q.s differ with type, and the evidence both from the point of view of somatotype and psychological type indicate that they do, then the notion of comparing people by I.Q. doesn't make much sense. If we line up a group of children and make them compete in the 100 yard dash, some will excel, and as the study of professional athletes has shown, these people have a certain kind of somatotype. But there is no way we can say that the children who excel are better than the children who do not in anything but running the 100 yard dash. There are differences, but we can't extrapolate from them to justify various social and political causes. This is a perennial temptation. It appeared, for example, in a virulent form in the eugenics movement of the first decades of this century in the U.S. There are human differences, and these differences will become more and more evident as our knowledge of biochemistry and genetics increases. But the real issue is not that human differences exist, but how we are going to handle them. We can't deny their existence, but we can't succumb to the temptation to justify various social programs on the meager knowledge we now possess.

On a more personal note I.Q.s seem rather pointless, a kind of tyranny of numbers. Our own children have never been tested, and we see no point in doing so. One would undoubtedly score higher than the other, but what would it prove? Simply that they had different kinds of intelligence, and there is no evidence that in life as a whole one kind is better than another. Each of us has a great deal of unused mental capacity, and this is where the emphasis should be, not whether one person is somehow smarter than another. The diversity of gifts that does exist is meant to serve the community, but instead, we often let it degenerate into mindless competition. This is one of the areas where Jung's work in psychological types holds great promise for the future.

Type and Gender

Beyond the obvious physical differences between men and women there are general somatotype differences. If we compare populations of men and women on the somatotype charts, men are distributed more widely, and women are less mesomorphic and more endomorphic. It's as if men are more experimental beings. Therefore, we could expect to see both a higher incidence of certain gifts and a higher incidence of certain defects, and there is evidence for both.

The distribution of women's somatotypes poses several problems for typology. It's harder to tell women apart on the basis of somatotype. The differences that separate one type from another are smaller, and it is also harder to decide how to divide the woman somatotype sample since the center has shifted more towards the endomorphic pole of the somatotype chart.

There are also differences in the distribution of the different psychological types between men and women. Jung noted some of these differences in passing in **Psychological Types.** When speaking of the extraverted thinking type, he says:

"In my experience this type is found chiefly among men, since, in general, thinking tends more often to be a dominant function in men than in women. When thinking dominates in a woman it is usually associated with a predominantly **intuitive** cast of mind." (p. 351)

And when speaking of the extraverted feeling type he comments:

"As feeling is undeniably a more obvious characteristic of feminine psychology than thinking, the most pronounced feeling types are to be found among women." (p. 356)

He also feels that the majority of the extraverted sensation types are men (p. 363) and that the extraverted intuitive type is more common among women (p. 369). Finally, he writes:

"It is principally among women that I have found the predominance of introverted feeling." (p. 388)

Our own experience bears out Jung's when it is a question of thinking and feeling, but we have not noticed any differences in the frequency of sensation and intuition. Summed up in its simplest form men with primary or secondary feeling or women with primary or secondary thinking are not common, to say the least. We take special notice when we meet one, and there is a real difference between a woman using her third function of thinking, a woman who is in the grip of the animus, and a woman whose thinking is typologically higher than her feeling. The same differences exist among men. This kind of development of thinking in a woman or feeling in a man is rare enough to cause special kinds of adjustment problems because of the expectations that society has. This area has gotten scarce attention, and among the different typological preferences, thinking and feeling are probably the most environmentally conditioned, making progress in this area more difficult. For example, when a new version of the Myers-Briggs Type Indicator was created, the only major adjustment was in the area of thinking and feeling. Before, the distribution among males had been 60% thinking and 40% feeling, and among females, 1/3 thinking and 2/3 feeling. In a 1972 study of university of Florida freshmen, there were only 44% thinking among males and 28% among females. The scales, therefore, had to be adjusted to match the old figures, but if the scales were that environmentally conditioned, we are certainly allowed to wonder whether the initial estimation of thinking and feeling and their different scoring for men and women were also environmentally conditioned. In short, it would not be surprising if there were a lot less thinking women and feeling men than the MBTI indicates.

The possibility remains, then, that the specially constructed and adjusted scales of the MBTI which, incidentally, differ more than the other scales when compared with the Grey-Wheelwright (MBTI Manual 1985, p. 209), are weighted more to produce thinkers among women and feelers among men. "On the TF (thinking-feeling) scale, it was evident that females, even those who in their behavior and attitudes indicated a clear preference for thinking, had a greater tendency to give certain feeling responses than did males. The difference was ascribed either to the possibility that certain feeling responses were more socially desirable for females than males, or to the effect of social training." (p. 149) But what if it were not environmental reasons but innate typological reasons that produced these tendencies?

One further note. Long before we knew anything about somatotypes we met some women who typologically appeared to be intuition thinking types, and they had a distinctive body type, a sort of husky build with a great deal of ectomorphy, as well. This brings to mind Jung's intuitive cast to thinking women.

The differences between the sexes in somatotypes and psychological types should eventually be brought into relationship with recent studies in sex differences in cognition and lateralization. For example, boys tend to score higher on tests of spacial ability and girls on tests of verbal abilities. These spacial abilities include maze performance, various exercises in mental rotation and chess. Bradshaw and Nettleton in their **Human Cerebral Asymmetry** surmised the list might also include musical composition and mathematics (p. 215). On the other hand, women are "less susceptible to language-related disorders such as developmental dysphasia, developmental dyslexia, stuttering and infantile autism." (p. 216)

There is a certain amount of evidence that suggests that females are less lateralized than males and therefore show less deficits after left hemisphere traumas. If the greater lateralization of males is confirmed, it would be an internal counterpart to Sheldon's observation of the wider distribution and more experimental nature of the male somatotypes. One would suspect, as well, that the psychological types of males not only differ in frequency of type from females, but might be more extreme within the particular type. In other words, women would show more balance in the use of the various functions while men would be more exclusively one-sided.

Whether this is true or not, or whether any analysis has been made or could be made of psychological type test data, I don't know.

Sheldon also indicated that the ectomorph was one of nature's most extreme experiments, and so we could expect to find both a higher incidence of these particular spatial-oriented gifts as well as developmental problems. As usual, both somatotype and psychological type are ignored in most of these studies. There are, however, several clues that point in this direction. Early maturing adolescents perform better on tests of verbal ability, and late-maturing adolescents score better on spatial ability. And since boys develop later than girls, it is suggested that "the prolonged maturation typical of males would ultimately lead to greater lateralization, greater separation of function and spatial (but not verbal) superiority, and a greater opportunity for language malfunction to occur." (Human Cerebral Asymmetry, p. 223) But as we will see in the studies on the maturation of the different somatotypes, it is the ectomorph who is the late maturer. This can be connected with studies of male rats outperforming female rats in mazes. There is also evidence "that females who are high and males who are low in the male sex hormone (androgen) score higher on spatial ability tests." (p. 218) And what males would be low in androgen if not those dwelling at the opposite poles of mesomorphy in the ectomorphic regions? From a psychological type viewpoint would Jung's women with thinking with an intuitive cast or women who are extraverted intuiters show higher androgen levels, higher spatial abilities, and more difficulties in traditional gender roles?

CHAPTER 12

TYPE AND NEUROSCIENCE

In type and psychopathology we saw that if we could understand just who from a typological point of view becomes a schizophrenic or manic-depressive, then it would be possible to begin to separate descriptions of the disease from the descriptions of the particular types that are mingled with them. Frankly, this particular problem is but one facet of a much wider one. Despite the enormous scientific progress that is taking place today it is rare when this scientific work averts to the question of human differences. It simply does not ask itself in an adequate way how its results are going to be skewed or obscured by the fact that there are important natural typological differences among the subjects they are examining.

For example, computerized tomography and magnetic resonance imaging, positron emission tomography, as well as other techniques, are unearthing potential differences between a schizophrenic brain and a normal brain in the form of ventricular enlargement, the number of dopamine D2 receptors and so forth. But we really have no idea how one normal brain differs from another. Will ectotonics have more frontal lobe activity than endotonics? Will introverted intuition types have more D2 receptors than extraverted sensation types? These questions are not far-fetched, and if they appear so to the neuroscientist it is because this is but another aspect of his own biologically founded psychiatry that has not yet been rescued from the environmentalism of the past.

Recently C. Robert Cloninger has described a

threefold typology based on novelty seeking, harm avoidance, and reward dependence. The person high in novelty seeking is impulsive and exploratory, and eager to take up new interests, but neglects details and quickly becomes distracted and bored. In contrast, the person low in novelty seeking is slow to make decisions, focuses on details, is frugal, orderly and slow tempered.

People high in harm avoidance are cautious, tense, inhibited, easily fatigable, shy and apprehensive worriers, while people low in harm avoidance are regarded as optimistic, outgoing, energetic and so forth.

The individual high in reward dependence is eager to please and help others, is warm, sympathetic and sensitive to social cues. The person low in reward dependence are tough minded, emotionally independent, socially detached, etc.

It is not farfetched to see in these descriptions, developed in more detail in three scales by Cloninger, similarities with Sheldon's three temperaments. The novelty seeker is closest to the mesotonic, the harm avoider to the ectotonic, and the reward dependent to the endotonic. It is also possible these descriptions have traces of Jung's psychological types. What kind of mesomorph is the novelty seeker? He looks like the extraverted intuition type. Cloninger describes the high rated novelty seeker: "Consistently seeks thrilling adventures and exploration; disorderly and unpredictable; intolerant of structure and monotony regardless of consequences; decisions and opinions based on vague global impressions and intuitions; consistently plays roles for dramatic effect so that real feelings and beliefs are uncertain; consistently spends on impulse in absence of external constraints; interests and friendships shift rapidly with the latest influence without any sustained commitments." ("A Systematic Method for Clinical Description and Classification of Personality Variants", p. 576)

But who is the person who is severely low in novelty seeking, who is disinterested in exploratory pursuits, and is highly orderly, highly frugal, slow to change interests and social attachments? We will not be far off if we look to the introverted sensation types, who are the typological opposites of the extraverted intuition types.

The person high in harm avoidance is inhibited by unfamiliar situations and strangers, and is easily fatigued. Here we find the ectotonic introverted intuition type. His opposite on the somatotype chart is the endomorphic-mesomorphic extraverted sensation thinking or feeling type, or extraverted thinking or feeling sensation type, that Cloninger describes as carefree meeting strangers and strange situations, and not fearful of risks, highly energetic, confident and optimistic, etc.

The reward dependent personality is closest to Jung's extraverted sensation type, and the low reward dependent person closest to the introverted thinking type, which is found opposite to the endomorphic pole on the somatotype chart.

While Cloninger does not relate his typology to Jung or Sheldon, he does give some indication of its biochemical foundations. He relates novelty seeking to dopamine and the brain's behavioral activation system, and harm avoidance to serotonin and behavioral inhibition: "Ascending serotonergic projections from the dorsal raphe nuclei to the substantia nigra inhibit nigrostriatal dopaminergic neurons and are essential for conditioned inhibition of activity by signals of punishment and frustrative nonreward." (p. 576) And reward dependence is correlated to norepinephrine and the acquisition and resistance to extinction of rewarded behavior.

Let's pursue this kind of neurobiological typology by looking at dopamine. The discovery of chlorpromazine led to the hope that its chemistry and that of other neuroleptic drugs would help us understand the

chemistry of schizophrenia. Scientists soon found that
chlorpromazine interferred with dopamine by binding
to the dopamine receptors, and preventing dopamine
from attaching to them. This led to the initial dopamine theory of schizophrenia which proposed that
schizophrenia was caused by too much dopamine.
However, post-mortem studies of schizophrenic brains
did not, for the most part, bear this out. This, in its
turn, led to the current dopamine theory in which
schizophrenics have an increased number of dopamine
D2 receptors. Dopamine research has been closely
connected with Parkinson's disease, which is a motor
disorder in which people have difficulty in initiating
action. It was found that the dopamine neurons in
the substantia nigra in Parkinson patients are fewer
and that they have less dopamine.

Today any number of dopamine theories of schizophrenia have been proposed, including a lack of
dopaminergic activity, or hyperdopaminergic activity
in the limbic system, and hypoactivity in the prefron-
tal cortex. But do introverts and extraverts differ
in dopamine activity? If dopamine helps initiate
action, then we would imagine extraverts would have
a higher level of it.

In 1975 Barchas, Ciaranello, Kessler and Hamburg
examined the genetic aspects of catecholamine synthesis in mice. The catecholamines include dopamine,
norepinephrine and epinephrine, which are important
in normal behavior and psychiatric disorders. They
stated:

"Strain differences exist in the activity of the
enzymes involved in the synthesis of the catecholamines in mice. This variation has a genetic basis.
Differential regulatory mechanisms of the enzymes
involved in catecholamine formation exist in different
strains and presumably the disvariation also has a
genetic basis." (p. 27)

And they concluded:

"The present studies, taken together, represent the

first demonstration that the activity of the enzymes involved in catecholamine biosynthesis are subject to the marked variation as a consequence of genetic differences. The experiments also provide the first suggestion that major differences in the physiological regulation of an enzyme involved in the formation of catecholamine exists within a single species." (p. 54)

But do these differences exist in humans? Roy King attempted to frame a hypothesis about dopamine function and temperament which can be summed up: "there may be genetic differences in mesolimbic dopamine cell numbers, as well as differences in dopamine release into the limbic striatum.", and "mesolimbic dopamine lowers the response threshold to affectively significant cues, thereby initiating action." ("Motivational Diversity and Mesolimbic Dopamine", p. 363)

Later King and his colleagues studied the dopamine levels in cerebral spinal fluid of 16 male patients suffering from depression who were also given the Eysenck Personality Inventory. They found a significant correlation (R=0.58, P less than 0.01) between the dopamine level and extraversion.

A strong positive correlation has also been observed between 5-HIAA, the metabolite of serotonin and HVA, the metabolite of dopamine, in human cerebro-spinal fluid. In one study by Hans Agren and his colleagues 175 men and women with depressive disorders show this relationship between 5-HIAA and HVA, which was confirmed by brain studies on dogs, which found "highly significant and positive correlations between dopamine and serotonin in areas of the brain stem and hypothalmus. In the basal ganglia (except the substantia nigra) the correlations are negative." (p. 183) What makes this study particularly interesting from our point of view is that in the group of women, the 5-HIAA was effected by age, height and body size: "women show highly significant correlations with age (positive) and height (negative) for both 5-HIAA and HVA. Dividing height with the cube root of weight (the ectomorphy index) strengthens the correlation coefficients even more." (p. 179) In short, the taller the women the lower the levels of 5-HIAA. Is it possible to relate this lower level of 5-HIAA in the more ectomorphic women to the lower levels of dopamine found in cerebral-spinal fluid of those who scored higher in introversion? If this relationship could be borne out we have both introversion and ectomorphy related to dopamine levels.

Now let's create a somewhat fanciful example to illustrate the potential interactions that might exist between type and a disease like schizophrenia. It would be an ectomorphic introverted intuitive type who lacked mesomorphy and exhibited what Sheldon called asthenic characteristics, i.e., a failure of the organism to reach its full flowering, that would be most at risk for schizophrenia. Is it possible that this type's inhibition in terms of action is related to a low level of dopamine? And could he have more D2 receptors to make the most of what dopamine he does possess? Then if he suffered a metabolic insult that effected the dopamine system he would be more likely than other types to cross the critical threshold that leads to the overt symptoms of schizophrenia. He would be unable to mobilize his already weak extraversion of action in order to stay in contact with the world. In short, he would become a hebephrenic schizophrenic. And when he is treated with neuroleptic drugs the suppression of the already low dopamine level in the motor centers could lead to Parkinson-like symptoms, or even tardive dyskinesis.

And if the already low dopamine levels of the introverted intuition type are lowered still more by the disease process, what will be the psychological effect on this type's already highly developed self-awareness? Will it reach a fever pitch as the introversion - extraversion balance is disrupted? Will the high arousal of the introvert go out of control, freewheeling without the normal enmeshment it has with everyday reality through its extraversion of action and affect?

Each of the salient characteristics of schizophrenia has to be evaluated according to the type of the person who has the disease. Schizophrenia has a heritable component, but what part of this component is due to genetic foundation of introversion and extraversion and somatotype? Schizophrenia seems to implicate the dopamine system, but what is the natural dopamine system like of those types most prone to it? Schizophrenia seems related to various brain abnormalities like ventricular enlargement and increased dopamine content in the amygdala on the left side of the brain, but what do normal introverted intuition brains look like?

These reflections on dopamine are indications that there are important and extensive biological foundations to introversion and extraversion, as well as the rest of our integrated typology. There may be even what could be called a biological introversion - extraversion axis. Why, for example, did Kretschmer describe the pyknic and the asthenic? We have already seen how Sheldon broke down these types into more fundamental components, but from an observational point of view Kretschmer was on to something. The pyknic, or endomorphic mesomorph, is the most dramatic kind of extravert, the most visible. He draws comments down upon himself. It is almost as if he is the most extraverted of the extraverts, while the introverted intuition type is the most introverted of the introverts. There is a certain affinity that endomorphy and mesomorphy have for each other in virtue of both being related to tempermental extraversion and mass while ectomorphy is opposed both to mass and extraversion. Sheldon's somatotype diagram is, as he realized, an idealization of the actual relationships that exist between the components. We should really shorten the distance between the endomorphic and mesomorphic poles, and lengthen the triangle in the direction of ectomorphy. Then, if we draw a line from the ectomorphic pole to the middle of the now shortened leg between endormophy and mesomorphy, this line would represent a tentative introversion - extraversion axis. On the extraverted end we find not only the pyknic, but the delinquent and criminal, the heart attack victim and the manic-depressive. All of them show a dynamic extraversion, often carried to the extreme. On the other end we have the extreme introversion of the introverted intuitive type and the schizophrenic.

If there is, indeed, a biological extraversion - introversion axis, it will appear in many places once we begin to look for it. For example, there have been any number of studies which have attempted, however tentatively, to relate temperament to ABO blood groups. Gille-Maisini, again drawing on the work of Leone Bourdel, as well as compiling the results of various studies, describes the rhythmic temperament as having a predisposition to blood group B, while the complex temperament, which is a mixture of the rhythmic, melodic and harmonic, is mostly AB. The rhythmics are closest to the extraverted thinkers. The harmonics, which he related to introverted intuition, are predisposed to group A, while the melodics, which are closest to the endomorphic mesomorphs, or pyknics, have a high frequency of type O. Eysenck relates the AB blood type to introversion, and finds that it has a much higher frequency in places like Japan and Egypt than in the United States and Italy. Our biological axis of introversion and extraversion would have at one end the O blood type, and at the other, the A and AB, while the B would represent a branching off closer to the O, but also having intermediate characteristics. There is a relationship between affective diseases and blood group O, and schizophrenia with A, and the predisposition to O among the affective diseases is especially strong in manic-depressives. There is also a relationship between O and duodenal ulcers. When Gille studied a group of male schizophrenics in Quebec, he found a greater frequency of paranoid schizophrenia among type O, and a greater frequency of A among what he describes as simple and hebephrenic-catatonic schizophrenics. Thus, he parallels the distinctions already made between these two basic classes of schizophrenics in virtue of differences in somatotype. There is some evidence, therefore, of an O-A dimension aspect in our introversion - extraversion axis, but it is overlaid with other tendencies and assertions that are hard to evaluate.

Goldin, Gershon and their coworkers found a possible genetic linkage between ABO locus and the locus for plasma dopamine-beta-hydroxylase, which is the enzyme that converts dopamine to norepinephrine. DBH has also been proposed as an index of sympathetic activity, and was one of the elements that went to make up the computer generated, biological profile faces we saw before. If there is, indeed, a connection between the ABO system and dopamine activity, it would be another element in the biological foundations of introversion and extraversion.

The Pineal Gland and Melatonin

Some of the most fascinating evidence about these biological foundations center around the pineal gland. In ancient times the pineal was associated with clairvoyance. Descartes, in the 17th century, thought it was the bridge between body and soul, and for several centuries after him attempts were made to discover evidence in the anatomy of the pineal for mental derangement. After these attempts proved fruitless interest in the pineal waned, and it has only been in recent times that it has made a strong

comeback. In 1958 Anton Lerner discovered a substance in the pineal that had a blanching effect on
the melanin in frog skins, and he called it melatonin.
    The pineal is a small, pea-sized, unpaired organ
in the brain with close links with the hypothalmus
and pituitary. Melatonin has a number of characteristics of great interest to the Jung-Sheldon typologist.
First of all, the action of the pineal is primarily
inhibitory. Melatonin, for example, diminishes the
weight of the thyroid, reduces the uptake of iodine
and inhibits thyroxin secretion. The pineal effects
adrenal and thyroid glands which are involved in
survival in the cold. Therefore, there are more complex pineal glands in penguins, seals, and walruses
than in crocodiles, armadillos and manatees. ("Pineal
Bodies and Thermoregulation", C.L. Ralph) Peak
melatonin values occur in winter and summer, and
lower levels in spring and autumn. Melatonin inhibits
ovary function and lowers testosterone levels. It is
lowest at ovulation and peaks at menstruation. It
induces sleep and exacerbates the symptoms of depressed patients and those with schizophrenia and
Parkinsonism, and is diminished by the anti-psychotic
drug propranalol. ("Melatonin in Human Body Fluids",
Waldhauser et al.) (P.E. Mullen) In line with the
transmethylaton theory of schizophrenia formulated
by Smythes and Osmond an abnormality in the biochemical machinery that produces melatonin could
lead, instead, to a hallucinagenic substance. LSD, in
fact, which increased MBTI scores in intuition, aug-
ments melatonin synthesis.
    The second major point is the close connection
the pineal has with light and the eyes by both normal visual pathways and non-visually. Melatonin has
an inverse relationship to light: the more light the
less melatonin that is produced. This leads to a 24-
hour melatonin rhythm in which melatonin levels peak
between one and three in the morning. Melatonin has
been found in the retina of several animals and can

be synthesized there. In the retina of rabbits it inhibits the release of dopamine so light which causes falling levels of melatonin leads, as well, to higher dopamine levels and to the down regulation of D2 dopamine receptors. (Dubocovich)

In order to see the implications of some of these facts let's look at the intriguing work of Morgan Worthy. Worthy was interested both in sports and in individual differences. He noticed that blacks and whites appeared to differ in their sport abilities, and then he went further and concluded that it was not really racial differences that were primary, but differences in eye color. Those sports which seemed to depend on quick and immediate reactions appeared to have a higher percentage of dark-eyed leaders, while the sports that were self-paced and demanded a certain inhibition before action seemed to have many light-eyed champions. For example, the light-eyed basketball players were significantly more accurate on shooting free throws than the dark-eyed. With this clue in mind Worthy ranged over an enormous variety of studies and eventually drew them together in his **Eye Color, Sex and Race: Keys to Human and Animal Behavior.** He found that light-eyed birds of prey differed from dark-eyed birds of prey in their methods of hunting, and two different survival patterns could be found among animals, as well. He called these patterns the react-approach-flee and the wait-freeze-stalk, with cats being a good example of the latter. He cites the work of Tyron, who in 1931 compared pigmented and albino rats on their maze learning ability. The rats with the lack of pigmented eyes did better, presumably because they could ignore extraneous stimuli. All in all, Worthy "found strong evidence of an eye darkness/reactivity relationship in such scattered areas as human athletic performance, hunting and escape tactics of birds and mammals, behavioral traits in different breeds of dogs, and laboratory studies of rodents." (p. 65)

But what was causing these differences? Wasn't eye color a relatively superficial characteristic? Perhaps not. Worthy felt that eyes with heavy pigmentation would have better visual acuity but less visual sensitivity, and be more responsive to the red end of the spectrum, while light-eyed creatures would respond to the blue end, and have more visual sensitivity than visual acuity. A certain amount of evidence has appeared linking light eyes with form perception and dark eyes with color perception. The dark eyed are described as more "interpersonally spontaneous and emotionally reactive". (p. 92)

In order to try to explain these kinds of findings Worthy turned to the early results of pineal research. Why did spring seem to bring about an outburst of sexual activity among Eskimos? Why were blind people and prisoners often obese? The answers all seem to lie in the pineal gland. He reports one experiment in which slow-running rats were distinguished from fast-running rats by observation of how much they used an activity wheel. Autopsies showed that the slow-running rats had higher cell densities in the pineal glands and lower cell densities in the adrenal glands compared to the fast-running group. He speculates that light-eyed people have a different level of pineal functioning than dark-eyed people, and he suggests a tentative link between eye color and height in terms of "an inverse relationship between eye darkness and height of human populations." And he pursues this possibility by examining the eye color and length in birds. Worthy also describes a New Zealand lizard, the tuatara, the sole survivor of an ancient line, who has a well developed pineal eye and takes an hour between breaths. Much like the view extraverts have of introverts!

Worthy's work is strengthened by other data. Raymond Cattell, for example, summarizes work on eye color that indicates the possibility of a relationship between light eye color and quantitative reasoning, and dark eyed color and quicker reaction time, and lower flicker fusion speed. The light-eyed are more highly field independent and the dark-eyed more susceptible to being influenced by the opinions of others. He reports that Havelock Ellis surveyed the British National Portrait Gallery, looking for relationships between eye and hair color and field of eminence. He found more mathematical and scientific performance among the light-eyed, and language and religious eminence among the dark-eyed. Perhaps melatonin, like dopamine, represents another area where an integrated typology of psychological types and somatotypes could begin to organize these disparate pieces into a coherent picture.

Let's speculate. Just who are the people who have high natural levels of melatonin? Just who are the most biologically inhibited types? Is it our old friend the introverted intuition type who anchors one end of the biological introversion - extraversion axis? Sheldon surmised that the ectotonia of the pronounced ectomorph kept his mesotonia and endotonia in check. Here we would expect to find a higher proportion of light-eyed people and a special manifestation of length which, as we remember, became one of the final criteria of ectomorphy in Sheldon's objectification of somatotypes. It is the ectomorph, as well, who is the late sexual maturer. David McNeill and Norman Livson found a positive relationship between endomorphy and sexual maturation and a negative relationship between ectomophy and sexual maturation. They felt that height over the cube root of weight accounted for most of the relationship between somatotype and sexual maturation.

Further, the administration of melatonin has been known to increase growth hormone levels and pineal hyperplasia manifests itself in dental and skin abnormalities, abdominal distensions, phallic enlargement, thickened nails, hirsutism and dental precocity, many of which point to the ectodermal layer of the embryo

from which the pineal itself derives. Melatonin induces sleep, lowers activity levels, and testosterone
levels. It is the ectomorph who sleeps more, acts
less, and is mesopenic. The more androgynous males,
in contrast to the more virilized males, have more
highly developed spatial ability, and Sheldon thought
the ectomorph more resistant to cancer than the
endomorphic-mesomorph, and melatonin does exert
an inhibitory effect on tumor growth.

The ectomorph also has difficulty tanning. Do the
higher levels of melatonin mediate this quality, as
well? Melanin deposited in human skin does not
change as rapidly as it does in certain animals, but
melatonin does inhibit the pituitary secretion of
melanocyte-stimulating hormone (MSH). It has been
suggested that in humans "the pineal hormones may
have shifted their target organ from the pigmentary
melanocyte cell to a cell sharing a common embryonic and evolutionary origin, the neurone" (Mullen and
Silman, p. 410) so while the melatonin does not
change skin color it could inhibit tanning. Interestingly, one of the diagnostic signs of Type A behavior
at the other end of the introversion - extraversion
axis is a "browning of skin of eyelids and of skin
immediately below the eyelids. This tan pigmentation
is due to a chronic excess discharge of a pigment-
inducing hormone (MSH) by the pituitary gland. Unlike
the tan coming after exposure to excess sunlight, this
type of periorbital pigmentation never seems to disappear. Although it is by no means common to all
persons exhibiting Type A behavior, its presence in
Caucasians invariably indicates severe Type A behavior and usually a relatively high level of serum cholesterol." (Friedman and Ulmer, p. 58) In women it
is the lower eyelid that is more likely to be involved. (p. 95)

In X-linked ectodermal dysplasia males show an
absence of teeth and sweat glands, and Darwin described a case "of a Hindoo family in Scinde, in which

ten men, in the course of four generations, were furnished in both jaws taken together, with only four small and weak incisor teeth and with eight posterior molars." (McKusick, 1985, 1347/30510) And it is intriguing that many of these patients are short and have hyperpigmentation around the eyes. Are there some light-eyed ectomorphs who are hypopigmented around the eyes?

In another X-linked disease, steroid sulfatase deficiency or ichthyosis, a drying and scaling of the skin, certain cases show deep corneal opacities. And it has been suggested that there is a reduction of cholesterol content of the stratum corneum. (McKusick, 1985, 1400/30810)

Gary and Glover report some anecdotal information on the relationship between light eyes and various illnesses. These included the higher incidence of hypoglycemia among light-eyed, light-haired and fair-skinned children (p. 112) and the story of a mother who said that when her autistic child was very withdrawn "her eyes which were normally brown became lighter in color, had no depth, lacked luster and seemed fuzzy." (p. 114) But when the eyes became darker the child would learn rapidly. In a study of learning disabilities, despite the fact that following Morgan Worthy they would have expected that light-eyed students would be better at tasks of discrimination and dark-eyed students better at problems that have to do with resolving power, they found that dark-eyed students are less likely to be learning disabled than light-eyed students, which we can relate to the possibility of their lower lateralization.

Happy and Collins investigated 25 autistic children and 65 normal children in Australia and found that there was an over-representation of hypopigmented children among the autistic group and under-representation of hyperpigmented children. They hypothesized that autism represented extreme introversion and that introversion was connected with the ascending reticular activating system, especially in connection with its dopamine and melanin content, and therefore was related to eye, skin and hair color.

The removal of the pineal gland results in higher blood sugar and blood pressure levels, and the pineal probably plays a role in the immune system. If high melatonin levels are connected with ectomorphy we would expect them to be connected to more psychological ectotonic qualities, as well. Rosenthal and his colleagues studied 29 patients who suffered depressions in the fall and winter which disappeared in the spring or summer. Their study grew out of their experience with a woman patient who suffered winter depressions and summer manias, which were effected by the latitude of where she was living. The winter depression would disappear if she went south for a vacation. She was treated with light therapy with good effect. When the research team advertised for people with similar problems by means of an article in the Washington Post, they got more than 2,000 replies. The resultant 29 subjects contained a large proportion of manic-depressives, and those who were treated with light therapy benefited from it.

Did manic-depressives in this sample suffer from an inability to handle melatonin, which induced in them lethargy and depression? In other studies patients suffering from depression and who stayed up all night were more talkative in the morning. Did a similar reduction in melatonin levels play a role here, as well?

Tyron's albino-eyed rats did better than pigmented rats in mazes, and in another study melatonin itself was connected to maze ability. Given the proclivities of the light-eyed and presumably more highly pineal active people for science and mathematics which we have already seen connected with the introverted intuition thinking and the introverted thinking intuition types, is intuition a prerequisite for maze ability? If it is, then the myth of Daedalus, who built the maze to contain the Minotaur, and Icarus, his son, the archetypal intuitive, would take on a new meaning. Perhaps the ancient link between the pineal and clairvoyance has its biological foundation in the connection between high melatonin levels and the introverted intuition type.

In Turner's syndrome where a woman suffers a partial or complete loss of one of her X chromosomes, there is often an impairment of visualizing ability. Can this be connected with the diminished melatonin levels that have been found in Turner's syndrome patients? Higher ranges of melatonin have been found in boys than in girls, and might point to a similar link with visual abilities.

Again we have strayed in fanciful flights of speculation, but the underlying point is important. Once we link Jung's psychological types to Sheldon's somatotypes we become sensitized to the issue of a complementary biological typology, the pieces of which are emerging all around us.

CHAPTER 13
TYPE AND GENETICS

There is considerable evidence that whatever the biological foundations to introversion and extraversion are, they have a genetic basis. The various studies of Sheldon in which the trunk index remained constant are a good indication of this. And they can be complemented by Susan Faber's **Identical Twins Reared Apart.** What better test of the stability of somatotypes could there be than to look at how different these identical twins have become by living in different environments? There has been any amount of publicity about the seemingly uncanny coincidences between identical twins brought together after many years of separation. Their wives might have the same first name, or their dogs, or they like the same kind of foods, or meet for the first time wearing the same kind of clothing and so forth. But it is their identical physical appearance that is often the key to their finding each other. Just how close are they physically? They are within 2/3 of an inch in height, and they usually agree in weight within 10 pounds, with women more labile than men due, perhaps, to their higher endomorphy. These twins shared the same shape ears, eyes, nose, distribution of hair and pigmentation, and the "shape of the skull varied by little more than the width of a pencil lead". (p. 69) They are so identical in electroencephalogram patterns that these patterns have sometimes been used to determine whether they are identical twins or not. In one case a neurologist studying a pair of twins saved himself time by using only one report. The twins appear alike in electrocardiogram patterns and blood pressure, and they are highly concordant in eye characteristics. In fact, we so expect these twins to look alike that it takes us a moment to reflect on the fact that their similarities are a confirmation of Sheldon's somatotype work. Some other evidence for a genetic basis to somatotype has been summarized by Rees (1968), and there is growing evidence that temperament, too, has a substantial genetic foundation, as can be seen in the work of Buss and Plomin (1975) and Thomas and Chess (1977), and is implied by Walker's studies of the temperament of young children that we already saw, and more recent studies, for example, Kagan and his coworkers' "Biological Bases of Childhood Shyness".

Introversion and extraversion has also been the subject of innumerable studies that have indicated a large genetic component. In 1956 Eysenck, for example, in a study of identical and paternal twins, found that identical twins resembled each other more closely than fraternal twins in extraversion and introversion. He summarized the evidence for the heritability of personality in "The Biological Basis of Personality" (1967). Scarr (1969), studying the results of ten twin studies including Eysenck's and her own found moderate to high genetic contributions to social introversion - extraversion, and Horn, Plomin and Rosenman (1976) found that talking to strangers, which is a good indicator of introversion - extraversion, was the strongest of all the traits in which identical twins were more concordant than fraternal twins.

We could cite many more studies on the genetic foundation to somatotype, temperament and introversion and extraversion, but it is more interesting to ask about the genetic mechanism by which these traits are transmitted, and here virtually nothing is known. Therefore the stage is set for another and final one of our speculative flights of fancy with the hope that this one, as well, will help us begin to

think of psychological types and somatotypes in terms
of biochemistry and genetics.

My wife and I have over our years of studying
types noticed a pattern of introversion and extraversion in families. Put in its simplest form, the daughters seem to follow the attitude, i.e. the introversion
or extraversion, of the father, while the sons follow
the attitude of the mother. For example, in one
family the father was extraverted and the mother
introverted, and the two sons introverted and the two
daughters extraverted. In another the father was
extraverted, the mother introverted, the four daughters extraverted and the two sons introverted. And
in still another the mother was extraverted, the
father introverted, and the daughter introverted. This
brings to mind the old saying, "Like father like
daughter, like mother like son." By now we have
observed this pattern so many times we are sure
something substantial is there, and have gone on to
ask ourselves just what it implies.

At the very least it means that even though
somatotypes, temperament and psychological types
are polygenic, that is, controlled by many genes,
there is probably a substantial X-linked factor. The
X chromosome is a very interesting one in which
more than 120 genes have already been found, but
whose secrets have not been fully deciphered. Mary
Lyon, for example, discovered that in women one of
their two X chromosomes is randomly inactivated so
they do not receive a double dose of the various X
genes. But recent research shows that this inactivation is not complete.

Once we became sensitized to the X-linked nature
of introversion and extraversion, we began to see
various pieces of this genetic puzzle. Morgan Worthy,
for instance, had suggested various reasons for an
X-linked factor in eye color reactivity. They included
sex differences in reactivity itself, the fact that one
of the genes for eye color is on the X chromosome,

and that some endocrine functions are X-linked, and here he cites work showing that biological clock functions in fruitflies are influenced by a gene on the X chromosome.

In **Eye Color, Sex and Children's Behavior** Gary and Glover, following Worthy, describe a somewhat informal but fascinating study in which university graduate students stopped every fifth pedestrian on the street and asked them questions like, "I enjoy the company of people a. always, b. sometimes, c. never." or "I enjoy parties a. always, b. sometimes, c. rarely." And along with the question they tried to determine by asking and observing what color eyes these people had. In answer to the first question, among the dark-eyed people 130 responded always, 5 sometimes and 1 never, while among the light-eyed people 14 said always, 88 sometimes and 8 never. For the second question it was dark eyes 63 always, 39 sometimes and 34 rarely, and light eyes 16 always, 41 sometimes, and 53 rarely.

Winge (1921) found a tendency for the eye color of the child to take after that of the parent of the opposite sex. Brues (1946) found some evidence for the occurence of dominant or partially dominant eye color genes on the X chromosome. We can speculate that both introversion and extraversion, or put in another way, the biochemical mechanism underlying introversion and extraversion and eye color, could be X-linked dominant characteristics. This would explain the patterns that Gary and Glover found.

Another piece of this puzzle can be found in the evidence. connecting manic-depressive (bi-polar) disease with X-linked dominant transmission. (Cadoret and Winokur, 1976; Winokur and Tanna, 1969). Sheldon described manic-depressives as failing in the mechanisms of inhibition. They lack ectomorphy-ectotonia, or put in another way, they could be called deficient in introversion. It is highly suggestive, then, that a disease that appears like a failure of the introversion

- extraversion mechanism should be associated with the X-linked dominant transmission.

If introversion and extraversion are X-linked dominant characteristics, then we would expect the somatotypes of the mother and son, or father and daughter, to agree to the extent that both would fall within the territories we have delineated for introversion and extraversion on the somatotype chart. If we look at the major cases that Sheldon described in the **Varieties of Temperament,** and determine the psychological attitude of the men and their mothers simply on the basis of somatotype, they agree in all 6 cases. A further comparison of the siblings of the subjects also shows agreement between child and the parent of the opposite sex with one exception. However, in most cases it appears that the parents share the same attitudinal type, so that the agreement of the children with this attitude is not particularly striking. If we remember the description of Kretschmer's parents we would say that his mother was an extravert and his father was an introvert, and Kretschmer, himself, following his mother, was an extravert.

Parnell (1958) in a study of 45 families, found a strong tendency for the child's somatotype to fall on or near a line drawn between the somatotypes of the parents when plotted on the basic somatotype chart. If we take this line principle as an expression of the polygenic nature of somatotypes, then we would expect it would also, in some fashion, express the X-linked nature of introversion and extraversion within this polygenic framework. If we examine the 45 cases and tentatively determine the introversion and extraversion of the child in relationship to that of the parent of the opposite sex by plotting the somatotypes on our chart that shows both somatotypes and psychological type, we find that out of the 45, 42 are in fairly close agreement and can be interpreted in terms of the child and the parent of the opposite sex sharing either introversion or extraversion. The cases that show a notable departure are cases 11, 19 and 20. Parnell found a number of cases that departed from his line principle. One of the cases that he pointed out as departing from it was case 11. Cases 19 and 20 also depart from the line principle.

Parnell (1959) reported on another study where men entering Birmingham University (Great Britain) were somatotyped, and then chose the somatotype of their fathers and mothers from a series of photographs. He then plotted the somatotypes of the parents for the men who had chosen their own somatotype correctly. The results are in fairly close agreement to our expectations that the somatotypes of the sons will fall in the introverted territories if the somatotype of the mother falls in the introverted territories, and vice versa for extraversion. For example, in a distribution of sons who chose 4-6-2 as the father's somatotype, and 2.5-2-6 as the mother's, 8 out of 11 fell in introverted territories. In a distribution of sons who estimated their father as 3-4-4 and their mother as 3-3-4, 9 out of 12 fell within the introverted territories. There are limitations to these kinds of comparisons. First there are obvious limitations springing from how the somatotypes of the parents were determined. Secondly, both father and mother were somatotyped, as is reasonable, on the same chart, but there is a strong possibility that the relationship between somatotype and psychological type is distributed differently in each case.

Brues (1950) in an article entitled, "Linkage of Body Build with Sex, Eye Color and Freckling" concluded that X-linked factors may be involved in the genetic foundation of body build. She felt it was fortuitous to have hit on a morphological index closely related "to a simple developmental reality". This index turned out to be our old friend height over the cube root of weight, which Sheldon used in his final objective method as an indication of ectomorphy. Tanner and his colleagues later wrote:

"We have investigated Brues' data on 83 families, and find no evidence for sex-linkage in genes controlling stature, but fairly conclusive evidence in the case of linearity of build as measured by height over the cube root of weight." ("The Genetics of Human Morphological Characters", p. 194)

Richard Stafford gave a spatial visualization test to 104 fathers and mothers and their 58 sons and 70 daughters, and found the highest correlations between father and daughter, and mother and son, which he considered compatible with an X-linked recessive pattern of inheritance. Stafford's work was reviewed by David Garron who compared it with the results of studies of women with Turner's syndrome in which a defect involving the X chromosomes is associated with a lack of spatial abilities, though it was not clear why an X-recessive trait would show as a defect in the absence of one of the X chromosomes.

In a recent Swedish study of risk factors for stroke in middle-aged men, Welin and his coworkers found three factors: increased blood pressure, abdominal obesity, and a maternal history of stroke. Could these men have inherited a more stroke-prone somatotype and psychological type from their mothers? Here, again, we see the difficulty in sorting out the disease itself and the underlying typological patterns.

If there are, indeed, X-linked eye color, linearity and spatial visualization traits, could they be signs of our deeper introversion - extraversion biological axis? This brings us to the possible mode of transmission of this X-linked introversion and extraversion. Our observations seem to indicate that this relationship between father and daughter, and mother and son, is rather consistent. To be absolutely sure of this is difficult because of the diagnostic problem of psychological types which, in this case, is exacerbated by the differences between men and women, and the fact that siblings can take on different typological roles in the family. The older child, for example, can appear more extraverted, and a younger more intro-verted. But let's look at the possible modes of transmission. In X-linked recessive traits almost all the effected people are males, and females transmit the trait to one-half of their sons. This diverges too much from our observations. In X-linked dominant behavior, while males transmit the trait to all of the daughters, heterozygous females transmit it to one-half of all their children and homozygous females transmit it to all their children. This is closer, but what would be ideal would be a mode of transmission in which the paternal X was always decisive for the attitude of the daughter, and both maternal Xs car-ried the gene for her dominant attitude so that this attitude was always expressed in the son.

Recent research in methylation imprinting suggests that "specific genes must be inherited from either the mother or father" (Marx, "A parent's sex may affect gene expression"), and this might shed light on this strange pattern of inheritance if it, indeed, exists.

The location for this putative introversion - extra-version gene is best sought on the terminal portion of the short arm of the X chromosome (Xpter). This segment of the chromosome contains the genes for the Xg blood group system, monoclonal antibody, steroid sulfatase and chondrodysplasia punctata. There is also evidence that links ocular albinism to the Xg blood group, though it is not on the Xpter itself.

The Xg(a) (McKusick 31470) acts like an X-linked dominant. The X chromosome, if not the Xg, has been linked to manic-depressive disease (Baron et al. 1987) and there is evidence that it is not inactiva-ted. Monoclonal antibody (31347), an antibody to human leukemia T cells, also escapes inactivation and along with the Xg is linked to the Y chromosome.

Steroid sulfatase deficiency (30810) or ichthyosis, a scaling of the skin, appears to avoid inactivation or lyonization as well. In some cases it is connected to deep corneal opacities. People with ichthyosis have increased plasma cholesterol sulfate levels which predominate in the low-density lipoprotein fraction of the plasma. Associated corneal problems have been connected to a reduction of cholesterol in the stratum corneum. Chondrodysplasia punctata (30295) may be an X-linked dominant. Patients can exhibit "hypoplasia of the distal phalanges" and "widespread atrophic and pigmentary lesions of the skin in a linear or whorled patterns" (McKusick 1986, p1335), and occasionally short stature.

This terminal of the short arm of the X chromosome exhibits pairing with corresponding loci on the Y chromosome. Among the genes on the Y chromosome is a testis-determining factor, which may be the same as the H-Y antigen which might be regulatory for a structural locus on the short arm of the X. There is also a gene relating to stature on the Y chromosome, and Tanner and his coworkers have argued that genes determining slower maturation must be on the Y. (McKusick 1986, plxxv-lxxvi; Tanner et al. "Genes on the Y chromosome influencing rate of maturation in man").

Is it possible that in the descriptions of these X and Y terminals we are catching a fleeting glimpse of our biological introversion-extraversion axis, which embrace manic-depressive disease, cholesterol levels, eye and skin pigmentation, stature and maturation rate?

Goodenough and his colleagues in "A Survey of X Chromosome Linkage with Field Dependence and Spatial Visualization" examined 67 families with three sons, and found a possible link between the Xg and the portable Rod and Frame Test, and the Embedded Figure Test. Both tests are measures of field dependence which is the degree a person is effected by the surroundings of a particular task to be accomplished, and probably are fairly good indicators of certain sorts of introversion and extraversion. These results bring to mind similar studies on form and color perception. Worthy found evidence that light-eyed people were better at form perception than color perception, and dark-eyed people were the reverse. Studies of Kretschmer's cyclothymia and schizothymia found pyknics (Sheldon's endomorphic-mesomorphs) did better at color than form perception, while the schizothymes were the opposite. (Eysenck, "Cyclothymia and Schizothymia as a Dimension of Personality").

The short stature of Turner's syndrome patients appears connected to a deletion on the short arm of the X chromosome. Can this be related to their visualizing disabilities and thus to a lack of ectomorphy? If the defect were on the non-inactivated Xpter it would help explain why a defect on one X chromosome could manifest itself despite the lyonization of most of the chromosome.

The Xq, or long arm, seems to have its own area of lack of inactivation and a defect in it can lead to problems of ovarian function. As Daniel Federman nicely puts it:

"The ovary is the most precisely doomed structure in the human body: it carries in its makeup the destruction of its own seeds. When the fetal ovaries differentiate, they contain about 7 million oocytes. Through an unknown process, these oocytes begin immediately to disappear, by birth there are about 3 million left, by the menarche about 400,000, and the menopause occurs when under 10,000 remain. Menses never occur in the patient with 45,X Turner's syndrome, but not because she is born without oocytes. Rather, it is that after appearing, her oocytes disappear at an accelerated rate and are gone by the age of two, i.e., the menopause occurs before the menarche. Thus, something on the normal female's second X chromosome slows the disappearance of ovarian follicles and allows menstrual function and fertility to occur." ("Mapping the X-Chromosome", p. 162)

This can be viewed as a startling contrast to the slow sexual maturation of the ectomorph, not to mention our friend the tuatara lizard with the well developed pineal eye from the last chapter. The "tuatara reproduce only once every four or five years. It takes two or three years for the female to manufacture eggs. After mating, she holds the eggs in her oviduct for another seven months before laying them. 12 to 16 months later, tuatara babies finally hatch." (**Discover,** April '89, p. 14)

The X chromosome has any number of other interesting genes that may hold the potential to add to the picture of the biological introversion - extraversion axis. These include: retinitis pigmentosa (31260) with visual defects and lumps of pigment, reduced flicker sensitivity and sometimes a rare blue-yellow color defect. (Worthy comments that light-eyed people are more receptive to blue light.); ocular albinism (30050) with the eyes and skin showing macromelanosomes and "stripe-like areas of retinal hypopigmentation in carrier"; and the anhidrotic ectodermal dysplasia (30510) we saw in the previous chapter.

It is possible that the lack of inactivation of this Xpter and its links with the Y chromosome play a role in the strange inheritance pattern of introversion and extraversion. And what could be the reason for such a pattern? It would tend to overcome some of the physical and psychological differences between the members of the family, for each parent could more easily recognize her or himself in the child of the opposite sex, and this would tend to bind the family closer together. This kind of inheritance would also shed an interesting light on discussions of the Oedipus and Electra complexes.

But the matter might go deeper than this and be a way of safeguarding our basic patterns of adaptation to life. Jung suggested that introversion and extraversion themselves had their roots in two basic ways of procreating. One was a broadcasting of many offspring with the hopes that a few would survive, while the second was the birth of a few offspring raised in highly protective conditions. In short, introversion and extraversion would represent two kinds of evolutionary adaptation, two viable ways of surviving in this world. And this kind of inheritance would guarantee that neither one of these patterns would die out, and as a result mankind would maintain the plasticity and adaptability, which is one of its most valuable attributes. This would be a confirmation on the psychological plane of Ohno's law of the evolutionary conservation of the X chromosome of mammals.

FINAL CONCLUSIONS

After the typological odyssey of the preceding chapters it is time for general impressions and conclusions.

Jung's psychological types should remain firmly rooted in the process of individuation. A split between types taken interpersonally, and types taken intrapersonally, impoverishes them both.

Type diagnosis is a critical issue, but its solution lies principally, not in the direction of the reformulation of psychological types, or the creation of more refined type tests, but in the realization that we are dealing with very complex natural phenomena and we have to school ourselves to see them correctly. To abdicate working at this kind of carefully cultivated seeing that both Jung and Sheldon possessed in favor of a type test is certainly easier, but in the long run will do us a disservice, for it will not be as accurate or as far seeing.

Cultivating seeing is the foundation of a genuine observational method in psychology which ought to interact in lively dialogue with the experimental method. Again, any split will impoverish them both.

Sheldon's somatotypes and temperament types represent one of the finest achievements of psychology. The most promising way to save them from oblivion is to integrate them with Jung's psychological types. Then somatotypes will gain by being seen in relationship to the whole psyche and its dynamics, and psychological types will begin to come to grips with their biological foundations. The most weighty evidence for a relationship between somatotypes - temperament types and psychological types is not in material of the sort collected in Chapter 8, but will be based on our own ability to look at individuals from both points of view and see these relationships for ourselves. Exactly which somatotypes go with which psychological types is an issue for the future to refine. But there are no psyches walking around without bodies, and there are no psychological types without their highly distinctive body and temperament types. Any lingering Cartesian dualism should give way to the realization that, as Jung said, "Somewhere the psyche is living body, and the living body is animated matter."

The future of typology holds out the promise that an integrated typology of body - temperament and psychological types will be completed by a biochemical typology. If this promise is fulfilled, we will see that our particular type is rooted in the very chemistry of our bodies and brains, and stretches to the innermost recesses of our psyches. Such a growing awareness seems inevitable, but will we find the wisdom to use this knowledge not to reinforce our prejudice, but enrich our human community? Jung, by describing how each of us is in a certain way all the types and must strive to become all of them, holds out to us the promise of an understanding of human differences that will become the foundation for tolerance and compassion.

ACKNOWLEDGEMENTS

Over the years many people helped my wife and me in our pursuit of knowledge about typology, whether by their writings, or in response to our questions and letters, or by being such interesting types themselves! I would like to mention just some of those whose contributions stay warmly in my memories.

John Beebe and Wayne Detloff, Jungian analytical and typological experts, for encouragement and fascinating conversations. Jess Groesbeck, also a Jungian analyst and type expert, for his thought provoking letters. Humphrey Osmond, who bridges the worlds of Sheldon, Jung and biochemical typology with his well developed intuition, for delightful letters and his reminiscences about carrying the **Atlas of Men** to Jung. Joan Albert for the hospitality of the C.G. Jung Library in San Francisco.

In studying Sheldon the help of his colleagues was vital. Helen and Wes Dupertuis who made the long journey out to our forest home with their "fat pinchers" that tickled the children and who gave us an example of people who could actually see via Sheldon's somatotypes and temperaments, and who generously shared their valuable unpublished findings. Roland Elderkin, for 40 years Sheldon's court jester and companion who patiently responded over the years to our inquiries. I can still see him efficiently and quickly answering question after question and crisply saying, "Next." Emil Hartl and Edward Monnelly in Boston for their unstinting help and efforts to smooth our way. Louise Ames who wrote a valuable paper on Sheldon to guide us. Ashton Tenney for his informative letters, and Edward Humphreys for his help, encouragement and warm hospitality. Robert

Lenski for his letters. The William Sheldon Trust for permission to reprint Sheldon's somatotype photos, diagrams and check list of temperament. Juan Cortés for permission to reprint his temperament quiz. Mr. and Mrs. L.H. Knowles, Sheldon's nephew and his wife, for their encouragement and information. James Glen for his welcome at the Smithsonian Anthropological Archives where Sheldon's files are now deposited. The long suffering librarians of the Klamath County Library, especially Marguerite Webb, Louise Bates, and Betty Emmert who helped us through their interloan system to find many of the books and articles we needed. And finally, our children and friends who put up with us talking endlessly about types, and testing and interviewing them.

BIBLIOGRAPHY

This bibliography, while not by any means exhaustive, already verges on becoming unwieldy. For the most part it consists of material actually commented upon in the text, or used in preparing it. This has been augmented by references I have not had the opportunity to examine. This latter material falls into at least four headings: references cited in the text, while commenting on an author who made use of them, interesting items I have not been able to obtain, for example, F. Jordan's **Character As Seen in Body and Parentage,** and E. Hanhart's **Konstitution und Psychotherapie,** references I would like to have pursued if I had not already felt dazed by daunting piles of texts, and something like the article of Brown-Sequard which deserves to be cited for the brilliance of its title alone.

Abravanel, Elliot D. and Elizabeth A. King. (1983) **Dr. Abravanel's Body Type Diet and Lifetime Nutrition Plan.** Bantam Books.

_____ (1986) **Dr. Abravanel's Body Type Program for Health, Fitness, and Nutrition.** Bantam Books.

Adams, Iain C. (1985) "Personality and Somatotype of Trainee Pilots" in **Psy. Reports, 56,** 835-840.

Adams, I.E. and W.W. Bolonchuk. (1985) "A Canonical Analysis of the Relationship Between Personality and Somatotype" in **J. Hum. Mov. Stud.** 11 (3), 159-167.

Adcock, C.J. (March 1948) "A Factorial Examination of Sheldon's Types" in **J. of Personality,** 16, 3, 312-319.

Adler, G. (1961) **The Living Symbol:** A Case Study in the Process of Individuation. NY: Pantheon

Books, Inc.

Agren, Hans, Ivan N. Medford, et. al. (1986) "Interacting Neurotransmitter Systems, A Non-Experimental Approach to the 5HIAA-HVA Correlation in Human CSF" in **J. Psychiat. Res.**, Vol. 20, No. 3, 175-193.

Akiskal, Hagop S., Robert M.A. Hirschfeld and Boghos I. Yerevanian. (July 1983) "The Relationship of Personality to Affective Disorders" in **Arch. Gen. Psychiatry**, Vol. 40, 801-810.

Allport, G.W. (1937) **Personality**: A Psychological Interpretation. NY: Holt, as cited in Hall and Lindzey, **Theories of Personality.**

Alpert, Sherry L. "Diamonds in the Rough: A Fifty-Year Narrative History of the Hayden Goodwill Inn School.

Ames, Louise Bates. (1950) Review of W.H. Sheldon's **Varieties of Delinquent Youth** in **J. Gen. Psy.**, 77, 139-147.

_____ (1987) "Comments about Dr. William H. Sheldon." Privately circulated.

Andreasen, Nancy C. (1984) **The Broken Brain**: The Biological Revolution in Psychiatry. NY: Harper & Row.

_____ (March 18, 1988) "Brain Imaging: Applications in Psychiatry" in **Science**, Vol. 239, 1381-1388.

Ansley, H.R., W.H. Sheldon, A.M. Tenney and R.D. Elderkin. (Nov. 1957) "Preliminary Report on Cytopathology of Erythrocytes of Schizophrenic Patients" from **Diseases of the Nervous System,** Vol. 18, No. 11.

Arehart-Treichel, J. (1980) **Biotypes - The Critical Link Between Your Personality and Your Health.** Time Books.

Arieti, S. (1974) **Interpretation of Schizophrenia.** Basic Books.

Aristotle. "Physiognomonica" in **The Works of Aristotle,** trans. into English by W.D. Ross, M.A.,

Oxford at the Clarendon Press, 1913.

Arraj, James. (1986) "Jung's Forgotten Bridge" in **J. of Anal. Psy.**, 31, 173-180.

_____ (1986) **St. John of the Cross and Dr. C.G. Jung.** Chiloquin, OR: Inner Growth Books.

Arraj, Tyra and James Arraj. (1987) **A Jungian Psychology Guide.** Chiloquin, OR: Inner Growth Books.

_____ (1988) **Tracking the Elusive Human,** Volume I. Chiloquin, OR: Inner Growth Books.

"Athletes and Steroids" (1984) in **The Science Almanac,** 1985-86 Edition, edited by Bryan Bunch. NY: Anchor Books, 473-474.

Ball, R.J. (1932) "Introversion-extroversion in a group of convicts." in **J. Abn. & Soc. Psychol.,** 26, 422-428.

Baltimore, David. (March 28, 1983) "Can Genetic Science Backfire? "That's the Chance We Take"." in **U.S. News & World Report,** 52-53.

Barchas, J.D., R.D. Ciananello, S. Kessler and D.A. Hamburg. (1975) "Genetic Aspects of Catecholamine Synthesis" in **Genetic Research in Psychiatry,** edited by R.R. Fieve, D. Rosenthal and H. Brill. Baltimore: John Hopkins Univ. Press.

Baron, M. Neil Risch, et al. (March 19, 1987) "Genetic linkage between X-chromosome markers and bipolar affective illness" in **Nature,** Vol. 326, 289-292.

Bash, K.W. (1961) **Introduction to General Clinical Psychopathology.** Zurich: C.G. Jung Institute.

Bauer, J. (1923) **Vorlesungen über allgemeine Konstitutions-Vererbungslehre.** Berlin: Springer.

Baumann, U., J. Angst, A. Henne and F.E. Muser. (1975) "The Gray-Wheelwright Test" in **Diagnostica** XXI/2, 66-83.

Bean, R.B. (1912) "Morbidity and morphology" in **Johns Hopk. Hosp. Bull.,** 23, 363.

Beebe, John. (1984) "Psychological Types in Transference, Countertransference, and the Therapeutic

Interaction" in **Chiron** 1984.

Beesing, Maria, Robert J. Nogosek and Patrick H. O'Leary. (1984) **The Enneagram:** A Journey of Self Discovery. Denville, NJ: Dimension Books.

Bernstein, M., E. Martinez and M. Gustin. (May-June, 1961) "Physical and Psychological Variation and the Sex Ratio" in **J. Heredity,** Vol. 52, No. 3, 109-112.

Bessonet-Favre, A. (1910) **Le Typologie, Méthode d'Observation des Types Humains.** Paris.

Bieler, Henry G. (1965) **Food Is Your Best Medicine.** NY: Vintage Books.

Bisbee, C. R. Mullaly and H. Osmond. (1982) "Type and Psychiatric Illness" in **Res. in Psychol. Type,** T.G. Carskadon, editor, Vol. 5, 49-68.

Blake, M.J.F. (1967) "Relationship between Circadian Rhythm of Body Temperature and Introversion-Extraversion" in **Nature,** 215, 896-897.

Bower, B. (Aug. 31, 1985) "Childhood Origins of Type A Behavior" in **Sci. News.**

Bradshaw, John L. and Norman C. Nettleton. (1983) **Human Cerebral Asymmetry.** Englewood Cliffs, NJ: Prentice-Hall, Inc.

Bradway, K. (1964) "Jung's Psychological Types: Classification by Test vs. Classification by Self." in **J. Analyt. Psychol.,** 9, 2, 129-135.

Bradway, K. and W. Detloff. (1976) "Incidence of Psychological Types" in **J. Analyt. Psychol.,** 135-146.

Bradway, K. and J. Wheelwright. (1978) "The Psychological Type of the Analyst." in **J. Analyt. Psychol.,** 211-225.

Brawer, F.B. and J.M. Spiegelman. (1964) "Rorschach and Jung" in **J. Analyt. Psychol.,** 9, 2, 137-149.

Bronks, R. and A.W. Parker. (July 1985) "Anthropometric observation of adults with Down syndrome" in **Am. J. Mental Deficiency,** Vol. 90(1), 110-113.

Brown-Sequard. (1889) "Des effects produits chez l'homme par des injections sous-cutanées d'un liquide retiré des testicules frais de cobaye et de chien." Compter-rendus hebdomadaires. **Des séances et mémoires de la société de biologie.** 9th series.

Browne, J.A. (1971) "Extraversion in Search of a Personality Dimension". A Ph.D. dissertation from the Univ. of Alberta.

Brues, A.M. (1964) "A Genetic Analysis of Human Eye Color" in **Am. J. Phys. Anthro.**, 4, 1-36.

_____ (1950) "Linkage of Body Build with Sex, Eye Color, and Freckling" in **Am. J. Human Genetics,** Vol. 2, No. 3, 215-238.

Bryant, J. (1914) "The carnivorous and herbivorous types of man" in **Boston Med. & Surg. J.,** 1914, 170, 795, 1915, 172, 321, 1915, 173, 384.

Burdick, J. Alan and D. Tess. (1983) "A Factor Analytic Study Based on the **Atlas of Men**" in **Psy. Reports,** 52, 511-516.

Burney, Jr. C.E. (1975) "A Study in Jungian Psychological Types: Body Characteristics, Value Preference and Behavior Preference." Doct. Diss. U.S. Int. Univ.

Buss, A. and R.A. Plomin. (1975) **A Temperament Theory of Personality Development.** NY: Wiley.

Buss, A. and W. Poley. (1976) **Individual Differences:** Traits and Factors. NY: Gardner Press, Inc.

Cabot, P.S. de Q. (1938) "The relationship between characteristics of personality and physique in adolescents" in **Genet. Psychol. Monogr.,** 20, 3-120.

Cadoret, R.J. and G. Winokur. (1976) "Genetics of Affective Disorders" in **Psychiatry and Genetics,** edited by M. Sperber and L. Jarvik. Basic Books.

Calcraft, L.G.A. (1980) "Aldous Huxley and the Sheldonian Hypothesis" in **Annals of Science,** 37, 657-671.

Campbell, K.J. (1929) "The application of extroversion-introversion tests to the insane" in **J. Abn. & Soc. Psychol.,** 23, 479-481.

CAPT (Center for the Application of Psychological

Type) (1982) **Myers-Briggs Type Indicator Biblio-graphy.** Gainesville, FL.

Carlson, R. (1980) "Studies of Jungian Typology: II. Representations of the Personal World" in **J. Personality & Soc. Psychol.,** Vol. 38, No. 5, 801-810.

Carlsson, Arvid. (Jan. 23, 1987) "Biological Issues in Schizophrenia" in **Science,** Vol. 235, 430-433.

Carter, J.E.L. (1971) "Somatotype characteristics of champion athletes" in **Anthropological Congress Dedicated to Ales Hrdlicka** edited by V.V. Novotny. Prague: Academia, 241-252.

_____ (1984) "Somatotypes of Olympic Athletes from 1948-1976" in **Medicine and Sport Science,** Vol. 18.

_____ (1985) "A comparison of ratings by Heath and Sheldon of Somatotypes in "Atlas of Men"." in **Humanbiol.** Budapest. 16: 13-22.

Castellino, P. (1927) **Le Costituzione Individuale:** La Personnalità. Naples.

Cattell, R.B. (1982) **The Inheritance of Personality and Ability.** Academic Press.

Cheek, J. (10/31/83) "Shyness: How It Hurts Careers and Social Life" in **U.S. News & World Report.**

_____ (1984) **A Source Book on Shyness Research and Treatment.**

Child, Irvin L. and William H. Sheldon. (Sept. 1941) "The Correlation Between Components of Physique and Scores on Certain Psychological Tests" in **Character and Personality,** Vol. X, No. 1, 23-34.

Child, Irvin L. (June 1950) "The Relation of Somato-type to Self-Ratings on Sheldon's Temperamental Traits" in **J. Personality,** Vol. 18, No. 4.

Ciovirnache, M., I. Florea, V. Ionescu and H. Popescu (1984) "Somatotype of Children with Gonadal Dys-genesis and Structural Anomalies of Genitalia" in **Rev. Roum Med. Endocrinol.,** 22 (3), 199-210.

Claessens, A., G. Beunen, J. Simons, P. Swalus, M. Ostyn, R. Renson and D. van Gerven. (1980) "A Modification of Sheldon's Anthroposcopic Somatotype Technique" in **Anthrop. Közl**, 24, 45-54.

Claessens, A.L.M., G.P. Beunen et. al. (1984) "Body structure somatotype and motor fitness of top-class Belgian judoists" in the 1984 Olympic Scientific Congress Proceedings, Vol. 1, J.A.P. Day (Ed.) Champaign, IL: Human Kinetics Pub.

Claessens, A., G. Beunen and J. Simons. (1985) "Anthropometric Principal Components and Somatotype in Boys Followed Individually from 13 to 18 years of Age" in **Humanbiol.** Budapest. 16, 23-36.

_____ (1986) "Stability of anthroposcopic and anthropometric estimates of physique in Belgian boys followed longitudinally from 13 to 18 years of age" in **Annals of Human Biology**, Vol. 13, No. 3, 235-244.

Cloninger, C. Robert. (24 April 1987) "Neurogenetic Adaptive Mechanisms in Alcoholism" in **Science,** Vol. 236, 410-416.

_____ (June 1987) "A Systematic Method for Clinical Description and Classification of Personality Variants" in **Arch. Gen. Psychiatry**, Vol. 44.

Conklin, E.S. (1923) "The definition of introversion, extroversion and allied concepts" in **J. Abn. & Soc. Psychol.**, 17, 367-382.

Cook, D.A. (1971) "Is Jung's typology true? A theoretical and experimental study of some assumptions implicit in a theory of personality types." Doctoral dissertation, Duke Univ. Dissertation Abstracts International, 1971, 31, 2979B-2980B.

Côrtes, J.E. and Gatti, F.M. (1965) "Physique and Self-Description of Temperament" in **J. Consulting Psychol.**, Vol. 29, No. 5, 432-439.

_____ (Oct. 1970) "Physique & Propensity" in **Psychology Today.**

_____ (1972) **Delinquency and Crime:** A Biopsychosocial Approach, Empirical, Theoretical and Practical Aspects of Criminal Behavior. NY and London: Seminar Press.

Coughlan, Robert. (June 25, 1951) "What Manner of Morph Are You?" in **Life.**

Damon, Albert, Edmund P. Fowler, Jr., and William H. Sheldon. (July-Aug. 1955) "Constitutional Factors in Otosclerosis and Meniere's Disease" reprinted from the Transactions American Academy of Ophthalmology and Otolaryngology.

Damon, A. (1965) "Delineation of the body build variables associated with cardiovascular diseases" in **Ann. NY Acad. Sci.,** 126, 711-727.

Danby, P.M. (1953) "A Study of the Physique of Some Native East Africans" in **J. Roy. Anth. Inst.,** 83, 194-214.

Danzer, John. "Balanced Somatotypes and the Sanguine Temperament". Privately circulated.

Davenport, C.B. (1923) "Body build, its development and inheritance" in Carnegie Institute of Washington, Publication 329.

Davidson, M.A., R.G. McInnes and R.W. Parnell. (1957) "The distribution of personality traits in seven-year-old children" in **Brit. J. Educ. Psychol.,** 27, 48-61.

Deabler, H., E. Hartl and C. Willis. (Oct. 1975) "Physique and Personality, Somatotype and Vocational Interest" in **Percep. & Motor Skills,** Vol. 41(2), 382.

Detloff, W. (1971) "Psychological Types: Fifty Years After" in **Spring,** 62-73.

Diamond, D. (1957) **Personality and Temperament.** NY: Harper and Bros.

Dicks-Mireaux, M.J. (1964) "Extraversion-Introversion in Experimental Psychology" in **J. Analyt. Psychol.,** 117-127.

Domey, R.B., J.E. Duckworth and A.J. Morandi. (1964) "Taxonomies and correlates of physique" in **Psychol. Bull.,** 62, 411-426.

Draper, G., C.W. Dupertuis and J.L. Caughey, Jr. (1944) **Human Constitution in Clinical Medicine.** NY: Harper and Bros.

Dubey, G.P., S. Agrawal and K.N. Udupa. (Sept. 1968) "^{131}I Profile Scan in Different Human Constitutions by Whole Body Counter" in **Indian J. Med. Res.**, 466-469.

Dubocovich, Margarita L. (1983) "Melatonin is a potent modulator of dopamine release in the retina" in **Nature,** Vol. 306 22/29 Dec.

Dupertuis, C. Wesley. "The Physique of Criminals". Privately circulated.

Dupertuis, C. Wesley and Helen S. Dupertuis. (Summer, 1967) "Be Your Physical Self" in **Outlook.** (Case Western Reserve Alumni)

_____ (1968) **The Role of the Somatotype in Survivorship Among Cardiac Patients.** School of Medicine, Case Western Reserve University.

_____ (1974) **The Structural Profile.** Privately circulated c/o C. Wesley Dupertuis, Case Western Reserve University, University Archives, 301 Quail Building, Cleveland, OH 44106.

_____ (1977) "Are You Sure You're Overweight?" Privately circulated.

Eaves, L. and H.J. Eysenck. (1975) "The Nature of Extraversion: A Genetical Analysis" in **J. Pers. & Soc. Psychol.,** 32, 102-112.

Ekman, G. (1951) "On the number and definition of dimensions in Kretschmer's and Sheldon's constitutional systems" in **Essays in Psychology Dedicated to David Katz.** Uppsala.

Elderkin, Roland. "Salvation in Modern Dress - Fifty Years Later". CTS 1934-37. Privately circulated.

Ellenberger, Henri F. (1970) **The Discovery of the Unconscious.** NY: Basic Books.

Enke, W. (1968) "Ernst Kretschmer" in **International Encyclopedia of Social Sciences,** Vol. 8, Mac-Millan, 450-452.

Epps, P. and R.W. Parnell. (1952) "Physique and temperament of women delinquents compared with women undergraduates" in **Brit. J. Med. Psychol.,** 25, 249-255.

Evans, Elizabeth C. (1969) "Physiognomics in the Ancient World" in **Transactions of the American Philosophical Society,** Vol. 59, Part 5.

Evans, Joan. (1979) **Taste and Temperament:** A Brief Study of Psychological Types in their Relation to the Visual Arts.

Eysenck, H.J. (Dec. 1950) "Cyclothymia and Schizothymia as a Dimension of Personality. I. Historical Review" in **J. Person.,** Vol. 19., No. 2, 123-152.

_____ (1956b) "The Inheritance of Intraversion-Extraversion" in **Acta Psychologica,** 12, 95-110.

_____ (1967) **The Biological Basis of Personality.** Springfield, IL: Charles C. Thomas Pub.

_____ (1970) (ed.) **Readings in Extraversion-Introversion.** Vol. I: Theoretical and Methodological Issues. Vol. 2: Fields of Application. Vol. 3: Bearings on Basic Psychological Processes. NY: Wiley-Interscience.

_____ (1970) **The Structure of Human Personality.** London: Methuen & Co., Ltd.

_____ (Oct. 1982) "The Biological Basis of Cross-Cultural Differences in Personality: Blood Group Antigens" in **Psychol. Reports,** Vol. 51(2), 531-546.

Eysenck, H.J. and Michael W. Eysenck. (1985) **Personality and Individual Differences.** NY: Plenum Press.

Farber, Susan L. (1981) **Identical Twins Reared Apart.** A Reanalysis. NY: Basic Books.

Fierz, H.K. (1959) "The Clinical Significance of Extraversion and Introversion" in **Jung's Typology** by Daryl Sharp. Inner City Books.

Fiske, D.W. (1942) "The relation between physique and measures of intelligence, temperament and personality in superior adolescent boys" in **Psychol. Bull.,** 39, 459.

Fordham, M. (1972) "Note on Psychological Types" in **J. Analyt. Psychol.,** 17, 2, 111-115.

Fosbroke, Gerald Elton. (1967) **Know Others - and**

Yourself.

_____ (1914) **Character Reading Through Analysis of the Features.**

Franz, Marie-Louise von. (1971) "The Inferior Function" in **Jung's Typology.** NY: Spring Pub.

Fraschini, F., R. Collu and L. Martini. (1971) "Mechanisms of Inhibitory Action of Pineal Principles on Gonadotropin Secretion" in **The Pineal Gland,** edited by G.E.W. Wolstenholme and J. Knight. Edinburgh: Churchill Livingstone, 259-273.

Freyd, N. (1924) "Introverts and extraverts" in **Psychol. Review,** 31, 74-87.

Friedman, M. and R.H. Rosenman. (1974) **Type A Behavior and Your Heart.** NY: A Fawcett Crest Book.

Friedman, Meyer and Diane Ulmer. (1984) **Treating Type A Behavior - and Your Heart.** NY: Alfred A. Knopf.

Gale, A., M. Coles and J. Blaydon. (1969) "Extraversion-Introversion and the EEG" in **Br. J. Psychol.,** 60, 2, 209-223.

Garron, D.C. (1970) "Sex-Linked, Recessive Inheritance of Spatial and Numerical Abilities, and Turner's Syndrome" in **Psychol. Review,** Vol. 77, No. 2, 147-152.

Gary, A.L. and J. Glover. (1976) **Eye Color, Sex and Children's Behavior.** Chicago: Nelson-Hall.

Gattaz, W.F., M. Seitz and H. Beckmann. (1985) "A possible association between HLA B-27 and vulnerability to schizophrenia" in **Person. Indiv. Diff.,** Vol. 6, No. 2, 283-285.

Gentry, Thomas A., K.M. Polzine and J.A. Wakefield, Jr. (1985) "Human genetic markers associated with variation in intellectual abilities and personality" in **Pers. Indiv. Diff.,** Vol. 6, No. 1, 111-113.

Gertler, M.M., P.D. White et. al. (1954) **Coronary Heart Disease in Young Adults.** Cambridge, MA: Harvard Univ. Press.

Gille-Maisani, J.-Ch. (1978) **Types de Jung et**

Tempéraments Psychobiologiques. Paris: Maloine S.A. éditeur.

Giorgi, Amedeo. (1970) Psychology as a Human Science. NY: Harper and Row.

Glueck, Sheldon and Eleanor Glueck. (1956) Physique and Delinquency. NY: Harper.

Godbey, Karolyn L. (1975) "The Use of the Myers-Briggs Type Indicator with Delinquent and Non-Delinquent Adolescents". A Thesis for the Univ. of Florida.

Goldin, L.R., E.S. Gershon et. al. (1982) "Segregation and Linkage Studies of Plasma Dopamine-Beta-Hydroxylase (DBH), Erythrocyte Catechol-O-Methyltransferase (COMT), and Platelet Monoamine Oxidase (MAO): Possible Linkage between the ABO Locus and a Gene Controlling DBH Activity" in Am. J. Hum. Genet. 34:250-262.

Goldthwait, J.E. (1915) "An anatomic and mechanistic conception of disease" in Boston Med. & Surg. J., 172, 881.

Goodenough, D.R., E. Gandini et. al. (1977) "A Study of X Chromosome Linkage with Field Dependence and Spatial Visualization" in Behav. Genet., Vol. 7, No. 5, 373-387.

Gorlow, L., N.R. Simonson and H. Krauss. (1966) "An empirical investigation of the Jungian typology" in Brit. J. Soc. and Clin. Psychol., 5(2), 108-117.

Gould, S.J. (1981) The Mismeasure of Man. NY: W.W. Norton & Co.

Graves, R. (1963) "The Whitaker Negroes" in Encounters (anthology from the first ten years of Encounter magazine) NY: Basic Books.

Gray, H. (Aug.-Nov. 1946) "Jung's Psychological Types in Relation to Occupation, Race, Body-Build" in Stan. Med. Bull., 100-103.

_____ (1948) "Jung's Psychological Types in Men and Women" in Stan. Med. Bull., 6, 29-36.

_____ (1949) "Jung's Psychological Types: Ambiguous Scores and Their Interpretation" in J.

Gen. Psychol., 40, 63-88.

Gray, H. and J.B. Wheelwright. (Feb. 1944) "Jung's Psychological Types and Marriage" in Stan. Med. Bull., Vol. II, No. 1, 37-39.

_____ (1946) "Jung's Psychological Types, Their Frequency of Occurrence" in J. Gen. Psychol., 34, 3-17.

Gray, H., J.H. Wheelwright and J.B Wheelwright. "Jungian Type Survey".

Groesbeck, C.J. (1978) "Psychological Types in the Analysis of the Transference" in J. Analyt. Psychol., Vol. 23, 23-53.

Grotevant, H., S. Scarr and R.A. Weinberg. (1977) "Patterns of Interest Similarity in Adoptive and Biological Families" in J. Pers. and Soc. Psychol., 35(9), 667-676.

Guthrie, E.R. (1927) "Measuring introversion and extroversion" in J. Abn. and Soc. Psychol., 22, 82-88.

_____ (1957) "The constancy of physical types as determined by factorial analysis" in Human Biol., 29, 40-61.

_____ (1957) "The status of physical types" in Hum. Biol., 29, 223-241.

"Hair and Violence" (1984) in The Science Almanac 1985-86 Edition, edited by Bryan Bunch. NY: Anchor Books, 457-458.

Hall, C.S. and G. Lindzey. (1970) Theories of Personality (2nd edition) NY: Wiley.

Hammond, W.H. (1953) "Measurement of physical types in children" in Human Biol., 25, 65-80.

Hanley, C. (1951) "Physique and reputation of junior high school boys" in Child Devel., 22, 247-260.

Hanson, J.R. and Silver. Teacher Self-Assessment Manual. Hanson Silver & Asso., Morristown, NJ.

Happy, R. and J.K. Collins. (Dec. 30, 1972) "Melanin in the ascending reticular activating system and its possible relationship to autism" in The Med. J. Australia, 1484-86.

Haronian F. and A.A. Sugerman. (1965) "A comparison of Sheldon's and Parnell's methods for quantifying morphological differences" in **Am. J. Phys. Anthrop.**, 23, 135-142.

Hart, J.J. (1982) "Psychology of the scientist: XLVI: correlation between theoretical orientation in psychology and personality type" in **Psychol. Reports**, 50, 795-801.

Hartl, E., E. Monnelly and R. Elderkin. (1982) **Physique and Delinquent Behavior**: A Thirty Year Follow-Up of W.H. Sheldon's Varieties of Delinquent Youth. Academic Press.

Hartl, Emil M. "The Constitutional Base of Personality (the Somatotype) as a Dimension for Investigation in the Study of the Group.

Hartl, Emil M. and others. (9/9/77) "Comments at Gravesite of Dr. Wm. H. Sheldon, Pawtuxet, RI"

Haslam, D.R. (1967) "Individual Differences in Pain Threshold and Level of Arousal" in **Brit. J. Psychol.**, 58, 139-142.

Havice, D.W. (1977) **Personality Typing, Uses and Misuses.** Univ. Press of Am.

Heath, Barbara Honeyman. (June 1963) "Need for Modification of Somatotype Methodology" in **Am. J. Phys. Anthrop.**, N.S. Vol. 21, No. 2, 227-233.

Heath, Barbara Honeyman and J.E.L. Carter. (1967) "A Modified Somatotype Method" in **Am. J. Phys. Anthrop.**, V. 27, No. 1, July, 57-74.

Heidbreder, E. (1926) "Measuring introversion and extraversion" in **J. Abn. & Soc. Psychol**, 21, 120-134.

Henderson, J.L. (1955) "The Inferior Function: A Study of the Application of Psychological Types in Psychotherapy" in **Studien zur analytischen Psychologie.** C.G. Jung, Zurich: Rascher.

Heston, L.L. (1973) "The Genetics of Schizophrenic and Schizoid Disease" in **Orthomolecular Psychiatry** (Treatment of Schizophrenia), edited by D. Hawkins and L. Pauling. San Francisco: W.H.

Freeman and Co., 54-70.

Hill, D.O. (1970) "Extraversion-introversion: An investigation of typological theory (Doctoral Dissertation, Texas Tech Univ.) Dissertation Abstracts International, 1970, 31, 6257B.

Hillman, James. (1971) "The Feeling Function" in **Jung's Typology.** Spring.

_____ (1980) "Egalitarian Typologies verses the Perception of the Unique" in **Eranos Lectures 4,** Dallas TX: Spring.

Hinkle, Beatrice M. (1923) **The Re-Creating of the Individual:** A Study of Psychological Types and Their Relation to Holiness. NY: Harcourt, Brace & Co.

Hippchen, L.J., ed. (1978) **Ecologic-Biochemical Approaches to Treatment of Delinquents and Criminals.** NY: Van Nostrand Reinhold Co.

Hogle, G.H. (1971) "Family Therapy: When Analysis Fails" in **Success and Failure in Analysis,** edited by G. Adler. NY: G.P. Putnam's Sons, 167-177.

Holden, Constance. (7 Aug. 1987) "The Genetics of Personality" in **Science,** Vol. 237, 598-601.

Hoop, J.H. van der. (1939) **Conscious Orientation:** A Study of Personality Types in Relation to Neurosis and Psychosis. London: Kegan Paul, Trench, Trubner & Co. Ltd.

Hooper, J. and D. Teresi. (1986) **The Three-Pound Universe.** NY: MacMillan Pub. Co.

Horn, J., R. Plomin and R. Rosenman. (1976) "Heritability of Personality Traits in Adult Male Twins" in **Beh. Genet.,** 6(1), 17-30.

Horn, Joseph M. (15 July 1983) "Delinquents in Adulthood". A review of **Physique and Delinquent Behavior** in **Science,** Vol. 221, 256-257.

Howells, W.W. (1952) "A factorial study of constitutional types" in **Am. J. Phys. Anthrop.,** 10, 91-118.

Huarte, J. Navarro. (1969) **The Examination of Men's Wits.** NY: Da Capo Press.

Huemer, Richard P. (1986) **The Roots of Molecular Medicine.** A Tribute to Linus Pauling. NY: W.H. Freeman and Co.

Humphreys, Ed. (July 1955) Book review of **Atlas of Men** by Wm. H. Sheldon in **Am. J. Mental Deficiency,** Vol. 60, No. 1.

Humphreys, L.G. (1957) "Characteristics of Type Concepts with Special Reference to Sheldon's Typology" in **Psych. Bull.,** 54, 218-228.

Hunt, E.E., Jr., (1949) "A Note on Growth, Somatotype and Temperament" in **Am. J. Phys. Anthro.,** 79-90.

Hunt, E.E., Jr. and W.H. Barton. (1959) "The inconstancy of physique in adolescent boys and other limitations of somatotyping" in **Am. J. Phys. Anthrop.,** 17, 27-35.

Huxley, Aldous. (Nov. 1944) "Who Are You?" in **Harper's Magazine,** NY: Harper & Bros., 512-522.

Irwin, J.R. (1947) "Galen on the Temperaments" in **J. Gen. Psychol.,** 36, 45-64.

Iselin, H.K. (1981) **Zur Entstehung von C.G. Jungs "Psychologischen Typen".** Aarua, Verlag Sauerländer.

Janoff, I.Z., L.H. Beck and I.L. Child. (1950) "The relation of somatotype to reaction time, resistance to pain, and expressive movement" in **J. Pers.,** 18, 454-460.

Janssen B. and H.T.A. Whiting. (1984) "Sheldon's Physical-Psychical Typology Revisited" in **J. Research in Pers.,** 18, 432-441.

Jenkins, C.D. (1975) "The Coronary Prone Personality" in **Psychological Aspects of Myocardial Infarction and Coronary Care.** (Ed. W.D. Gentry and R.B. Williams, Jr.) Mosby.

Jung, Carl G. (1913) "A Contribution to the Study of Psychological Types" in **Coll. Works, 6.**

_____ (1916/1957) "The Transcendent Function" in **Coll. Works, 8.**

_____ (1919) "On the Problem of Psychogenesis

of Mental Disease" in **Coll. Works, 3.**
_____ (1921) "Psychological Types" in **Coll. Works, 6.**
_____ (1928) "The Relations Between the Ego and the Unconscious" in **Coll. Works, 7.**
_____ (1929) "The Significance of Constitution and Heredity in Psychology" in **Coll. Works, 8.**
_____ (1931) "A Psychological Theory of Types" in **Coll. Works, 6.**
_____ (1934/1950) "A Study in the Process of Individuation" in **Coll. Works, 9, Part I.**
_____ (1950) "Concerning Mandala Symbolism" in **Coll. Works, 9, Part I.**
_____ (1952) "Synchronicity: An Acausal Connecting Principle" in **Coll. Works, 8.**
_____ (1961) **Memories, Dreams, Reflections.** NY: Vintage Books.
_____ (1968) **Man and His Symbols.** NY: Dell.
_____ "The Symbolic Life" (Miscellaneous Writings) in **Coll. Works, 18.**
_____ **Letters.** Vol. 1: 1906-1950 and Vol. 2: 1951-1961, Princeton Univ. Press.
C.G. Jung Speaking. (1977) edited by W. McGuire and R.F.C. Hull. Princeton Univ. Press.
Kagan, J., J.S. Reznick and N. Snidman. (April 1988) "Biological Bases of Childhood Shyness" in **Science,** Vol. 240, 167-171.
Keen, Sam. (Dec. 1974) "The Golden Mean of Roberto Assagioli" in **Psychology Today,** 97-107.
Keirsey, D. and M. Bates. (1978) **Please Understand Me:** An Essay on Temperament Styles. Del Mar, CA: Promethean Books.
Kelley, W.D. (1974) **One Answer to Cancer.** The Kelley Foundation.
_____ (1981) "Metabolic Typing - Medicine's Missing Link".
_____ (1982) **Metabolic Typing.** International Health Institute, P.O. Box 358A, Winthrop, WA 98862.

King, Roy. (1986) "Motivational Diversity and Meso-limbic Dopamine: A Hypothesis Concerning Temperament" in **Emotion**, Vol. 3, edited by R. Plutchik and H. Kellerman. Academic Press, 363-380.

King, R.J., I.N. Mefford, C. Want, et. al. (1986) "CSF Dopamine Levels Correlate With Extraversion in Depressed Patients" in **Psychiat. Research**, 19, 305-310.

Kirsch, Thomas B. (1978-80) "Reflections on Introversion and/or Schizoid Personality in **J. Analyt. Psychol.**, 145-152.

Kline, N.S. and A.M. Tenney. (1950) "Constitutional Factors in the Prognosis of Schizophrenia" in **Am. J. Psychiat.**, 107, 432-441.

Kline, Nathan S. (1974) **From Sad to Glad.** NY: Ballantine Books.

Konapaka, R.J. and S. Benzer. (1971) "Clock mutants of Drosophilia melanogaster" in **Proceedings of the National Academy of Science, U.S.A.**, 68, 2112-2116.

Kraus, B.S. (1952) "Male Somatotypes Among the Japanese of N. Honshu" in **Am. J. Phys. Anthrop.**, 10, 347-364.

Kretschmer, E. (1936) **Physique and Character:** An Investigation of the Nature of Constitution and of the Theory of Temperament. Harcourt Brace.

_____ (1931) **The Psychology of Men of Genius.** NY: Harcourt.

_____ (1963) **Körperbau und Charakter.** Berlin. 23rd ed.

_____ (Sept. 23, 1968) "Ernst Kretschmer (1888-1964) Body and Mind", editorial in **JAMA**, Vol. 205, No. 13.

_____ (1971) **Gestalten und Gedanden.** Stuttgart: Thieme.

Kroeger, O. and J. Thuesen. (1988) **Type Talk** (Or How to Determine Your Personality Type & Change Your Life) Delacorte Press.

Lasker, G.W. (1947) "The effects of partial starvation on somatotype: An analysis of material from the Minnesota starvation experiment" in **Am. J. Phys. Anthrop.**, 5, 323-341.

Latter, B.D.H. (Aug. 1980) "Genetic Differences Within and Between Populations of the Major Human Subgroups" in **Am. Naturalist**, Vol. 116, No. 2, 220-237.

Laverty, S.G. (1958) "Sodium Amytal and Extraversion" in **J. Neurology & Neurosurg. & Psychiat.**, 21, 50-54.

Lawrence, G. (1979) **People Types & Tiger Stripes.** CAPT.

Lehrke, R. (1972) "A Theory of X-linkage of Major Intellectual Traits" in **Am. J. Mental Defic.**, Vol. 76, No. 6, 611-619.

Lenski, R. (Sept. 1977) "Eye Color's Contribution to National Temperament" in **Body and Mind**: A Journal of Constitutional Psychology, Vol. 1, No. 4.

_____ (1981) **Toward a New Science of Man:** Quotations for Sociobiology. Washington, DC: Pimmit Press.

Lester, D. (1981) "Ectomorphy and Suicide" in **J. Soc. Psychol.**, 135-136.

_____ (1986) "A Cross-Cultural Test of Sheldon's Theory of Personality" in **J. Soc. Psychol.**, 126(5), 695-6.

_____ (1976) "Preferences Among Sheldon's Temperaments" in **Psychological Reports**, 38, 722.

_____ (1977) "Deviation in Sheldonian Physique-Temperament Match and Neuroticism" in **Psychological Reports**, 41, 942.

Lewak, R.W., J.A. Wakefield, Jr., and P.F. Briggs. (1985) "Intelligence and Personality in Mate Choice and Marital Satisfaction" in **Pers. Indiv. Diff.**, Vol. 6, No. 4, 471-477.

Lillyquist, Michael J. (1985) **Sunlight and Health.** NY: Dodd & Mead & Co.

Lindegard, Bengt, editor. (1956) **Body-Build, Body-**

Function, and Personality. Lund: C.W.K. Gleerup.

Lindzey, G. (1967) "Behavior and Morphological Variation" in **Gen. Div. & Hum. Behav.,** (ed. by J.N. Spuhler) Chicago: Aldine Pub. Co., 227-240.

Livson, N. and D. McNeil. (1962) "Physique and Maturation Rate in Male Adolescents" in **Child Dev.,** 33, 145-152.

Loehlin, J.C., L. Willerman and J.M. Horn. (1982) "Personality Resemblances Between Unwed Mothers and Their Adopted-Away Offspring" in **J. Pers. & Soc. Psychol.,** Vol. 42, No. 6, 1089-1099.

Loomis, M. and J. Singer. **The Singer-Loomis Inventory of Personality.** Center for the Study of Cognitive Processes, Psy. Dept., Wayne State Univ., Detroit, MI 48202.

Loomis, M. and J. Singer. (1980) "Testing the Bipolar Assumption in Jung's Typology" in **J. Analyt. Psychol.,** 351-356.

Loomis, M. (1982) "A New Perspective for Jung's Typology: The Singer-Loomis Inventory of Personality" in **J. Analyt. Psychol.,** 27, 59-69.

Lubin, A. (1950) "A note on Sheldon's table of correlations between temperamental traits" in **Brit. J. Psy.,** 3, 186-189.

Lucas, W.P. and H.B. Pryor. (Nov. 1933) "The Body Build Factor in the Basal Metabolism of Children" in **Am. J. Diseases of Chil.,** Part I, Vol. 46, No. 5, 941-948.

Lynn, R. and H.J. Eysenck. (1961) "Tolerance for Pain, Extraversion and Neuroticism" in **Percep. and Motor Skills,** 12, 161-162.

Lynn, R. (1982) "IQ in Japan and U.S. shows a growing disparity" in **Nature,** 297, 222-223.

Macdad, G., M. McCaulley and R. Kainz. **Myers-Briggs Type Indicator: Atlas of Type Tables.**

Malone, Michael P. (1977) **Psychetypes.** NY: E.P. Dutton & Co.

Mangan, G.L. (1982) **The Biology of Human Conduct.** East-West Models of Temperament and Personality. NY: Pergamon Press.

Mann, H., M. Siegler and H. Osmond. (1968) "The Many Worlds of Time" in **J. Analyt. Psychol.**, Vol. 13, 1, 33-55.

Maritain, J. (1959) **The Degrees of Knowledge.** NY: Charles Scribner's Sons.

Marsh, Thomas O. **Roots of Crime.** A Bio-Physical Approach to Crime Prevention and Rehabilitation. Newton, NJ: Nellen Pub. Co.

Marshall, I.N. (1968) "The Four Functions: A Conceptual Analysis" in **J. Analyt. Psychol.**, 13, 1, 1-32.

Martiny, M. (1948) **Essai de Biotypologie Humaine.** Paris: Peyronnet.

Marx, Jean L. (22 Jan. 1988) "A Parent's Sex May Affect Gene Expression" in **Science**, Vol. 239, 352-353.

Mattoon, Mary Ann. (1981) **Jungian Psychology in Perspective.** NY: The Free Press.

_____ (Jan. 1977) "The neglected function of analytical psychology" in **J. Analyt. Psychol.**, Vol. 22(1), 17-31.

McBroom, P.M. (1980) "Behavioral Genetics" in **Monographs 2,** Bethesda, MD. Nat. Insti. of Mental Health.

McCaulley, M.H. (1978) **Application of the Myers-Briggs Type Indicator to Medicine and Other Health Professions: Monograph I.** CAPT.

_____ (1980) **Isabel Briggs Myers: Her Life.** MBTI News.

_____ (1981) "Jung's Theory of Psychological Types and the Myers-Briggs Type Indicator". Paul McReynold, editor. Advances in Psychological Assessment V, Jessey Bass, 294-352.

McDougall, W. (1929) "The Chemical Theory of Temperament Applied to Introversion and Extraversion" in **J. Abnor. Soc. Psychol.**, 24, 393-409.

McKusick, V.A. (1964) **On the X Chromosome of Man.** Am. Insti. of Bio. Sciences. Baltimore, MD: Waverly Press.

_____ (1986) **Mendelian Inheritance In Man:** Catalogs of Autosomal Dominant, Autosomal Recessive, & X-Linked Phenotypes. Johns Hopkins. 7th ed.

McNeil, D. and N. Livson. (1963) "Maturation Rate and Body Build in Women" in **Child Dev.,** 34, 25-32.

Meier, C.A. and M.A. Wozny. (1978) "An Empirical Study of Jungian Typology" in **J. Analyt. Psychol.,** 23, 3, 226-230.

Meier, C.A. (1971) "Psychological Types and Individuation: A Plea for a More Scientific Approach in Jungian Psychology" in **The Analytic Process:** Aims, Analysis and Training. (Ed. J.B. Wheelwright) NY: G.P. Putnam, 297-308.

_____ (1983) Personal communication.

Metzner, R. (1980) "Correlations Between Eysenck's, Jung's and Sheldon's Typologies" in **Psy. Reports,** 47, 343-348.

_____ (1979) **Know Your Type.** Anchor Books.

Metzner, R., C. Burney and A. Mahlberg. (1981) "Towards a Reformulation of the Typology of Functions" in **J. Analyt. Psychol.,** 26, 33-47.

Michener, James A. (Aug. 19, 1984) "Living with an Ailing Heart" in **The N.Y. Times Magazine,** 26ff.

Miller, Julie Ann. (Nov. 9, 1985) "Eye to (Third) Eye" in **Sci. News,** Vol. 128, 298-299.

Mills, R.W. (1917) "The relation of body habitus to visceral form, position, tonus, and motility" in **Am. J. Roentgenology,** 4, 155.

Monnelly, E.P., E.M. Hartl and R. Elderkin. (1983) "Constitutional Factors Predictive of Alcoholism in a Follow-Up of Delinquent Boys" in **J. Studies on Alcohol,** Vol. 44, No. 3, 530-537.

Montemayor, R. (1978) "Men and Their Bodies: The Relationship between Body Type and Behavior" in **J. Soc. Issues,** Vol. 34, No. 1, 48-64.

Moore, T. (Mar. 30, 1987) "Personality Tests Are Back" in **Fortune.**

Moore, L.W. (1979) **Extraversion and Introversion:** An Interactional Perspective. NY: John Wiley & Sons.

Mueller, W.H. and S.K. Joos. (1985) "Android Centralized Obesity and Somatotypes in Men: Association with Mesomorphy" in **Ann. Hum. Biol.** 12(4), 377-382.

Mullen, P.E. and Silman, R.E. (1977) "The Pineal and Psychiatry: A Review" in **Psy. Medicine, 7,** 407-417.

Myers, I.B. (1962) **The Myers-Briggs Type Indicator Manual.** Palo Alto, CA: Consulting Psychologists Press.

_____ (1976 rev.) **Introduction to Type.** CAPT.

Myers, I.B. and Myers, P.B. (1980) **Gifts Differing.** Palo Alto, CA: Consulting Psychologists Press.

Myers, I.B. and M.H. McCaulley. (1985) **Manual for the Myers-Briggs Type Indicator.** Palo Alto, CA: Consulting Psychologists Press.

Neumann, E. (1969) **Depth Psychology and a New Ethic.** NY: Harper & Row.

Newman, R.W. (1952) "Age changes in body build" in **Am. J. Phys. Anthrop.,** 10, 75-90.

Niederman, J.C., H.M. Spiro and W.H. Sheldon. (April 1964) "Blood Pepsin as Marker of Susceptibility to Duodenal Ulcer Disease" in **Arch. of Envir. Health,** Vol. 8, 540-546.

O'Gorman, J.G. and J.E.M. Lloyd. (1985) "Is EEG α a consistent measure of individual differences?" in **Person. Indiv. Diff.,** Vol. 6, No. 2, 273-275.

Oppenheim, J. (1931) **American Types:** A Preface to Analytic Psychology. NY: Knopf.

Ornstein, R. and R.F. Thompson. (1984) **The Amazing Brain.** Boston: Houghton Mifflin Co.

Osborne, R.H. and F.V. DeGeorge. (1959) **Genetic Basis of Morphological Variations.** Cambridge, MA: Harvard Univ. Press.

Osmond, H. (1965) in **Aldous Huxley** (1894-1963), edited by Julian Huxley. NY: Harper & Row.

Osmond, H. with J.A. Osmundsen and J. Agel. (1974)

Understanding Understanding. NY: Harper & Row.
Osmond, H., M. Siegler and R. Smoke. (1977) "Typology Revisited: A New Perspective" in Psychol. Perspec., Vol. 8, 2, 206-219.
Osmond, H. (1983) Personal Communcation.
Ostow, M. (1959) "The Biological Basis of Human Behavior" in American Handbook of Psychiatry, edited by S. Arieti. NY: Basic Books.
Ott, J.N. (1976) Health and Light. NY: Pocket Books.
Paepe, A. De and M. Matton. (1985) "Turner's Syndrome: Updating on Diagnosis and Therapy" in Endocrine Genetics and Genetics of Growth edited by C.J. Papadatos and C.S. Bartsocas. NY: Alan R. Liss, Inc., 283-300.
Parnell, R.W. (1958) Behavior and Physique: An Introduction to Practical and Applied Somatometry. London: Edward Arnold.
_____ (1959) "Physique and Family Structure" in Eugenics Review, 51, 75-88.
Petersen, A.C. (1979) "Hormones and Cognitive Functioning in Normal Development" in Sex-Related Differences in Cognitive Functioning, edited by M.A. Wittig and A.C. Petersen. NY: Academic Press.
Petersen, G. (1967) Atlas for Somatotyping Children. NY: Charles C. Thomas.
Philpott, W.H. and D.K. Kalita. (1980) Brain Allergies: The Psycho-Nutrient Connection. New Canaan, CT: Keats Pub.
Pillsbury, W.B. (1939) "Body Form and Introversion-Extraversion" in J. Abn. & Soc. Psychol., 34, 400-401.
Plattner, W. (1938) "Das Körperbauspektrum" in Zisch. f.a.ges. Neurol. Psychiat., 160, 703-712.
Plaut, A. (1972) "Analytical Psychologists and Psychological Types (Comment on Replies to a Survey)" in J. Analty. Psychol., 17, 2, 137-149.
Quenk, Alex. (1984) Psychological Types and Psychotherapy. Gainesville, FL: CAPT.

Quenk, N.L. (1978-80) "On Empirical Studies of Jung-
    ian Typology" in **J. Analyt. Psychol.**, 219-225.
Ralph, C.L. (1984) "Pineal Bodies and Thermoregula-
    tion" in **The Pineal Gland** edited by R.J. Reiter.
    NY: Raven Press.
Rees, L. (1961) "Constitutional Factors and Abnormal
    Behavior" in **Handbook of Abnormal Psychology**
    edited by H.J. Eysenck. NY: Basic Books, 344-392.
    _____ (1968) "Constitutional Psychology" in **Inter-
    national Ency. of the Soc. Sciences,** Vol. 13,
    edited by D.L. Sill. NY: Macmillan, 66-76.
Richek, H.G. and O.H. Bown. (1968) "Phenomenolo-
    gical Correlates of Jung's Typology" in **J. Analyt.
    Psychol.**, Vol. 13, 57-65.
Richek, H.G. and J. Van Rhodes. (1978-80) "A Note
    on Existential Adjustment and Jung's Typology"
    in **J. Analyt. Psychol.**, 357-362.
Roberts, D.F. and D.R. Bainbridge. (1963) "Nilotic
    Physique" in **Amer. J. Phys. Anthro.**, 21, 341-371.
Robertson, E.A., A.C. Van Steirteghem et al. (1980)
    "Biochemical Individuality and the Recognition of
    Personal Profiles with a Computer" in **Clin.
    Chem.**, Vol. 26, No. 1, 30-36.
Rosenthal, D., P.H. Wender et al. (1968) "Schizo-
    phrenics' Offspring Reared in Adoptive Homes"
    in **The Transmission of Schizophrenia,** edited by
    D. Rosenthal and S.S. Kety. Oxford: Pergamon,
    377-391.
Rosenthal, N.E., D.A. Sack et al. (Jan. 1984)
    "Seasonal Affective Disorder" in **Arch. Gen. Psy-
    chiat.**, Vol. 41, 72-80.
Ross, J. (1966) "The Relationship Between a Jungian
    Personality Inventory and Tests of Ability, Person-
    ality and Interest" in **Australian J. Psy.**, Vol. 18,
    No. 1, 1-17.
Rossi, E. (1977) "The Cerebral Hemispheres in Analy-
    tical Psychology" in **J. Analyt. Psychol,** Vol. 22,
    32-58.
    _____ (1986) **The Psychobiology of Mind-Body**

Healing. NY: W.W. Norton & Co., Inc.

Rubin, Z. (May 1981) "Does Personality Really Change After 20?" in **Psychology Today,** 18-27.

Saltus, C. (1986) **Bodyscopes:** Your guide to how body structure reveals the secrets of personality. NY: Bantam Books.

Samuels, Andrew. (1985) **Jung and the Post-Jungians.** Boston: Routledge & Kegan Paul.

Scarr, S. (1969) "Social Introversion-Extraversion as a Heritable Response" in **Child Dev.,** 40, 823-832.

Schachter, S. "Some Extraordinary Facts About Obese Humans and Rats" in **Amer. Psychol.,** 129-144.

Seltzer, C.A., F.L. Wells and E.B. McTernan. (June 1948) "A Relationship Between Sheldonian Somatotype and Psychotype" in **J. Personality,** 16, 4, 431-436.

Shapiro, K.J. and I. Alexander. (1975) **The Experience of Introversion.** Durham, NC: Duke Univ. Press.

Sharp, D. (1987) **Personality Types:** Jung's Model of Typology. Inner City Books.

Sheldon, W.H. (Feb. 2, 1924) "The Intelligence of Mexican Children" in **School & Society,** Vol. 19, No. 475, 1-9.

_____ (1924) "A Christmas Letter" in **The Scroll,** 122-124.

_____ (March 1927) "Morphologic Types and Mental Ability" in **The Personnel J.,** Vol. V, No. 11.

_____ (June 1927) "Social Traits and Morphologic Types" in **The Personnel J.,** Vol. VI, No. 1, 47-55.

_____ (Aug. 1927) "Ability and Facial Measurements" in **The Personnel J.,** Vol. VI, No. 2, 102-112.

_____ (1936) **Psychology and the Promethean Will.** NY: Harper.

Sheldon, W.H. with S.S. Stevens and W.B. Tucker. (1940) **The Varieties of Human Physique:** An Introduction to Constitutional Psychology. NY: Harper.

Sheldon, W.H. (Sept. 1941) See Irvin L. Child.

Sheldon, W.H. with S.S. Stevens. (1942) **The Varieties of Temperament:** A Psychology of Constitutional Differences. NY: Harper.

Sheldon, W.H. (Sept. 1945) A review of **Mainsprings of Civilization** by E. Huntington in **Am. J. Phys. Anthrop.,** Vol. 3 N.S., No. 3.

Sheldon, W.H. and Walter Alvarez correspondence. (1947-1969) in the Archives of the Smithsonian Institute.

Sheldon, W.H. (Dec. 1948) See P. Wittman.

Sheldon, W.H. with E.M. Hartl and E. McDermott. (1949) **Varieties of Delinquent Youth:** An Introduction to Constitutional Psychiatry. NY: Harper.

Sheldon, W.H. with H.K. Downing and M.H. Sheldon. (1949) **Early American Cents (1793-1814)** NY: Harper.

Sheldon, W.H. and Ernst Kretschmer correspondence. (May 26, 1950) in The Archives of the Smithsonian Institute.

Sheldon, W.H. and R. Ball. (1950) "Physical Characteristics of the Y Twins and Their Relation to Hypertension" in **Res. Publ. Ass. Nerv. Ment. Dis.,** 29, 962-975.

Sheldon, W.H. (July 1951) "Integration in the Biological and Social Sciences" in **Proceedings of the Am. Acad. of Arts and Sciences,** Vol. 80, No. 1, 31-36.

_____ (1951) "The Somatotype, the Morphophenotype and the Morphogenotype" in **Cold Spring Symposia on Quan. Biol.,** Vol. 15, 373-382.

Sheldon, W.H. with C.W. Dupertuis and E. McDermott. (1954) **Atlas of Men:** A Guide for Somatotyping the Adult Male at All Ages. NY: Harper.

Sheldon, W.H. (July-Aug. 1955) See Albert Damon.

_____ (May 1957) "Mesomorphs in Mischief", a review of **Physique and Delinquency** by S. Glueck and E. Glueck in **Cont. Psy.,** II, 5.

Sheldon, W.H. (Nov. 1957) See H.R. Ansley.

Sheldon, W.H. (March 13, 1961) "History of the Constitution Research Project and Objectification of the Somatotype". Lecture given at Children's Medical Center, Boston, MA.

_____ (1963) "Constitutional Variation and Mental Health" in **Ency. of Mental Health,** Vol. 2, NY: Franklin Watts, 355-366.

Sheldon, W.H. (April 1964) See J.C. Niederman.

Sheldon, W.H. (May 13, 1965) "Informal Communication on Psychiatry and Somatotyping". Maudsley Bequest Lecture read by E.M. Hartl at the Royal Society of Medicine in London, Eng.

Sheldon, W.H., N.D.C. Lewis and A.M. Tenney. (1969) "Psychotic Patterns and Physical Constitution: A Thirty-Year Follow-Up of Thirty-Eight Hundred Psychiatric Patients in New York State" in **Schizophrenia:** Current Concepts and Research edited by D.V. Siva Sankar. NY: PJD Pub., 838-912.

Sheldon, W.H. (April 1971) "The New York Study of Physical Constitution and Psychotic Patterns" in **J. & Hist. of Behav. Sci.,** 115-126.

_____ (1975) **Prometheus Revisited.** Cambridge, MA: Schenkman.

Sheldon, W.H. Television interviews with William Sheldon. (Videotaped)

Sherman, R.G. (1981) "Typology and Problems in Intimate Relationships" in **Res. in Psychol. Type,** Vol. 4, edited by T.G. Carskadon, 4-23.

Shields, J., L.L. Heston and I.I. Gottesman. (1975) "Schizophrenia and the Schizoid: The Problem for Genetic Analysis" in **Genet. Res. in Psychiat.** edited by R.R. Fieve et al. Baltimore: The John Hopkins Univ. Press, 167-197.

Silberner, J. (Jan. 26, 1985) "It's all in the hips..." in **Science News,** Vol. 127.

Singer, June and Mary Loomis. (1984) **Interpretive Guide for The Singer-Loomis Inventory of Personality.** Palo Alto, CA: Consulting Psychologists Press.

_____ (1984) **The Singer-Loomis Inventory of**

Personality (SLIP) Palo Alto, CA: Consulting Psychologists Press.

Smith, D.W. (1957) "The relation between ratio indices of physique and selected scales of the Minnesota Multiphasic Personality Inventory" in **J. Psychol.**, 43, 325-331.

Smith, S.L. (1968) "Extraversion and Sensory Threshold" in **Psychophysiology**, 5, 293-299.

Spain, D.M., V.A. Braders and G. Huss. (1953) "Observations on atherosclerosis of the coronary arteries in males under age of 46: a necrophy study with special reference to somatotypes" in **Ann. Int. Med.**, 38, 254.

Sparacino, J. (Dec. 1979) "The Type A Behavior Pattern: A Critical Assessment"

Sperber, M. and L. Jarvik, eds. (1976) **Psychiatry and Genetics.** NY: Basic Books.

Stafford, R.E. (1961) "Sex Differences in Spatial Visualization as Evidence of Sex-Linked Inheritance" in **Percep. and Motor Skills**, 13, 428.

Stein, Murray, editor. (1984) **Jungian Analysis.** Boulder & London: Shambhala.

Stephenson, W. (March 1939) "Methodological Consideration of Jung's Typology" in **J. Mental Sci.**, Vol. 85, No. 355.

Stern, M.B. (1982) "Bibliographical Essay" in **A Phrenological Dictionary of 19th Century Americans.** Westport, CT: Greenwood Press.

Stevens, A. (1982) **Archetypes.** A Natural History of the Self. NY: William Morrow & Co.

Stevens, J. (1987) **Storming Heaven:** LSD and the American Dream. NY: **Atlantic Monthly Press.**

Stewart, H. (1982) "Body Type, Personality Temperament and Psychotherapeutic Treatment of Female Adolescents" in **Adolescence,** Vol. 17, No. 67.

_____ (1980) "Body Type, Personality Temperament and Psychotherapeutic Treatment of Male Adolescents" in **Adolescence,** Vol. 15, 60, 927-932.

Stoute, H.M. (1971) Un nuevo recurso técnico para
la somatotipología. Tesis Profesional de la Escuela
Nacional de Antropología e Historia. México.
(Inédito)

Stricker, L.J. and J. Ross. (1964) "An Assessment of
Some Structural Properties of the Jungian Personality Typology" in **J. Abn. & Soc. Psychol.**, 68,
62-71.

Stockard, C.R. (Jan. 1923) "Human Types and Growth
Reactions" in **Am. J. Anatomy.**

Swengel, E.M. (1966) A Scale for Rating Traits of
Temperament. UCLA.

Sykes, G. (1962) "William Sheldon and the Human
Physique" in **The Hidden Remnant.** NY: Harper,
109-116.

Tanner, J.M. (1954) "Lack of sex-linkage and dominance in genes..." in **Carylogia,** Vol. Supp., 933-934.

Tanner, J.M. and M.J.R. Healy. (1956) "The Genetics
of Human Morphological Characters" in **Advancement of Science,** No. 51, 192-194.

Tanner, J.M., A. Prader et al. (Aug. 1959) "Genes
on the Y chromosome influencing rate of maturation in man" in **The Lancet,** ii, 141-144.

Tanner, J.M. with R.H. Whitehouse and S. Jarman.
(1964) **The Physique of the Olympic Athlete.**
London: George Allen and Unwin Ltd.

Tanner, J.M. (1964) "Human Growth and Constitution"
in **Human Biology** by G.A. Harrison et al. NY and
Oxford: Oxford Univ. Press.

_____ (1981) **A History of the Study of Human
Growth.** Cambridge: Cambridge Univ. Press.

Tanner, J.M. and R.H. Whitehouse. (1982) **Atlas of
Children's Growth:** Normal Variation and Growth
Disorders. London: Academic Press.

Tanner, J.M. (1985) "Growth Regulation and the
Genetics of Growth" in **Endo. Genet. & Genet. of
Growth,** 19-32.

Taylor, W.N. (1985) **Hormonal Manipulation:** A New
Era of Monstrous Athletes. Jefferson, NC &

London: McFarland & Co.

_____ (May 1985) "Super Athletes Made to Order" in **Psychology Today**, 63-66.

Thomas, A. and S.B. Chess. (1977) **Temperament and Development.** NY: Mazel.

Thurstone, L.L. (1959) **The Measurement of Values.** Chicago: Univ. of Chicago Press.

Toynbee, Arnold. (1954) **A Study of History,** Vol. VII, 716-736. Oxford Univ. Press.

Tucker, L.A. (Jan. 1983) "Self-Concept: A Function of Self-Perceived Somatotype" in **J. Psychol.,** Vol. 113(1), 123-133.

_____ (June 1982) "Relationship between perceived somatotype and body cathexis of college males" in **Psychol. Reports,** Vol. 50(3, Pt. I), 983-989.

Tucker, W.B. and W. Lessa. (1940) "Man: A Constitutional Investigation" in **Quar. Rev. Biol.,** 15, 3 & 4.

Turner, W.J. (1979) "Genetic Markers for Schizotaxia" in **Biol. Psychiat.,** Vol. 14, No. 1.

"Type A Minus" (May 26, 1986) in **Time,** 60.

Valentine, Tom & Carole. (1986) **Metabolic Typing:** Medicine's Missing Link. Wellingborough & NY: Thorsons Pub. Group.

Vandenberg and Kuse. "Spatial Ability: A Critical Review" in **Sex-Related Differences in Cognitive Functioning.** NY: Academic Press.

Verghese, A., P. Large and E. Chiu. (1978) "Relationship Between Body Build and Mental Illness" in **Brit. J. Psychiat.,** 132, 12-15.

Villanueva, Sagrado, María. (1979) **Manual de Técnicas Somatotipológicas.** Mexico: Univ. Nacional Autonoma de México.

Waldhauser, F., H.J. Lynch and R.J. Wurtman. (1984) "Melatonin in Human Body Fluids: Clinical Significance" in **The Pineal Gland** edited by R.J. Reiter. NY: Raven Press, 345-370.

Walker, R.N. (1962) "Body Build and Behavior in Young Children: I. Body Build and Nursery School

Teachers' Ratings" in **Mono. of Soc. for Res. in Child Dev.**, Vol. 27, No. 3.

_____ (1963) "Body Build and Behavior in Young Children: II. Body Build and Parents' Ratings" in **Mono. of Soc. for Res. in Child Dev.**, 34, 1-23.

_____ (1974) "Standards for somatotyping children: II. The prediction of somatotyping ponderal index from children's growth data" in **Ann. Hum. Biol.**, 1(3), 289-299.

_____ (1978) "Pre-School Physique and Late-Adolescent Somatotype" in **Ann. Hum. Biol.**, 5, 113-129.

Walker, R.N. and J.M. Tanner. (1980) "Prediction of Adult Sheldon Somatotype I and II from Ratings and Measurements at Childhood Ages" in **Ann. Hum. Biol.**, Vol. 7, No. 3, 213-224.

Welin, L., K. Svardsudd et al. (Aug. 27, 1987) "Analysis of Risk Factors for Stroke in Men Born in 1913" in **New Eng. J. Medi.**, Vol. 317, No. 9.

Wertheimer, F.I. and F.E. Hesketh. (1926) "The significance of the physical constitution in mental disease" in **Med. Monogr.**, Vol. 10.

Westman, A.S. and F.M. Canter. (1979) "Relationship Between Certain Circadian Behavior Patterns and Jungian Personality Types" in **Psy. Reports**, 44, 1199-1204.

Wheelwright, J.B., J.H. Wheelwright and J.A. Buehler. (1964) **Jungian Type Survey**: The Gray-Wheelwright Test Manual. (16th revision) San Francisco: Soc. of Jungian Analysts of No. CA.

Wheelwright, Joseph. (a lecture given May 19, 1971) "Psychological Types". Published by the C.G. Jung Institute of San Francisco.

Willeford, W. (Jan. 1977) "The Primacy of Feeling. II. Relations among the functions" in **J. Analyt. Psychol.**, Vol. 22, No. 1, 1-16.

Williams, R.J. (1956) **Biochemical Individuality**: The Basis for the Genetotrophic Concept. Texas: Univ. of TX Press.

Wilson, J.Q. and R.J. Herrnstein. (1985) **Crime & Human Nature.** NY: Simon and Schuster.

Winge, O. (1921) "On a Partial Sex-Linked Inheritance of Eye Colour in Man" in **Compt. Rend. Lab.** Carlsberg, Copenhagen, 14, 1-4.

Winokur, G. and V.L. Tanna. (1969) "Possible Role of X-Linked Dominant Factor in Manic Depressive Disease" in **Dis. of Nerv. Sys.,** Vol. 30, 89-93.

Wittman, P., W.H. Sheldon and C.J. Katz. (Dec. 1948) "The Study of the Relationship Between Constitutional Variations and Fundamental Psychotic Behavior Reactions" in **J. Nerv. and Ment. Dis.,** Vol. 108, No. 6, 470-476.

Witzig, J.S. (1978) "Jung's Typology and Classification of the Psychotherapies" in **J. Analyt. Psychol.,** 23, 4, 315-331.

Woodruff, G.N., J.A. Poat and P.J. Roberts, editors. (1986) **Dopaminergic Systems and Their Regulation.** VCH.

Worthy, M. (1974) **Eye Color, Sex and Race:** Keys to Human and Animal Behavior. Anderson, SC: Droke House Hallux.

Zerssen, D. von. (1965) "Eine biometrische Überprufung der Theorien von Sheldon über Zusammenhänge zwischen Körperbau und Temperament" in **Zeitschrift fur experimentelle und angewandte Psychologie,** 12, 521-548.

_____ (1976) "Physique and Personality" in **Human Behavior Genetics** edited by A.R. Kaplan. Springfield, IL: Charles C. Thomas.

Zimbardo, P.G., P.A. Pilkonis and R.M. Norwood. (May 1975) "The Social Disease Called Shyness" in **Psy. Today,** 69-72.

Zuk, C.H. (1958) "The Plasticity of the physique from early adolescence through adulthood" in **J. Genet. Psychol.,** 92, 205-214.

INDEX

ST. JOHN OF THE CROSS AND DR. C.G. JUNG
CHRISTIAN MYSTICISM IN THE LIGHT OF JUNGIAN PSYCHOLOGY by James Arraj

Many current attempts to revitalize the life of prayer are inspired by either the writings of St. John of the Cross or the psychology of Dr. C.G. Jung. Both are excellent choices. Even better would be a program of renewal under their joint inspiration.

Yet such a program faces three serious challenges: theological misgivings about the compatibility of Jung's psychology with Christian belief, long-standing misinterpretations of St. John's doctrine on contemplation, and the need to clarify the relationship between Jung's process of individuation and contemplation.

Parts I and **II** are devoted to resolving these first two problems, while **Part III** gives a practical demonstration of the relationship between individuation and contemplation in St. John's life and writings and in a variety of contemporary spiritual problems.

"The story of Jung's encounter with Fr. Victor White suggests the difficulties of a task which nevertheless must be carried out: the collaboration of psychology and theology...very complete bibliography." **Choice,** June 1987

"This book deserves to be read. It is well written, well documented, easy to follow, and on occasion fascinating..." **Spirituality Today,** Summer 1988

"Arraj has presented both Jung and John of the Cross in a competent manner. He relates the two figures in a deeply thoughtful way, and challenges the reader to reflect along with him..." John Welch, O.C.D., author of **Spiritual Pilgrims:** *Carl Jung and Teresa of Avila*

208 pages, paperbound, index, bibliography, notes, ISBN 0-914073-02-8, $11.95

TRACKING THE ELUSIVE HUMAN

VOLUME I:
A Practical Guide to C.G. Jung's Psychological Types, W.H. Sheldon's Body and Temperament Types and Their Integration

by Tyra and James Arraj

TRACKING THE ELUSIVE HUMAN

VOLUME I
A PRACTICAL GUIDE TO
C.G. JUNG'S PSYCHOLOGICAL TYPES
W.H. SHELDON'S BODY AND
TEMPERAMENT TYPES
AND THEIR INTEGRATION

TYRA ARRAJ and JAMES ARRAJ

Volume I gives clear descriptions of C.G. Jung's eight psychological types, and the body and temperament types of William Sheldon, interwoven with an actual account of what it is like to go on the inner journey of individuation by way of typology. These typologies are seen in their true light as practical ways of dealing with daily life. It treats of type recognition, type development, how types play a role in falling in love, marriage, and bringing up children. It puts special emphasis on the crucial role of our fourth or least developed function. The descriptions are enlivened by line drawings, cartoons and self-discovery quizzes. **Tracking** presents a compassionate and tolerant view of what makes people different that will serve you well both at home and on the job.

"Discussions of Jung's psychology are often bogged down in theoretical interpretations: the beauty of this volume is in its practical applications to daily life...Tracking...takes Jung's concepts and Sheldon's work, combines the two, and leads non-psychologically trained readers past the maze of jargon and analysis and on the road to practical self-discovery."   **The Midwest Book Review**

184 pages, paperbound, index,
ISBN 0-914073-16-8, $11.95.

IS THERE A SOLUTION TO THE CATHOLIC DEBATE ON CONTRACEPTION?
by James Arraj
128 pages, paperbound, bibliography,
index, ISBN 0-914073-19-2, $9.95

More than twenty years after Pope Paul VI's encyclical **Humanae Vitae,** contraception remains a deeply divisive problem in the Catholic Church. It absorbs energy that could be applied to other pressing issues, and it alienates Catholics from the life of their Church.

Is there a solution to the question of contraception? Is a reconciliation possible between the two sides of the debate? This book proposes such a solution. This would be a presumptuous undertaking except for the fact that many of the elements for a solution already exist, and what is needed is a way to bring them all together.

HOW TO USE JUNG'S PSYCHOLOGICAL TYPES
by James Arraj
Audio Cassette   60 minutes $7.95

A good introduction to psychological types that goes beyond type terminology and explores how typology is connected to the process of individuation. The heart of psychological types is learning to see what Jung was talking about so that we can use types as a practical tool in our marriages and family life, and in all our relationships.

ARE THERE REALLY CONTEMPLATIVES TODAY?
by James Arraj
Audio Cassette   60 minutes $7.95

An overview of today's interest in contemplation or mystical experience that uses John of the Cross, the Spanish mystic and poet, to address the questions of what contemplation is, whether people still experience it today, what to do if we are called to contemplation, and what to do if we are not.

A JUNGIAN PSYCHOLOGY RESOURCE GUIDE

Compiled by
Tyra and James Arraj

A JUNGIAN PSYCHOLOGY RESOURCE GUIDE

LOCAL ᴀɴᴅ PROFESSIONAL GROUPS
PSYCHOLOGICAL TYPES
CONFERENCES
PERIODICALS • PUBLISHERS
MAIL ORDER BOOK SOURCES
LIBRARIES ᴀɴᴅ
BIBLIOGRAPHICAL TOOLS
BASIC READING LIST ᴀɴᴅ FILMS
JUNGIAN ANALYSIS
TRAINING PROGRAMS

COMPILED BY
JAMES ᴀɴᴅ TYRA ARRAJ

A unique reference work to Jungian Psychology today that describes:
local and professional groups in the U.S., Canada and around the world; psychological types organizations; conferences; periodicals; book publishers; mail order book sources; libraries and bibliographical tools; basic reading list and films; and Jungian analysis and training programs.

"...the first ever book of information about all things Jungian...as a librarian I am genuinely enthusiastic about the Guide. It is conscientiously compiled, well-organized, and thorough. These attributes, combined with the long-time and considerable need for such a publication, make the Guide a very welcome tool for Jungian professionals, laymen and scholars."
                    The San Francisco Jung Institute **Library Journal**

"This volume provides a valuable set of lists to the reader interested in the psychology of Carl G. Jung."
                    American Reference Books Annual, 1988, Vol. 19.

"Most psychological discussions of Jungian theory focus upon theory rather than reference guides: this compilation...offers the Jungian researcher and interested layman precise references to Jungian practitioners which are often hard to come by, gathering all the information in easily-located chapters for quick reference...Readers seeking a concise reference to Jungian practitioners and resources will find this an invaluable handbook, not to be missed."
                    The Midwest Book Review

144 pages, paperbound, index,
ISBN 0-914073-05-2, $11.95

THE INNER NATURE OF FAITH

A MYSTERIOUS KNOWLEDGE

COMING THROUGH THE HEART

by James Arraj

THE
INNER
NATURE
OF
FAITH

A MYSTERIOUS
KNOWLEDGE
COMING
THROUGH
THE HEART

JAMES ARRAJ

Faith is a highly distinctive kind of knowledge, a knowledge that works through love, through the heart and because we misunderstand the nature of this knowledge we resist it, or fail to respond fully to its mysterious call.

Part I is a reflection on how I first heard this call of faith coming through an experience of human love, and struggled to respond to it and understand it.

Part II describes three ways in which this knowledge is in the process of being rediscovered in the 20th century: the debates of the theologians on the nature of faith, wisdom and gnosis in the Scriptures and Fathers, and Jacques Maritain on knowledge through connaturality.

Part III is an attempt to understand the inner nature of faith, after the pattern of human love.

144 pages, paperbound, bibliography, notes, index, ISBN 0-914073-22-2, $10.95

THE TREASURES OF SIMPLE LIVING

A FAMILY'S SEARCH FOR A SIMPLER AND MORE MEANINGFUL LIFE IN THE MIDDLE OF A FOREST

by Tyra and James Arraj

At first glance this is the kind of story that feeds fantasies: a family, tired of suburban living, finds itself in the middle of a forest. There, beyond paved roads and power lines, they built their own house, grow salads year-round in a solar greenhouse, and teach their children at home, all in a setting of towering trees, wild animals, and winters in which the snow gets four feet deep.

It is a book about the gifts that simplicity can bring that far outweigh the material disadvantages involved. It includes a discussion of basic skills useful in simple living, as well as an annotated guide to resources in the field of alternative lifestyles.

The Treasures of Simple Living "*is engrossing reading - a new Swiss Family Robinson in the late 20th Century!*"
Catholic Sentinel

"*An idyllic but passionately challenging account of transition from middle-class, city turmoil to taking personal control...*"
Learning Unlimited Network of Oregon

"*...full of practical tips and resources for creating your own simple living adventure.*" **The Mail Order Catalog**
The Farm, Summertown, Tennessee

Readers' comments: "*I received it in yesterday's mail and stayed up much too late...*" "*I greatly enjoyed The Treasures...It was like living through the whole experience with you...*" "*I picked up your book at my local library last night. I can hardly put it down!*" "*...such a free-flowing easy read - an encouragement in down to earth practicality without getting overburdened with detail.*"

216 pages, paperbound, resource guide, index, ISBN 0-914073-04-4, $9.95

ORDER FORM

Telephone orders: (503) 783-3126 - have your Visa or
MasterCard ready.

Please send the following: Amount

[ ] Tracking the Elusive Human, Vol. I @ $11.95 ..... _____
[ ] Tracking the Elusive Human, Vol. II @ $15.95 .... _____
[ ] St. John of the Cross and Dr. C.G. Jung @ $11.95 _____
[ ] A Jungian Psychology Resource Guide @ $11.95 .... _____
[ ] God, Zen and the Intuition of Being @ $10.95 .... _____
[ ] The Inner Nature of Faith @ $10.95 .... _____
[ ] Is There a Solution to the Catholic Debate
      on Contraception? @ $9.95 .... _____
[ ] The Treasures of Simple Living @ $9.95 .... _____
[ ] Are There Really Contemplatives Today?
      Cassette @ $7.95 .... _____
[ ] How to Use Jung's Psychological Types
      Cassette @ $7.95 .... _____

                                        Subtotal: _____

Postage: $1.25 for first item and 50¢ for each addi-
tional item. Foreign orders: $1.75 for first
item and $1 for each additional item. .... _____

                                           Total: _____

Name _____

Address _____

City _____ State _____

[ ] Here is my check, payable to **Inner Growth Books**, in the
amount of $_____.
[ ] Please charge my [ ] Visa or [ ] MasterCard

Card number _____

Signature _____

Expiration date _____ / _____

INNER GROWTH BOOKS, BOX 520
CHILOQUIN, OR 97624, (503) 783-3126